Intro...
Cont...

Introduction to Contemporary Political Theory

Colin Farrelly

SAGE Publications
London • Thousand Oaks • New Delhi

First published 2004

SAGE Publications Ltd
6 Bonhill Street
London EC2A 4PU

SAGE Publications Inc.
2455 Teller Road
Thousand Oaks, California 91320

SAGE Publications India Pvt Ltd
B-42, Panchsheel Enclave
Post Box 4109
New Delhi 100 017

British Library Cataloguing in Publication data

A catalogue record for this book is available
from the British Library

ISBN 0 7619 4907 0
ISBN 0 7619 4908 9 (pbk)

Library of Congress Control Number 2003110019

Typeset by C&M Digitals (P) Ltd., Chennai, India
Printed in Great Britain by TJ International, Padstow, Cornwall

For Lori. Words cannot express my depth of gratitude.

Contents

Preface   ix

Part One: Contemporary Liberal Theory   1

1 Rawls and Justice as Fairness   3
   1.1 Introduction   3
   1.2 The original position   7
   1.3 Equal opportunity   10
   1.4 Cohen's egalitarian critique   15
   1.5 The principles that apply to individuals   17
   1.6 Who are the least advantaged?   21
   1.7 Beitz on global justice   23
   1.8 A political conception of justice   26

2 Nozick and the Entitlement Theory of Justice   33
   2.1 Introduction   33
   2.2 The state: is it necessary?   35
   2.3 Wilt Chamberlain and the entitlement theory   39
   2.4 The principle of intial acquisition   41
   2.5 The principle of rectification   46
   2.6 Conclusion: self-ownership and private property   49

3 Gauthier and Justice as Mutual Advantage   53
   3.1 Introduction   53
   3.2 Hobbes and the state of nature   54
   3.3 Gauthier and the compliance problem   57
   3.4 What is a rational bargain?   63
   3.5 The limits of justice as mutual advantage   67

4 Dworkin on Equality   73
   4.1 Introduction   73
   4.2 Dworkin on equality of resources   75
   4.3 Welfare reform and the basic income proposal   80
   4.4 Political equality and democracy   85
   4.5 Against luck egalitarianism   89

Part Two: Alternative Traditions   95

5 Communitarianism   97
    5.1 Introduction   97
    5.2 Deontological liberalism and the unencumbered self   99
    5.3 State neutrality   102
    5.4 Walzer and complex equality   106
    5.5 Miller on nationalism   110
    5.6 Conclusion   115

6 Multiculturalism   119
    6.1 Introduction: the politics of recognition   119
    6.2 Kymlicka and the rights of national minorities   122
    6.3 Polyethnic rights   127
    6.4 Barry against multiculturalism   131

7 Deliberative Democracy   137
    7.1 Introduction: the importance of democracy   137
    7.2 Moving beyond the aggregative model of democracy   139
    7.3 How substantive are the principles of democracy?   144
    7.4 Retaining the critical edge of deliberative democracy 148
    7.5 Critically assessing the ideal of deliberative democracy 150

8 Feminism   157
    8.1 Introduction   157
    8.2 Liberal feminism   159
    8.3 The public/private dichotomy   164
    8.4 The politics of difference   169
    8.5 Conclusion   174

Bibliography   177

Index   183

Preface

What is 'political theory'?

I suppose the obvious place to begin a textbook entitled *An Introduction to Contemporary Political Theory* is to stipulate what I take to count as 'contemporary' and, more importantly, what counts as 'political theory'. This is not as easy as it sounds. Let me begin with the second and more difficult of these two questions – that of defining what political theory is. I am hesitant to stipulate a concise, all-encompassing definition; any such definition is bound to alienate someone and thus result in the charge that my definition is not inclusive. There is no consensus among political theorists as to what, exactly, constitutes the discipline. When one surveys the journals in political theory and the books written by those who call themselves 'political theorists' one sees a variety of topics being addressed. These range from the history of political thought to analyses of political concepts like freedom, equality and democracy. Topics from such diverse traditions as feminism, socialism, anarchism and liberalism all fall under the general rubric of 'political theory'. The fact that political theory is thriving as a discipline makes it all the more difficult to provide an inclusive definition of the discipline. The areas of enquiry that political theorists explore are constantly changing, and with this, our understanding of what qualifies as political theory.

However, having said that, I think it is accurate to say that what unites these diverse traditions under the rubric of 'political theory' is their concern for how we *ought*, collectively, to live together. More than forty years ago John Plamenatz described political theory as the 'systematic thinking about the purposes of government' (Plamenatz, 1960: 37) and I think this definition is just as apt today as it was then. I doubt a more inclusive definition could be constructed that would cover the vast array of concerns which contemporary political theorists have.

Political theory is thus a *normative* discipline, it is primarily concerned with how things ought to be as opposed to how things actually are. Of course this does not mean that theorists should not take seriously the realities of the current social and political arrangements. This is essential as one cannot determine what we should be aspiring towards if one does not know where we currently are and thus what the pros and cons of the current arrangement are. But political theorists do not engage in the descriptive or explanatory project that the political scientist engages in. The political scientist tackles questions like How is the American political system different from that of other countries?, or Who *actually* wields political power in America? Whereas the political theorist will ask Who *should* wield political power in society and what ideals, principles and institutional arrangements best secure the diverse demands of justice? A diverse range of political arrangements can be, and have been, defended by reference to values such as justice, freedom, equality and democracy. The job of the political theorist is to bring some precision to these vague and contested concepts so that one can provide convincing arguments for the particular social arrangements they believe we should be aspiring towards. Ideas are powerful things, they exert great influence on the real world and help determine the fate of the lives of billions of people. So the political theorist has a very important role to play, one that has an influence on the real world of politics.

This textbook focuses exclusively on debates in *contemporary* political theory. Deciding on which topics and theorists to address in this book was not easy. I focus primarily on the central theories and debates of the past thirty years. The publication of John Rawls's *A Theory of Justice* marked a turning point in political theory and this textbook seeks to cover the main positions and issues that have been central to political theory since the publication of Rawls's influential book. That is not to say that articles and books written prior to the publication of *A Theory of Justice* are unimportant or outdated. Such an inference would clearly be mistaken. But when writing a textbook on contemporary theories and issues one must draw a line somewhere and I think it is fair to say that the post-*A Theory of Justice* line is the most practical one to impose.

The design of the book

My approach to designing this textbook has been inspired by three concerns I believe instructors have when they put together a course in political theory. Firstly, they want to expose students to the main theoretical traditions, which will allow them to explore the diverse approaches theorists take to the issue of how society should be arranged. I believe this book accomplishes this. It covers the main positions in contemporary political theory – liberalism, communitarianism, multiculturalism, deliberative democracy and feminism. Rather than discuss and analyse these different theoretical positions in a very general and abstract form, I have sought instead to address specific theories and theorists in some detail. Thus I feel it is important to stress that the various labels one encounters in political theory, such as 'liberalism', 'communitarianism' and 'feminism', are just that – they are *labels*. They serve a pedagogical purpose but they should not be the main preoccupation. To design a textbook around contrived stipulated definitions of 'liberalism', 'multiculturalism', etc. would result in a book that not only grossly simplified contemporary debates but, I believe, such a book would be pretty boring to read (and write!). Instead of doing this, I often reinforce how these various traditions complement each other and point out, where appropriate, the common ground shared between alleged theoretical 'opponents' as well as the areas of genuine disagreement. Many liberals are deliberative democrats, for example, and many feminists are multiculturalists. So students should take the various *'isms'* of the chapters with a pinch of salt and recognize that the complexities of contemporary political theory run much deeper than the simple category schema conveyed in the table of contents of this book.

The second concern behind the design of this book is that it is important for students (and instructors!) to develop the critical skills necessary to assess the different arguments theorists advance and to decide for themselves which of these positions they find most promising or problematic. I have sought to do this by incorporating boxed-text exercises in each chapter to help stimulate class discussion and further study on the issues addressed. I have also tried to give a 'fair hearing' to each of the positions covered in this book, so that students can decide for themselves what they think of the different arguments.

Thirdly, I believe that the most effective way of motivating students to engage in these abstract theoretical debates is to emphasize their practical significance. Political theorists study what they study because they believe the answers to the questions they examine have an important impact of what goes on in the real world. This book is inspired by this view of political theory. I believe theory does, and ought to, inform public policy and public debate in general and thus political theorists have an important contribution to make to a wide variety of practical issues. From the issues of global justice and welfare reform to minority rights and gender quotas for political representatives, this book links theoretical debates to practical issues of concern so that students see why political theory is important.

Part One of the book focuses on contemporary liberal theory. I know that some will have reservations about the extensive treatment liberalism receives here but let me attempt to alleviate these concerns. Firstly, as I mentioned above, I believe that the division of political theory into various 'isms' is largely artificial. That is, many theorists who are labelled 'communitarians' or 'feminists' also share many of the same commitments that liberals have, and vice versa. So the fact that I spend four chapters on liberalism does not mean that I think liberalism is four times as important as the positions covered in the second part of the book. Given that liberalism is the main target of criticism for the four traditions examined in Part Two, one actually gains a better understanding and appreciation of those arguments only after one is familiar with the different liberal theories they are critical of. So by spending half of the book on four liberal theories of justice one is covering the background necessary for introducing communitarianism, multiculturalism, deliberative democracy and feminism. Once one has examined the different principles of justice liberals have advocated (for example, the difference principle, minimax relative concession, etc.) one can better appreciate the claims that liberalism fails to take seriously the importance of community, cultural membership and democracy; or that the distributive paradigm is ill-equipped to eliminate the oppression of women.

Furthermore, the inclusion of the four liberal theories of justice in Part One is useful because it permits one to cover some of the most important debates in contemporary political theory. By focusing on these four theories, I was able to address methodological issues (for example, the contrast between Rawls's method of reflective equilibrium and Gauthier's foundationalism) as well as effectively bring out the practical relevance of the abstract theoretical debates. A diverse range of applied topics are covered in the first part of the textbook, ranging from civil disobedience and global justice to the welfare state and campaign expenditures.

Many more applied topics are addressed in Part Two. For example, in the chapter on communitarianism the practical significance of the communitarian critique is illustrated by considering the issues of state neutrality and nationalism. In Chapter 6 we examine multiculturalist arguments for national minority rights and polyethnic rights. The practical significance of deliberative democracy is brought out by linking it with other themes addressed in the textbook, such as constitutionalism, and by considering the proposal for creating a new national holiday called Deliberation Day. And finally, in the chapter on feminism, we examine the practical significance of feminist internationalism, the feminist slogan 'the personal is political' as well as consider the argument for gender quotas for political representatives.

Writing this book has been a very enlightening experience. Writing a textbook forces one to emerge from their own entrenched theoretical perspective and to give an impartial and fair presentation of the positions that they might, in their other research, have attacked vigorously. I am happy to admit that working on this book has had a profound impact on my own political convictions. I am now much more critical of the theoretical tradition I align myself with and I have a much greater appreciation of the sophistication and insights of those whom I believed were my opponents. I suspect it is too much to hope that my readership will undergo a similar transformation but I do hope the textbook raises new questions for them to consider, presents familiar arguments in a new and interesting light and encourages them to engage in issues and traditions they perhaps have tended to ignore.

Taking on a project like this is a laborious task and I could not have written this book without the support of a number of people. I am grateful to the referees from Sage, who provided useful comments on both the initial designs of the book and on some of the chapters. I owe a special debt of gratitude to the referee who suggested that I also do *Contemporary Political Theory: A Reader* (as a companion volume to this textbook). Lucy Robinson and David Mainwaring from Sage have given me unwavering support and enthusiasm on both the textbook and the *Reader* and I am very grateful for this. Students on my courses at both the Universities of Birmingham and Manchester utilized drafts of some of the chapters of the textbook and I received useful feedback from them. I also benefited from the political theory reading groups I participated in at the Universities of Birmingham and Manchester, which helped me to stay abreast of the recent literature. I am particularly grateful to Hillel Steiner and Stephen De Wijze for many 'lively' and memorable debates about justice and the family that helped motivate me to get through the final stages of this book.

I also owe a special debt of gratitude to my family. I wish to thank my parents for their support over the years. During the time I worked on this book my two sons, Connor and Dylan, were born. Balancing the demands of work and family has proved to be an enormous challenge, a challenge that I could not even entertain tackling if it were not for the support of my wife, Lori, to whom this book is dedicated. Without her unfailing support not one word of it would have been written.

Colin Farrelly

Part One:

Contemporary Liberal Theory

1 Rawls and Justice as Fairness

Summary Contents

1.1	Introduction	3
1.2	The original position	7
1.3	Equal opportunity	10
1.4	Cohen on incentives	15
1.5	The principles that apply to individuals	17
1.6	Who are the least advantaged?	21
1.7	Beitz on global Justice	23
1.8	A political conception of justice	26

1.1 Introduction

John Rawls is arguably the most important political philosopher of the twentieth century. In his two most important books, *A Theory of Justice* (1971)[1] and *Political Liberalism* (1993), he defends his theory entitled 'justice as fairness'. Justice as fairness is primarily concerned with 'the way in which major social institutions distribute fundamental rights and duties and determine the division of advantages from social cooperation' (Rawls, 1999: 6). As such, justice as fairness is a theory designed to apply to what Rawls calls the 'basic structure' – the political, social and economic institutions of society. It provides a normative ideal by which we are to judge the political constitution of society and the principal economic and social arrangements. The just society, according to justice as fairness, is one governed by the two principles of justice. These principles are:

- Each person has the same indefensible claim to a fully adequate scheme of equal basic liberties, which scheme is compatible with the same scheme of liberties for all (*equal basic liberties principle*).
- Social and economic inequalities are to satisfy two conditions. First, they are to be attached to offices and positions open to all under conditions of fair equality of opportunity (*fair equality of opportunity principle*); and second, they are to be to the greatest benefit of the least-advantaged members of society (*difference principle*).

The principles are presented in *lexical order*. This means that they are listed in order of priority. The equal basic liberties principle must be satisfied before the second principle is invoked and the fair equality of opportunity principle must be satisfied before the difference principle can be invoked.

In this chapter we shall consider the main components of Rawls's liberal theory and some of the objections raised against it. Many of the theorists we shall examine in later chapters will also raise objections to Rawls's liberal theory of justice. In constructing his theory of 'justice as fairness' Rawls appeals to the idea of the social contract. His theory is inspired by contractarians like John Locke, Jean-Jacques Rousseau and Immanuel Kant. The main rival of the contractarian tradition is utilitarianism and Rawls offers his theory as an alternative to utilitarianism, which had been the dominant tradition prior to the publication of *A Theory of Justice*. It is perhaps best to begin then with a brief discussion of utilitarianism and Rawls's objections to it.

In *Contemporary Ethics: Taking Account of Utilitarianism* William Shaw claims that two fundamental ideas underlie utilitarianism: 'first, that the results of our actions are the key to their moral evaluation, and second, that one should assess and compare those results in terms of the happiness they cause (or more broadly, in terms of their impact on people's well-being)' (Shaw, 1999: 2). When stated like this, it is easy to see why utilitarianism has enjoyed an eminent list of devotees, which include David Hume, Adam Smith, Jeremy Bentham and John Stuart Mill. It captures some of our most basic moral intuitions concerning the importance of, for example, impartiality and human welfare. Utilitarians have put forth diverse accounts of what qualifies as 'human happiness', or 'utility', but they share the belief that the best outcome is the one that *maximizes* overall happiness or utility.

It is important to note that utilitarianism can be utilized as both an ethical theory designed to answer the question 'what should I do?' and as a political theory that applies to the conduct of political affairs – the decisions we make regarding how we are, collectively, to live together. It is this appeal to utilitarianism as a public philosophy that Rawls criticizes and thus I shall focus only on its viability as a normative political theory.

In *A Theory of Justice* Rawls invokes two main concepts of ethics – the right and the good – in order to illustrate how his contractarian theory differs from utilitarianism. 'The structure of an ethical theory is, then, largely determined by how it defines and connects these two basic notions' (Rawls, 1999: 21). Rawls distinguishes between the following two ways of relating the right and the good. The first way is to define the good independently from the right, and then the right as that which maximizes the good. Suppose, for example, one defines the good as material prosperity. If we accept this definition of the good then we can determine which laws and policies are the right ones by simply choosing the institutional arrangement that will bring about the greatest level of material prosperity. Institutions and acts are right if, of the available alternatives, they produce the most good. Rawls calls this type of theory a *teleological theory*. It is contrasted with a *deontological theory*. Deontological theories can be defined as a theory 'that either does not specify the good independently from the right, or does not interpret the right as maximising the good' (Rawls, 1999: 26). Rawls wants to defend a theory that is deontological in this second sense, that is, it gives a priority to the right over the good.

The appeal of the deontological position can be brought out by considering the example noted above. A teleological theory instructs us to maximize the good. If we define the good as material prosperity, for example, the institutions of our society will be designed to maximize overall material prosperity. But such a goal may be pursued by measures we think are unjust. Maximizing overall material prosperity might justify restricting the number of children people can have or denying the terminally ill expensive health care provisions. By asserting a priority of the right over the good Rawls seeks to avoid the injustices that may be made in the name of maximizing utility. As Rawls puts it, 'each person possesses an inviolability founded on justice that even the welfare of society as a whole cannot override' (Rawls, 1999: 3).

The main target of Rawls's critique is the classical utilitarian doctrine espoused by Jeremy Bentham and Henry Sidgwick. This version maintains that 'society is rightly ordered, and therefore just, when its major institutions are arranged so as to achieve the greatest net balance of satisfaction summed over all the individuals belonging to it' (Rawls, 1999: 20). Such an approach extends what is a commonsensical approach to the principle of choice for one person to the principle of choice for an association of people. Rawls explains how, as a principle of choice for one person, the utilitarian ethic seems like a rational ethic:

> Each man in realizing his own interests is certainly free to balance his own losses against his own gains. We may impose a sacrifice on ourselves now for the sake of a greater advantage later. A person quite properly acts, at least when others are not affected, to achieve his own greatest good, to advance his rational ends as far as possible. (Rawls, 1999: 21)

But the reasoning that is appropriate for the choice of one person should not, argues Rawls, be extended to the choice for an association of people. This is what utilitarianism does. In doing so it does not take seriously the distinction between persons. There are some things we should not do to people, even if doing it 'achieves the greatest net balance of satisfaction for all'. In particular, Rawls argues that 'in a just society the basic liberties are taken for granted and the rights secured by justice are not subject to political bargaining or to the calculus of social interests' (Rawls, 1999: 25).

Utilitarianism treats questions of distributive justice as questions of efficient administration. 'The nature of the decision made by the ideal legislator is not, therefore, materially different from that of an entrepreneur deciding how to maximize his profit by producing this or that commodity, or that of a consumer deciding how to maximize his satisfaction by the purchase of this or that collection of goods' (Rawls, 1999: 24). But justice, claims Rawls, must trump the virtue of efficiency. The right is prior to the good. Justice denies that the loss of freedom for some is made right by a greater good shared by others.

Rawls's method

The task of determining which principles should govern the main institutions of our society is a monumental one and Rawls believes that we must begin this task with some criteria for assessing the viability of the principles on offer. Rawls claims that there is 'a definite if limited class of facts against which conjectured principles can be checked …'(Rawls, 1999: 44). This class of facts comprises the considered judgements we have concerning what constitutes a just society. Our moral sensibilities tell us that acts of murder, slavery and discrimination, for example, are acts that our institutions should seek to prevent and, in cases where they do occur, the perpetrators should be appropriately punished. Any theory of justice that conflicts with these judgements will fail to be compelling. For example, a theory that permits denying ethnic minorities the right to vote will fail to secure our approval. One of our most firmly entrenched beliefs concerning justice is that all citizens should be entitled to the right to vote, regardless of their race, religion or gender. A theory that fails to accommodate such a widely shared belief fails to be a viable account of the demands of justice.

This appeal to a shared understanding of what justice demands is an important aspect of Rawls's theory. When constructing a theory we must start somewhere, and Rawls wants to start with general and widely accepted premises, premises that reflect the considered judgements citizens of a democratic society have. These judgements serve as the *moral data* from which we are to construct and test a theory of justice. A theory that blatantly violates one of these convictions will fail to be a viable theory. While Rawls endorses appealing to some shared beliefs in the initial stages of his theory, he is quick to point out that he does not appeal to values that violate what he calls the *fact of reasonable pluralism*. 'This is the fact of profound and irreconcilable differences in citizens' reasonable comprehensive religious and philosophical conceptions of the world, and in their views of the moral and aesthetic values to be sought in human life' (Rawls, 2001: 3). Citizens affirm diverse and often competing conceptions of what is of value in life. An appeal to contentious claims concerning, for example, what the Bible says concerning the sexual relations between a man and a woman, goes well beyond the shared judgements citizens of a free and democratic society have.

Rawls does not provide an exhaustive list of what these initial shared assumptions are. Nor does he claim that our initial convictions are exempt from scrutiny. On the contrary, once we begin to consider the complexities of issues raised by different conceptions of justice, we will find that we revise or perhaps even abandon some of the initial convictions we began with. What we seek is a *fit* between the principles of justice and our considered judgements. This is what Rawls calls *reflective equilibrium*. We will not find a perfect fit between these two things, but by striving for such a fit we can rule out various contending principles of justice as well as clarify what our considered judgements are regarding the demands of justice.

While Rawls does not provide an exhaustive list of what these initial assumptions are, he does invoke certain fundamental ideas he believes are embedded in the public political culture of a democratic society. These include the following:

1 *The idea of society as a fair system of social cooperation over time from one generation to the next.*
2 *The idea of citizens as free and equal persons.* As such, they are taken to possess two moral powers. Firstly, the capacity for a sense of justice. That is, the capacity to understand, to apply, and to act from (and not merely in accordance with) the principles of political justice that specify the fair terms of social cooperation. Secondly, persons have a capacity for a conception of the good. That is, the capacity to have, revise, and rationally to pursue a conception of the good. (Rawls, 2001: 18–19)

These fundamental ideas are, claims Rawls, viewed as being familiar from the public political culture of a democratic society.

> Even though such ideas are not often expressly formulated, nor their meaning clearly marked out, they may play a fundamental role in society's political thought and in how its institutions are interpreted, for example, by courts and in historical or other texts regarded as being of enduring significance. That a democratic society is often viewed as a system of social cooperation is suggested by the fact that from a political point of view, and in the context of the public discussion of basic questions of political rights, its citizens do not regard their social order as a fixed natural order, or as an institutional structure justified by religious doctrines or hierarchical principles pressing aristocratic values. (Rawls, 2001: 6)

If we begin with these fundamental organizing ideas, how are we to determine what the specific requirements of fair terms of cooperation actually are? To answer this question Rawls introduces the original position.

1.2 The original position

Appealing to our moral sensibilities concerning what we believe to be fair and just, Rawls constructs the original position. The original position is a hypothetical choice situation. It corresponds to the state of nature in traditional contract theories. Parties are placed in the original position and given two tasks. First, to choose the principles that are to govern the basic structure of society. And secondly, to choose the principles that are to apply to individuals. They are also given a limited list of principles from which to choose. This list includes Rawls's two principles of justice and their priority rules, utilitarianism and perfectionism.[2]

Rawls describes the original position as the *appropriate initial status quo*. It is one in which all people are treated as equals. In order to be so, certain conditions must hold. In everyday life a number of unfair factors influence agreements that we want to rule out in the original position. For example, unfair bargaining advantages, threats of force and coercion, and deception and fraud. In order to ensure that the choice of principles of justice is impartial and fair Rawls invokes the following two constraints:

1   The principles must fulfil what he calls *the formal constraints of the right*.
2   They must be chosen behind a *veil of ignorance*.

The formal constraints of the right impose five restrictions on the choice of principles. The principles must be *general* in form and *universal* in application, they are to be *publicly* recognized as a *final court of appeal* for *ordering the conflicting claims* of moral persons. Rawls provides an explanation for each of the five constraints of the right.[3] But none of the formal constraints of the right rule out the traditional conceptions of justice. What they do rule out are certain variants of egoism. The generality requirement, for example, rules out first-person dictatorships.

Further constraints are imposed on the choice situation by the veil of ignorance. By placing the parties behind a veil of ignorance Rawls believes that the choice situation will 'nullify the effects of specific contingencies that put men at odds and tempt them to exploit social and natural circumstances to their own advantage' (Rawls, 1999: 118). From behind the veil of ignorance the parties are denied certain information which will ensure that they evaluate principles solely on the basis of general considerations. The parties do not know the following information:

- Their place in society (for example, class or social status).
- Their race or gender.
- Their fortune in the distribution of natural assets and abilities (for example, intelligence, strength, etc.).
- Their conception of the good.
- The particular circumstances of their society (for example, its economic or political situation).
- The generation they belong to.

The only facts the parties do know are general facts about society (for example, principles of economic theory and laws of human psychology) and that their society is subject to the circumstances of justice.[4]

Having clarified the task facing the parties in the original position and the constraints placed on their choice by the formal constraints of the right and the veil of ignorance, Rawls turns to the issue of the *rationality of the parties*.

If the parties do not know what their conception of the good is, how are they to decide which principles to choose? Rawls claims that the parties have some rational plan of life, they just do not know what the details of this plan are. In order to ensure that individuals have the opportunity to pursue their conception of the good in the real world, once the veil is lifted, the parties in the original position seek to secure the largest share they can of what Rawls calls the *social primary goods*. These goods are rights and liberties, powers and opportunities, income and wealth and self-respect.

The argument for the two principles of justice

We are now in a position to consider Rawls's argument for the two principles of justice. The parties are presented with a shortlist of traditional conceptions of justice and must decide which of these will secure them the largest share of social primary goods. Rawls believes that it is rational for the parties to choose his two principles of justice over the rival principles. He defends this claim by arguing that the two principles of justice are the *maximin solution* to the problem of social justice. 'The maximin rule tells us to rank alternatives by their worst possible outcomes: we are to adopt the alternative the worst outcome of which is superior to the worst outcomes of the others' (Rawls, 1999: 133). Given that the parties do not know what their social position will be, or what their level of natural assets will be, it is rational, argues Rawls, for them to adopt the conservative attitude expressed by this rule. The maximin rule is 'a useful heuristic rule of thumb for the parties to use to organize their deliberations' (Rawls, 2001: 97 note 19).

The maximin rule, argues Rawls, instructs the parties to choose the two principles of justice for they guarantee the highest minimum payoff. As we have already noted, Rawls believes that utilitarianism permits the interests of some to be sacrificed for the greater good of others and thus the principle of utility would not be chosen as it does not satisfy the requirements of maximin. Some have questioned whether it is rational for the parties to adopt the conservative stance required by the maximin strategy. John Harsanyi (1975), for example, points out that the maximin principle has some very irrational conclusions.

> If you took the maximin principle seriously then you could not ever cross a street (after all, you might be hit by a car); you could never drive over a bridge (after all, it might collapse); you could never get married (after all, it might end in a disaster), etc. If anybody really acted this way he would soon end up in a mental institution. (Harsanyi, 1975: 595)

Now of course Rawls is not suggesting that real people should live their daily lives in accordance with the maximin principle. He argues that it is the appropriate strategy to invoke in the special case of the original position. But Harsanyi rejects even this claim. By evaluating institutional arrangements in

terms of the interests of the least advantaged Harsanyi argues that the
difference principle has some unacceptable moral implications.

> Consider a society consisting of one doctor and two patients, both of them
> critically ill with pneumonia. Their only chance to recover is to be treated
> by an antibiotic, but the amount available suffices only to treat one of the
> two patients. Of these two patients, individual A is a basically healthy
> person, apart from his present attack of pneumonia. On the other hand,
> individual B is a terminal cancer victim but, even so, the antibiotic could
> prolong his life by several months. Which patient should be given the
> antibiotic? According to the difference principle, it should be given to the
> cancer victim, who is obviously the less fortunate of the two patients.
> (Harsanyi, 1975: 596)

Harsayni's interpretation of what the difference principle requires is questionable. As we shall see, a lot depends on how one defines the least advantaged. Rawls does not adopt the position Harsayni implies in this example.
That is, that the least advantaged are those with the most serious illness. But
Harsayni's critique of the maximin principle has led many to question the
viability of Rawls's assumption that it is rational for the parties in the original position to adopt a conservative attitude.

1.3 Equal opportunity

In addition to the argument presented in the original position, Rawls offers
a second, direct argument, for the second principle of justice. This argument
is independent of the original position but is, Rawls claims, the same argument only presented in a different way. Appealing once again to our intuitions concerning what is fair and just, Rawls considers the issue of the
conditions under which socio-economic inequalities can be justified. The
moral intuitions Rawls appeals to when constructing the original position
are once again appealed to. In particular, he appeals to the ideal of equal
opportunity and argues that a commitment to this ideal entails a *prima facie*
commitment to equality of social primary goods. Rawls defends this position by considering increasingly stringent notions of the requirements of
equal opportunity. The first interpretation is the most lax and equates equal
opportunity with *careers open to talents*. This interpretation of equal opportunity is formal equality of opportunity. Formal equality of opportunity entails
that all have at least the same legal right of access to all advantaged social
positions. Rawls calls the kind of society that strives to achieve 'careers open
to talents' the *system of natural liberty*. It corresponds to the kind of society
Adam Smith defends in *The Wealth of Nations*. That is, a society of equal
liberty and a free market economy. Rawls argues that such a society will
bring about unjust distributive outcomes:

But since there is no effort to preserve an equality, or similarity, of social conditions, except insofar as this is necessary to preserve the requisite background institutions, the initial distribution of assets for any period of time is strongly influenced by natural and social contingencies. The existing distribution of income and wealth, say, is the cumulative effect of prior natural assets – that is, natural talents and abilities – as these have been developed or left unrealized, and their use favored or disfavored over time by social circumstances and such chance contingencies as accident and good fortune. (Rawls, 1999: 62–3)

Formal equality of opportunity does not capture the intuitive appeal of the ideal of equal opportunity. The elimination of arbitrary barriers (for example, policies of racial or gender discrimination) to advancement is a necessary but not sufficient measure for securing equal opportunity for all. The system of natural liberty permits morally arbitrary factors to greatly influence one's distributive share. Brian Barry (1989) refers to these factors as the result of three lotteries:

There is the natural lottery, which distributes genetic endowments; there is the social lottery, which distributes more or less favorable home and school environments; and there is what Hobbes called 'the secret working of God, which men call Good Luck' – the lottery that distributes illnesses, accidents, and the chance of being in the right place at the right time. (Barry, 1989: 226)

These three lotteries greatly influence one's life prospects. Those who fare well in these lotteries will have a much greater chance of succeeding in a system of natural liberty. But those who fare poorly in, for example, the natural and social lotteries of life, will not stand nearly as good a chance of succeeding. This is unfair: people do not deserve the genetic endowments they are born with nor the social position they are born into. Justice requires us to mitigate the influence of these morally arbitrary factors. We can do so through the basic structure of our society. But the system of natural liberty fails to do this. It is thus an inadequate interpretation of equal opportunity.

A second, more viable interpretation of equal opportunity is what Rawls calls *liberal equality*. Like formal equality of opportunity it maintains that arbitrary barriers to advancement must be eliminated. But it goes further than invoking the slogan 'careers open to talents' by adding the further condition of the principle of fair equality of opportunity. Fair equality of opportunity seeks to eliminate, or at least minimize as much as possible, the influence social contingencies (such as social class) have on people's opportunities.

More specifically, assuming that there is a distribution of natural assets, those who are at the same level of talent and ability, and have the same willingness to use them, should have the same prospects of success regardless of their initial place in the social system. In all sectors of society there should be roughly equal prospects of culture and achievement for everyone similarly motivated and endowed. The expectations of those with the same abilities and aspirations should not be affected by their social class. (Rawls, 1999: 63)

In order to ensure that the influence of the social lottery is mitigated our institutions have to preserve the social conditions for fair equality of opportunity. The system of natural liberty, with its free market economy, failed to do this. Liberal equality requires that excessive accumulations of property and wealth be prevented and that equal opportunities of education for all be maintained. Educational barriers such as parents' inability to pay for their child's education should be eliminated.

Liberal equality is more appealing than the system of natural liberty. It does a better of job of cohering to the intuitions that underlie our commitment to the ideal of equal opportunity. But, argues Rawls, it still does not go far enough. While it is fair that persons with identical talents should have similar life prospects, what about persons who have less talents? The natural lottery of life is just as morally arbitrary as the social lottery of life. If justice requires our institutions to mitigate the influence of factors such as social class then it should also mitigate factors such as our natural endowments. The abilities and talents we have are influenced by morally arbitrary factors such as our genetic endowment. Social factors and class attitudes also influence the extent to which our natural capacities develop and these cannot be mitigated by the principle of fair equality of opportunity. The principle of fair equality of opportunity can be only imperfectly carried out, claims Rawls, at least as long as some form of the family exists. Rawls claims:

> Even the willingness to make an effort, to try, and so to be deserving in the ordinary sense is itself dependent upon happy family and social circumstances. It is impossible in practice to secure equal chances of achievement and culture for those similarly endowed, and therefore we may want to adopt a principle which recognizes this fact and also mitigates the arbitrary effects of the natural lottery itself. That the liberal conception fails to do this encourages one to look for another interpretation of the two principles of justice. (Rawls, 1999: 64)

The systems of natural liberty and liberal equality are inadequate interpretations of equal opportunity because they do not go far enough in requiring society to mitigate the influences of the social and natural lotteries of life. Rawls puts forward a third and final interpretation which he feels succeeds in achieving this. This third interpretation is *democratic equality*. It is arrived at by 'combining the principle of fair equality of opportunity with the difference principle' (Rawls, 1999: 65). Rawls's analysis of equal opportunity has, so far, pushed us in the direction of objecting to any inequalities in social primary goods because such inequalities will reflect morally arbitrary factors. Formal equality of opportunity and liberal equality fail to provide us with compelling reasons why all citizens, especially the least advantaged, should accept the institutional arrangements such societies implement. Democratic equality thus amounts, claims Barry, 'to equality of outcomes' (Barry, 1989: 224).

It is perhaps more accurate to say that democratic equality amounts to a *presumption* in favour of equality of outcomes. Equality is a benchmark by which we are to judge other possible distributive arrangements. An equal distribution of social primary goods is not necessarily a good thing. If everyone is equal but extremely poor, it seems rather odd to say that that is the society we should strive for. Inequalities that benefit everyone, especially the least advantaged, are not objectionable. The underlying intuition behind egalitarianism is, for Rawls, a concern for the least advantaged. Why object to an unequal distribution if the least advantaged have more than they would in a situation of equality? Rawls does not believe that an egalitarian can give a convincing answer to this question. Thus he believes that egalitarians will opt instead for the difference principle. The difference principle permits inequalities provided such inequalities maximize the prospects of the least advantaged.

Consider the following questions:

- Does the original position help or hinder our understanding of what the demands of justice are?
- How viable is Rawls's claim that it is rational for the parties in the original position to adopt the conservative attitude of maximin?
- Is Rawls correct in assuming that the effects of the social and natural lotteries of life are extensive and deep and that justice requires mitigating these factors?
- Reflecting on your own situation, how have the social and natural lotteries of life affected your life prospects?

Efficiency

In order to understand how a move away from equality to inequality can satisfy the requirements of the difference principle one must consider the issue of efficiency. This aspect of Rawls's theory gets rather technical and I do not intend to consider all of these issues in detail. By making justice the *first* virtue of institutions Rawls seeks to ensure that other virtues, such as efficiency, do not trump considerations of fairness. But that does not mean Rawls wants to rule out all concerns relating to efficiency. It is important for a theory of distributive justice to consider this issue and Rawls attempts to do this by opting for the difference principle instead of strict equality of goods.

The importance of efficiency can be illustrated with the following example. Imagine that there are 100 units of goods that are to be distributed between

Bob and Mary. There are many possible *efficient* distributions of these goods. The following distributive outcomes are all efficient ones:

Bob:	0 units	Mary: 100 units
Bob:	100 units	Mary: 0 units
Bob:	99 units	Mary: 1 unit
Bob:	50 units	Mary: 50 units

Each of these distributive outcomes are *Pareto optimal*. That is, the outcome is such that it is not possible to move away from it in a way that makes one party better off without making another worse off. The fact that a distributive outcome is efficient does not guarantee that it is fair. For example, if we give Bob all 100 units and give Mary nothing we have an efficient distribution but an unfair one. Our egalitarian intuitions tell us that the closer the distribution comes to an equal one the better. But there are many possible equal distributions that are not efficient. Consider the following equal but inefficient distributive outcomes:

Bob:	2 units	Mary: 2 units
Bob:	10 units	Mary: 10 units
Bob:	25 units	Mary: 25 units
Bob:	49 units	Mary: 49 units

Each of these distributive outcomes are inefficient, that is, they are not Pareto optimal. In each case we could give extra goods to someone without reducing the amount of goods of the other person. This is so because we have a total of 100 units to distribute. Any distributive arrangement that does not total 100 units will be inefficient. A theory of justice should be guided not only by concerns of fairness and equality, but also by concerns of efficiency.

The real world does not have a fixed stock of commodities and thus we should not approach the issue of justice as if it were as simple as the two-person example noted above. The amount of goods to be distributed will be influenced by a number of factors. One important factor is that of *incentives*. The rewards we offer people, especially the most talented, will influence the level of our society's prosperity. This point can be illustrated by returning to the example of Bob and Mary. Instead of beginning with a fixed number of commodities let us assume that the amount of goods to be distributed will be determined by how well Bob and Mary can produce. Let us assume that if we tell Bob and Mary that they will get an equal share of whatever they produce then the total amount of goods they produce is 100 units. They thus each get 50 units. But suppose that it turns out that Mary is very talented and that she could produce a lot more if given the right incentives. For example, if we allot her 175 units her extra effort will raise the total amount of goods from 100 units to 300 units. This means that Bob can actually increase his initial 50 units of goods to 125 units if he permits the inequality-generating incentives that Mary requires in order to be more productive. This is the kind of scenario the difference principle envisions when it claims that inequalities are to be arranged so that they are to the greatest benefit of the least advantaged. This argument has been referred to as the *Pareto argument for inequality*.

1.4 Cohen's egalitarian critique

The Pareto argument for inequality is presented by Rawls as one that should win the support of egalitarians. While the difference principle does permit inequality it does so only when such inequalities benefit everyone, especially the least advantaged. Some egalitarians have challenged Rawls's argument and claim that the Pareto argument for inequality is not as egalitarian as Rawls presupposes. This critique is put forth most forcibly by G.A. Cohen.[5] What Cohen is critical of is Rawls's claim that the principles of justice only apply to the basic structure of society. The difference principle only requires the basic political and social institutions of our society be designed to maximize the prospects of the least advantaged members of society. But other factors beyond these institutions also contribute greatly to economic inequality. For example, the conventions of our society, the social ethos that shapes people's interpersonal attitudes, and the personal choices we make. These factors also, claims Cohen, play a significant role in determining the life prospects of the least advantaged but they are exempt from the demands of justice because, according to Rawls, the principles of justice only apply to social institutions.

In criticizing this aspect of Rawls's theory Cohen invokes the popular slogan 'the personal is political'. We shall encounter this slogan again in Chapter 8 when we consider feminism. The personal choices that Cohen is particularly concerned with are the self-seeking choices of talented individuals that induce inequality that is harmful to the badly off. Cohen provides a real policy example to illustrate his concerns. In 1988 Margaret Thatcher's Conservative government brought the top rate of income tax in Britain down, from 60 to 40 per cent. There were many distinct justifications for this tax cut. The most politically effective justification of the unequalizing policy of Thatcher Conservatism invoked the major premise that Rawls's Pareto argument for inequality invokes: that inequalities are justified when they render badly off people as well off as it is possible for such people to be. Defenders of the tax cut argued that by reducing the rate of income for top earners *all* people, including the worst off, would be better off. The extra income provided by the tax cut would cause these talented people to be more productive than they otherwise would. Their higher level of productivity would actually benefit everyone, including the worst off. Assuming that these factual claims are indeed true, it appears that such a policy is consistent with the demands of Rawlsian justice. The difference principle permits inequalities that are to the greatest benefit of the worst off. Lowering the rate of income tax for the highest earners will exacerbate the gap between the rich and poor but if such a tax cut benefits the worst off then it is consistent with Rawlsian justice.

Cohen rejects the conclusion that such tax cuts, even if they benefit the worst off, should be labelled *just*. He asks us to consider why the talented require the extra income the tax cut will give them before they will be more productive. Once we do this we see that the motives of such individuals are themselves unjust. Cohen distinguishes between incentives that are physically and/or psychologically necessary and those that are necessary only in an intention-relative sense. That is, incentives the talented *choose* not to work as productively without. While Cohen does not deny that there are genuine cases where incentives might be physically and/or psychologically necessary in order for people to perform certain tasks, these are not the kinds of incentives that high earners are appealing to when they demand their income tax be reduced from 60 to 40 per cent. It is the second category of incentives, those the talented choose not to work as productively without, that are at play in this instance and it is this category of incentives that Cohen wants to claim is morally suspect.

Within the category of incentives that are necessary only in an intention-relative sense further distinctions can be made. Cohen distinguishes between cases where people are motivated by self-interest to some reasonable extent and those where people are simply being selfish. Cohen does not wish to rule out a modest right of self-interest, but such a right could not justify the extremes of wealth and poverty that actually obtain in real capitalist societies. One major reason such extremes of wealth and poverty exist is that policies like Thatcher's tax cut appease the selfish choices of higher earners. The attitudes of such individuals, Cohen claims, are unjust. If these individuals truly cared about the least advantaged they would not need special incentives before they would be more productive. These individuals are not committed to the spirit of the difference principle. But this, for Rawls, is perfectly just. It is only institutions that must fulfil the requirements of the difference principle. As such, Cohen claims that Rawls's conception of justice is too narrow. The principles of justice must apply to *both* the legally coercive structure and the choices that people make within that structure.

Consider the following:

- Rawls presents his theory of justice as an egalitarian theory which embodies a fraternal ethos. Now Cohen argues that by permitting inequality-generating incentives Rawls permits people to engage in behaviour that runs counter to that ethos. But I think Cohen's position is untenable. If we agree with Cohen that the demands of justice apply to the decisions individuals make about career or spending this has counterintuitive consequences. For example, we should choose careers not that we find most rewarding, but those that will best benefit society. But isn't this 'thick' ethos simply too demanding? Does justice require us to be saints?

- Consider the case of Thatcher's tax cut in 1988. If such a tax cut actually benefited everyone, including the least advantaged, do you think such a tax cut should be called *just*? Reflect on your own attitudes toward taxation. Do you think you pay too much tax or not enough tax?
- David Estlund (1998) argues that there are a number of distinct reasonable motives which can cause inequality. For example, the pursuit of the interests of one's family, loved ones and friends. The talented may require extra pay so they can send their children to college, or can afford in-home care for an ageing parent. Which prerogatives do you think should be permitted and why?

1.5 The principles that apply to individuals

Cohen's critique of Rawlsian justice focuses exclusively on the principles that apply to social institutions. But Rawls does recognize that principles of justice also apply to individuals, but these principles are distinct from the ones that apply to the basic structure. This aspect of Rawls's theory is often overlooked by Rawls's critics and this is no doubt due in part to the fact that Rawls himself has said very little about them since the publication of *A Theory of Justice*. But the principles that apply to individuals are 'an essential part of a conception of right' (Rawls, 1999: 293). It is thus important that we consider this aspect of Rawls's theory. By doing so we shall see that Rawlsian justice requires individuals to fulfil a diverse array of duties.

In Chapter VI of *A Theory of Justice* Rawls considers the duties and obligations that apply to individuals. After choosing the principles that apply to institutions the parties in the original position are to choose the principles that apply to individuals. The parties must first choose the principles that apply to institutions for these determine, to a large extent, what the natural duties and obligations of individuals are. Rawls makes a distinction between *natural duties* and *obligations*. Let us first consider Rawls's discussion of obligations. Obligations are distinct from other moral requirements. Rawls emphasizes three characteristic features of obligations: (1) how they arise, (2) how their content is defined and (3) who they are owed to.

> For one thing, they arise as a result of our voluntary acts; these acts may be the giving of express or tacit undertakings, such as promises and agreements, but they need not be, as in the case of accepting benefits. Furthermore, the content of obligations is always defined by an institution or practice the rules of which specify what it is that one is required to do. And finally, obligations are normally owed to definite individuals, namely, those who are cooperating together to maintain the arrangement in question. (Rawls, 1999: 97)

All of the obligations that apply to persons, claims Rawls, can be derived from the principle of fairness. The principle of fairness imposes on us an obligation to do one's fair share in a system we benefit from. Free-riders are the obvious example of people who fail to fulfil this obligation. By accepting the benefits of cooperation but failing to fulfil the burdens of cooperation, free-riders lack a sense of fair play.

Rawls claims that the notion of obligations, as distinct from natural duties, helps us with the case of political officers. Members of political office, for example, must fulfil a number of moral requirements beyond those expected of the average citizen. Judges, members of parliament, etc. have voluntarily taken on their roles and thus are bound even more tightly to the scheme of just institutions.

Natural duties differ from obligations in that they do not have the three characteristics noted above. Natural duties apply to individuals without regard to our voluntary acts. Their content is not, in general, defined by the rules of these arrangements. And natural duties hold between all as equal moral persons, irrespective of their institutional relationships. Natural duties include both positive and negative duties. The former include the duty to uphold justice, the duty of mutual aid, and the duty of mutual respect. The negative duties include the duty not to injure and the duty not to harm the innocent. These are, claims Rawls, the principles (for individuals) that would be chosen in the original position.

The duty to uphold justice has two parts. First, we are to support and to comply with just institutions that exist and apply to us. And second, we are to assist in the establishment of just arrangements when they do not exist, at least when this can be done with little cost to ourselves. The duty of mutual respect requires us to 'show a person the respect which is due to him as a moral being, that is, as a being with a sense of justice and a conception of the good' (Rawls, 1999: 297). This mutual respect for others can be expressed in different ways. For example, when we are willing to see the situation of others from their point of view. Or when we are prepared to give reasons for our actions whenever the interests of others are materially affected. The parties in the original position would choose this duty because it is essential for the most important primary good – self-respect.

> Now the reason why this duty would be acknowledged is that although the parties in the original position take no interest in each other's interests, they know that in society they need to be assured by the esteem of their associates. Their self-respect and their confidence in the value of their own system of ends cannot withstand the indifference much less the contempt of others. Everyone benefits then from living in a society where the duty of mutual respect is honored. The cost to self-interest is minor in comparison with the support for the sense of one's own worth. (Rawls, 1999: 297)

The duty of mutual aid imposes on citizens 'a duty of helping another when he is in need or jeopardy, provided that one can do so without excessive risk or loss to oneself' (Rawls, 1999: 98). There are many distinct arguments for including this duty in an account of justice. Kant, for example, argues that the ground for proposing this duty is that situations may arise in which we will need the help of others.[6] But this is not, for Rawls, the most important reason for adopting the duty of mutual aid. The most important reason for adopting this duty is its pervasive effect on the quality of everyday life.[7]

Civil disobedience

After outlining the distinct duties of justice as fairness Rawls considers the case of civil disobedience. There are times when a conflict of duty arises. On the one hand we have a duty to comply with laws enacted by a legislative majority. On the other hand we have a right to defend our liberty and a duty to oppose injustice. What do we do when these two duties conflict? A theory of justice, argues Rawls, needs a theory of civil disobedience which provides some guidance for cases when the distinct duties of justice conflict. Let us consider and assess Rawls's account of civil disobedience.

Rawls sheds light on the content of the principles of natural duty and obligation by sketching a theory of civil disobedience. He considers the conflict of duties that can arise in what he calls a *nearly just society*. Rawls does not provide an exact definition of what qualifies as a nearly just society. What we are told is that such a society will be democratic and one that is 'well-ordered for the most part but in which some serious violations of justice nevertheless do occur' (Rawls, 1999: 319). In such a society the duty to comply with laws/policies enacted by a legislative majority can conflict with the right to defend one's liberties and the duty to oppose injustice. When such a conflict arises which duty should prevail? Rawls outlines a theory of civil disobedience in an attempt to shed some light on this question.

At first one may be surprised by the suggestion that a theory of justice should even consider the question of when the duty to comply with majority rule should be overridden. Does justice not require an unconditional commitment to majority rule? The answer to this question, at least for Rawls, is No. Suppose the majority passes an unjust law that violates the basic rights and freedoms of minority members of our society. Would we be *morally* bound to such an unjust law simply because the majority enacted it? Would we not have a moral obligation to *oppose* such an unjust law? Many of the most important progressive movements in human history challenged the legitimacy of laws enacted by the majority. The civil rights movement, for example, was instrumental in dismantling segregation laws. The weight we place on the value of democracy must be balanced against other fundamental values, such as freedom and equality.

The just society is, for Rawls, a *constitutional* democracy. The constitution ensures that the requirements of the first principle of justice are taken off the political agenda. The judicial branch of government serves as a check on majority rule to ensure that citizens' basic rights and freedoms are not violated. But a just and stable society will not be secured by placing this responsibility solely on judges. Citizens also have a responsibility to ensure that a legislative majority does not infringe on the demands of justice and a theory of civil disobedience outlines what is required of us as citizens when the duties of justice conflict.

Rawls defines civil disobedience as 'a public, nonviolent, conscientious yet political act contrary to law usually done with the aim of bringing about a change in the law or policies of the government' (Rawls, 1999: 320). By saying that civil disobedience is a public act Rawls means that it must be done openly with fair notice. This rules out acts that are secretive or covert. Rawls compares civil disobedience to public speech. 'By acting in this way one addresses the sense of justice of the majority of the community and declares that in one's considered opinion the principles of social cooperation among free and equal men are not being respected' (Rawls, 1999: 320). As a form of expression acts of civil disobedience must be non-violent. 'Any interference with the civil liberties of others tends to obscure the civilly disobedient quality of one's act' (Rawls, 1999: 321). The nonviolent nature of the act, coupled with the public nature of the act and the willingness to accept the legal consequences of one's conduct, expresses one's fidelity to the law.

What makes an act of civil disobedience *political* is not simply the fact that it is addressed to the majority that holds political power, but that it is guided and justified by political principles. The justification for the act in question must not appeal to principles of personal morality or to religious doctrines. Instead such acts must appeal to the commonly shared conception of justice that underlies the political order. When, for example, civil rights activists challenged the legitimacy of segregation laws they appealed to a common sense of justice when justifying their actions. Martin Lurther King, Jr often appealed to *Brown* v. *Board of Education* (1954) in which the Supreme Court of America ruled that segregation was unconstitutional. Such an appeal is a clear example of how a common sense of justice can be invoked to justify one's actions.

In order for acts of civil disobedience to be justified, argues Rawls, three conditions must be met. The first condition concerns the kinds of wrongs that are appropriate objects of civil disobedience. Rawls claims that these wrongs must be instances of *substantial* and *clear injustices*. These include serious infringements of the first principle of justice and blatant violations of fair equality of opportunity. But Rawls discounts violations of the difference principle because it is too difficult to ascertain to what degree it is violated. Unless a tax law is clearly designed to attack a basic equal liberty, argues Rawls, it should not normally be protested by civil disobedience.

The second condition that must be satisfied in order for acts of civil disobedience to be justified is that normal appeals to the political majority must have already been made in good faith and have failed. Legal protests and demonstrations, for example, must have been pursued and shown to be ineffective. Civil disobedience is a last resort. Rawls argues that there may be cases where this second condition need not be satisfied in order for civil disobedience to be justified. 'Some cases may be so extreme that there may be no duty to use first only legal means of political opposition' (Rawls, 1999: 328).

The third and final condition is a complicated one. In most cases, satisfying the first two conditions is sufficient to justify civil disobedience. But this may not always be the case. If a society has a number of unjust laws/policies then it may be the case that more than one minority is justified in being civilly disobedient. If all these people engage in civil disobedience simultaneously then this could pose a serious threat to respect for law and the constitution. In such a scenario respect for the rule of law would require one to abstain from engaging in acts of civil disobedience even though the first two conditions have been met.

Rawls does not intend his discussion of civil disobedience to provide precise principles that clearly decide actual cases but by considering some real examples you can assess the strengths and weaknesses of his account. Many activists engage in acts of civil disobedience to raise awareness about a number of causes ranging from animal liberation, gay rights and abortion to globalization and fuel tax.

- Which of these, if any, would satisfy Rawls's three conditions for justified civil disobedience?
- Do you agree with Rawls's account of civil disobedience?

1.6 Who are the least advantaged?

Rawls's difference principle requires the basic structure of society be organized so that social and economic inequalities are to the greatest benefit of the least advantaged. But who are the *least advantaged* in Rawls's theory? Rawls claims that the least advantaged are those who are least favoured by each of the three main kinds of contingencies.

Thus this group includes persons whose family and class origins are more disadvantaged than others, whose natural endowments (as realized) permit them to fare less well, and whose fortune and luck in the course of life turn out to be less happy, all within the normal range and with the relevant measures based on social primary goods. (Rawls, 1999: 83)

By saying 'all within the normal range' Rawls assumes that everyone has physical needs and psychological capacities within the normal range. Thus questions of health care and mental capacity do not arise. Such an idealization allows Rawls to construct a theory of justice for the simpler case of a society of 'normal, fully cooperating members'. Rawls's reason for making this assumption is not that such issues necessarily fall outside the scope of justice but that they should be dealt with 'at the legislative stage when the prevalence and kinds of these misfortunes are known and the costs of treating them can be ascertained and balanced along with total government expenditure' (Rawls, 1993: 184). One may question the adequacy of Rawls's bracketing of these issues. If Rawls's methodology is to appeal to our moral intuitions concerning what justice demands then one may find this idealization clause unsatisfactory. Many would argue that the greatest demands of justice come from those who are not 'normal, fully cooperating members of society' and thus Rawls's project is too narrowly conceived.[8]

Rawls does not attempt to provide a concise, definitive definition of who qualifies as the least advantaged in a society of full and active participants. He notes that 'it seems impossible to avoid a certain arbitrariness in actually identifying the least favored group' (Rawls, 1999: 84). But he does provide two possible definitions. Firstly, we may define the least advantaged as all those with approximately the income and wealth of the unskilled worker, or less. Alternatively, we could define the least advantaged as all persons with less than half of the median income and wealth.

Several critics of Rawls's theory have criticized his theory for permitting individuals who, through their own choices, qualify as members of the least advantaged and are thus entitled to the benefits demanded by the difference principle. In 'Primary Goods Reconsidered' Richard Arneson (1990) raises this objection against Rawls. Membership in the least advantaged class appears to be settled in terms of primary goods that individuals enjoy over the course of their lives and this, argues Arneson, has counterintuitive consequences. He illustrates this with the example of the life choices of four individuals – Smith, Black, Jones and Johnson. Smith and Black both graduate from an elite law school with high grades and can choose among several career options. Black chooses to be a Wall Street lawyer, the work is stressful but the income is high. Smith opts for the life of a bohemian artist, the income is meagre but the work is like play. Jones and Johnson did not go to college and both graduated from formal schooling with very little in terms of marketable skills. Jones chooses to be a bohemian artist and Johnson an unskilled labourer.

According to Rawls's definition of the least advantaged, Smith is one of the least advantaged. That is, his income falls below both the median income and that which the unskilled worker would get. The difference principle requires us to maximize the prospects of the least advantaged and both Smith and Johnson are members of this group. But our moral intuitions tell us that these two individuals should not be treated the same. Smith had lots of opportunities. With his law degree he could have chosen a variety of jobs that would have secured him a high income. But he *chose* to be a bohemian artist and the low level of subsistence that comes with it. This contrasts with Johnson. Due to his low level of marketable skills he never had a choice between high income and low income jobs. In addition to this, he chose to work for a living doing hard labour rather than live the life of a bohemian artist. Johnson is one of the deserving poor, argues Arneson, while Smith is not. Smith is poor by choice and thus should not receive the same benefits that Johnson receives. Justice does not require us to compensate individuals for inequalities they have voluntarily chosen.

In his later writings, Rawls proposes adding leisure to the index of primary goods in order to meet the type of concern raised by Arneson.[9] By including leisure in the index of primary goods Rawls argues that those who choose not to work will have extra leisure stipulated as equal to the index of the least advantaged. This means that such individuals would not be entitled to public funds. This suggestion raises some tricky conceptual difficulties for Rawls.[10] Firstly, we must ask what counts as work. Is work to be equated with paid employment? Or does it include unpaid work, like domestic work? Secondly, how should hours of work be made comparable? Is one hour of intensive, productive work equivalent to one hour of easy, inefficient work? If Rawls's proposal to include leisure in the index of primary goods is to be taken seriously then some of these tricky conceptual issues must be resolved. But even if such issues can be resolved, one would still have to assess how effectively it deflects the objection Arneson raises. That is, does it resolve the dilemma presented by the Smith–Black–Jones–Johnson example? Arneson thinks it does not and thus he argues 'that distributive justice should be concerned with the inequalities in the opportunity sets that individuals face, rather than what use presumably rational individuals make of their opportunities' (Arneson, 1990: 444).

1.7 Beitz on global justice

The main focus of *A Theory of Justice* is the issue of domestic justice. But Rawls's theory has also been extended to apply at the level of global justice.[11] In this section we shall consider one of the main proponents of this tactic – Charles Beitz. In *Political Theory and International Relations* Beitz makes a contractarian argument that 'persons of diverse citizenship have distributive obligations to one another analogous to those of citizens of the same state' (Beitz, 1979: 128). Beitz provides two arguments to defend this claim. Let us call these the *natural resources argument* and the *interdependence argument*.

The natural resources argument begins with the assumption, which Beitz actually believes is false, that nations are self-sufficient. That is, the production of goods and services in all countries is done entirely by its own labour and resources without trade of any kind. In such a scenario one might think that demands of distributive justice, at the global level, would not arise. No country can blame another country for its low level of prosperity. No other country *caused* a poor country to be poor. For example, the rich countries did not get rich from plundering the weaker countries. But this argument overlooks an important issue, argues Beitz. That issue is natural resources. Some areas have ample resources and some do not. Societies that are fortunate to be rich in resources like fertile land, oil, etc. are much more likely to prosper. Societies that are not so fortunate may, despite their best efforts, fail to fulfil their members' basic needs. Such a fact must figure into the reasoning of parties in an international original position. Like parties in the domestic original position who seek to mitigate the morally arbitrary distribution of natural talents, parties in an international original position would seek to mitigate the influence of the arbitrary distribution of natural resources over the world. 'Therefore, the parties would think that resources (or the benefits derived from them) should be subject to redistribution under a resource distribution principle' (Beitz, 1979: 138). Beitz does not explain how the countries rich in natural resources are to redistribute them to the poor countries but the main aim of this first argument is to establish that we do have moral ties to those with whom we do not share membership in a cooperative scheme.

Beitz's second argument considers the more realistic scenario where the world is one characterized by economic interdependence between countries. When there exists a flow of trade and services between countries, argues Beitz, there exists a global system of cooperation. 'If social cooperation is the foundation of distributive justice, then one might think that international economic interdependence lends support to a principle of global justice similar to that which applies within the domestic society' (Beitz, 1979: 144). Beitz advances this line of reasoning arguing that international interdependence involves a complex and substantial pattern of social interaction.

> Thus, for example, international property rights assign exclusive ownership and control of a territory and its natural resources to the recognized government of the society established on it, or reserve partial or total control of common areas (seas and outer space) to the international community. Also, laws and conventions established or codified by treaty, and thus guaranteed by the *pacta sunt servanada* rule of customary international law, protect private foreign investment against expropriation without compensation. Perhaps most important of all is the rule of nonintervention, which, when observed, has clear and sweeping effects on the welfare of people everywhere. (Beitz, 1979: 149)

These arrangements produce benefits and burdens that would not exist if countries were self-sufficient. They contribute to the wealth or poverty of a country and must be regulated by principles of global justice. National boundaries do not, argues Beitz, mark the limit of social obligations. 'Confining principles of social justice to domestic societies has the effect of taxing poor nations so that others may benefit from living in "just" societies' (Beitz, 1979: 150). By seeking to maximize the prospects of the least advantaged in their own society wealthy countries may deny providing aid to needy peoples in poor countries. Such a scenario is perverse, argues Beitz. The principles of domestic justice are only genuine principles of justice if they are consistent with principles of global justice. A fair distribution of the benefits and burdens of global cooperation requires satisfying a global difference principle that requires us to maximize the position of the globally least advantaged representative person (Beitz, 1979: 152).

Beitz recognizes that many will object to his argument on the basis that the analogy between international and domestic society is not as pronounced as Beitz would have us believe. One might argue that interdependence is a necessary but not a sufficient condition for the global application of principles of justice. That is, other conditions, in addition to global interdependence, must be satisfied before it is appropriate to talk about justice at the global level, conditions such as having effective decision-making and decision-enforcing institutions. Such institutions exist at the domestic level but not at the global level. One may also point to the fact that a sense of community is an important motivational basis for compliance with laws and official decisions and that, in international relations, no sense of community exists nor is it ever likely to exist. The world is just too large, and its culture too diverse, to support a global sense of justice.

Beitz responds to these objections by claiming that they misunderstand the relation between ideal theory and the real world. His argument is presented at the level of ideal theory. That is, he is concerned with prescribing standards that can serve as goals of political change in the nonideal world. The fact that, at the present time, there are no effective decision-making and decision-enforcing institutions at the global level nor a global sense of community does not establish the point that one would have to establish in order to refute Beitz's ideal theory. That is, that these things never could, in the future, be established. Beitz argues that 'there is no evidence that it is somehow given in the nature of things that people can neither develop sufficient motivation for compliance nor evolve institutions capable of enforcing global principles against offenders' (Beitz, 1979: 156).

In *The Law of Peoples* Rawls considers Beitz's argument and notes that, while he understands the appeal of Beitz's argument, its appeal is questionable.[12] Rawls argues that a duty of assistance is more satisfactory than a global egalitarian principle that lacks a clear target. He illustrates this with the following example. Consider the case of two liberal countries that have the same level of wealth and the same size of population. The first country decides to industrialize and to increase its rate of saving while the second country does not. The second country prefers a more leisurely society and, being content with the way things are, it does not adopt the changes that the other society opts for. In time the first country becomes twice as rich as the second country. Now, according to Beitz's argument, claims Rawls, a global egalitarian principle requires there always be a flow of taxes between the two countries as long as the wealth of one people is less than that of another. Such a result seems unacceptable, argues Rawls. This counterintuitive result is avoided if we opt for a duty of assistance. This duty does not require us to tax the wealth of people in the industrial country if those in the poorer country are able to determine the path of their own future for themselves.

The duty of assistance is a principle of transition that assists burdened societies to become full members of the Society of Peoples.

It is ironic that Rawls should raise this objection against Beitz's global difference principle for this is the same objection that Arneson raises against Rawls's domestic difference principle. Rawls objects to the global difference principle because it permits countries that, through the choices of their members, qualify as the least advantaged and are thus entitled to the benefits demanded by the global difference principle. But this is the same objection that Arneson raises against a domestic difference principle. Arneson's Smith–Black–Jones–Johnson example makes the same point that Rawls makes with his example of the two liberal societies. Namely, that it is inequalities in the opportunity sets that individuals or countries face that matters. If Rawls rejects the global difference principle on the grounds that it lacks a clear target than one could argue that he should also reject such a principle at the domestic level for the same reason.

Consider the following questions:

- How viable are Beitz's arguments for global justice?
- Given that we inherit distinct national identities, how plausible is it that we could achieve a global sense of community?
- Does Beitz's argument for global justice threaten the self-determination of national communities?
- If the demands of justice extend across national boundaries does that mean we should not give special attention to the interests of compatriots?

Further reading

Charles Beitz, *Political Theory and International Relations* (Princeton, NJ: Princeton University Press, 1979).
Peter Singer, 'Famine, Affluence, and Morality', *Philosophy and Public Affairs*, 1 (3), 1972: 229–43.
Thomas Pogge, 'An Egalitarian Law of Peoples', *Philosophy and Public Affairs*, 23 (3), 1994: 195–224.
David Miller, *On Nationality* (Oxford: Oxford University Press, 1995).

1.8 A political conception of justice

In the three decades following the publication of *A Theory of Justice* Rawls has continued to develop his account of justice as fairness. In *Political Liberalism* Rawls presents a revised version of justice as fairness. He remains faithful to many aspects of his earlier theory (for example, the two principles of justice and the original position) but claims that justice as fairness is now presented as what he calls a 'political conception of justice' instead of a 'comprehensive doctrine'.[13] In the introduction to *Political Liberalism* Rawls remarks:

> The aims of *Theory* ... were to generalize and carry to a higher order of abstraction the traditional doctrine of the social contract. I wanted to show that this doctrine was not open to the more obvious objections often thought fatal to it. I hoped to work out more clearly the chief structural features of this conception – which I called 'justice as fairness' – and to develop it as an alternative systematic account of justice that is superior to utilitarianism. I thought this alternative conception was, of the traditional moral conceptions, the best approximation to our considered convictions of justice and constituted the most appropriate basis for the institutions of a democratic society. (Rawls, 1993: xvii)

The aims of the theory outlined in *Political Liberalism* are very different, claims Rawls. The question he is primarily concerned with in this second book is this: How is it possible for those affirming a religious doctrine that is based on religious authority, for example, the Church or the Bible, also to hold a reasonable political conception that supports a just democratic regime? Rawls's 'shift' to a political conception of justice has divided supporters of his original work. Some remain faithful to his original project, others see his shift as an important improvement on the original formulation of the theory and others think that Rawls's shift does not really represent a substantial change to the original theory. The main issue which motivated Rawls to modify his theory was that of stability. A just democratic society must be stable. It must be able to exist over time and to secure the support of citizens who remain profoundly divided by reasonable religious, philosophical and moral doctrines. In order for this to be the case citizens must endorse the political arrangement for the right reasons. Rawls claims that the theory presented in *A Theory of Justice* violated this requirement. It required citizens to hold the same comprehensive doctrines and this included aspects of Kant's comprehensive liberalism.

Before considering some of the details of Rawls's revised formulation of justice as fairness, it is important that we consider closely the question of what the justification of his two principles of justice is, as presented in *A Theory of Justice*. This will help us to understand the different receptions Rawls's later work has received. If we ask why citizens should accept the two principles of justice as the standard for a just basic structure the following three answers can be found in *A Theory of Justice*:

1 We should accept the two principles of justice because they do a better job of matching our considered judgements about what is just and unjust than utilitarianism does.
2 We should accept the two principles of justice because they are the result of a fair choice. And as such, they can be justified to everyone.
3 We should accept the two principles of justice because acting from the principles of right and justice as having first priority expresses our freedom from contingency and happenstance.

Allen Buchanan labels these three justifications the *principles matching justification*, the *conditions matching argument* and the *Kantian interpretation*, respectively.[14] The first two justifications are based on appeals to considered moral judgements and the third on distinctively Kantian grounds. It is Rawls's invocation of this third justification that motivates Rawls to revise his original theory. This reason stipulates that our nature as a free and equal rational being can be ful-filled only by acting on the principles of right and justice as having first pri-ority. 'It is acting from this precedence that expresses our freedom from contingency and happenstance' (Rawls, 1999: 503). Rawls now claims that such a reason will not secure stability. Citizens who affirm other reasonable moral, religious or philosophical doctrines will not be moved by an appeal to Kantian metaphysics. What is needed, argues Rawls, is a *political conception* of justice. A conception that does not criticize any particular theory of the truth of moral judgements. A political conception adopts a restrained posture towards such questions and is thus presented as a free-standing view.

Critics of Rawls's revision have taken issue with the way Rawls has char-acterized his earlier view. Barry, for example, makes reference to Rawls's comment that 'while [a political] conception [of justice] is, of course, a moral conception, it is a moral conception worked out for a specific kind of subject, namely for political, social and economic institutions' (Rawls, 1993: 11). In reply to this comment Barry argues: 'On this definition of the political, it is hard to see why *A Theory of Justice* should not be said to contain a political conception of justice. *A Theory of Justice* is a moral theory, inasmuch as justice is an aspect of morality' (Barry, 1995: 877–8). Barry's comments do raise questions about the adequacy of Rawls's characterization of his original theory. Justice as fairness, as presented in *A Theory of Justice*, was designed to apply to the basic structure of society. While Rawls's invocation of the reason from the Kantian interpretation does raise problems for his theory, this justi-fication was never central to *A Theory of Justice*. In the concluding paragraph of *A Theory of Justice*, for example, Rawls asks why citizens should accept the principles chosen in the original position.

> [W]hy should we take any interest in [the original position], moral or other-wise? Recall the answer: the conditions embodied in the description of this situation are ones that we do in fact accept. Or if we do not, then we can be persuaded to do so by the philosophical considerations of the sort occasion-ally introduced. Each aspect of the original position can be given a support-ing explanation. Thus what we are doing is to combine into one conception the totality of conditions that we are ready upon due reflection to recognize as reasonable in our conduct with regard to one another. (Rawls, 1999: 514)

This passage is telling, for Rawls does not try to justify his theory by appealing to Kantian metaphysics. What he appeals to are the moral consid-erations embodied in the original position. These are considerations he believes diverse reasonable persons also accept (for example, impartiality and fairness).

An overlapping consensus

In *Political Liberalism* Rawls introduces some new vocabulary. He now talks about 'reasonable persons', 'public reason', 'the rational and the reasonable' and the 'burdens of judgement'. The extent to which these terms represent a substantial change to Rawls's theory as opposed to simply clarifying aspects of his original theory is debatable. One idea that has become more central to Rawls's revised theory is the idea of *an overlapping consensus*. Rawls claims that a political conception of justice is the object of an overlapping consensus of reasonable comprehensive doctrines. He describes a political conception as 'a module, an essential constituent part, that fits into and can be supported by various reasonable comprehensive doctrines that endure in the society regulated by it' (Rawls, 1993: 12).

Barry argues that Rawls's emphasis on an overlapping consensus threatens to undermine Rawls's two principles of justice, especially the difference principle. Barry claims:

> No doubt Christianity can be given an egalitarian slant. (We may think of levelling Protestant sects and the 'preferential option for the poor' of Liberation Theology.) But mainstream Christian denominations have always tolerated socioeconomic inequalities (including, in the past, slavery) vastly in excess of anything that could be justified by Rawls's 'difference principle'. Islam and Judaism embrace a similar spread of views, while Hindu and Confucian systems are inegalitarian to the core in a way that no monotheistic religion can be. It is therefore almost inconceivable that Rawls's second principle of justice could be presented as an inescapable implication of all the major religions. (Barry, 1995: 911)

The fact that most societies fall well short of meeting the requirements of the two principles of justice, especially the difference principle, suggests that Barry is right and that Rawls is being unrealistic if he assumes that existing comprehensive doctrines would endorse the main tenets of justice as fairness. Rawls claims that justice as fairness 'elaborates a political conception as a free-standing view working from the fundamental idea of society as a fair system of cooperation and its companion ideas' (Rawls, 2001: 189). But to what extent are the ideas Rawls invokes truly embedded in the public democratic culture of contemporary societies? There is a tension between the *descriptive* and *normative* claims of justice as fairness. One the one hand Rawls invokes ideals he believes diverse, decent people care about. Ideals such as equality and impartiality. But on the other hand Rawls recognizes that these ideals do not always guide everyday politics. Justice as fairness inspires a public philosophy that is, as Rawls puts it, *realistically utopian*. This phrase effectively captures the fundamental tension in Rawls's project. The tension between articulating a theory that is *realistic* in the sense that it appeals to the moral sensibilities of real people, here and now, and yet one that inspires us to transcend the status quo and move closer to a more decent political order. As we shall see in the next chapter, other political theorists appeal to our moral sensibilities but they come to very different conclusions concerning how our institutions are to be arranged. The ideas of society as a fair system of cooperation and citizens as free and equal persons could be invoked to justify a radically different type of political regime. To see how this is so we shall consider the libertarian argument advanced by Robert Nozick in *Anarchy, State and Utopia*.

SUMMARY

- In constructing his account of justice Rawls appeals to general and widely shared moral convictions. The original position represents a fair choice situation that incorporates and clarifies many of these convictions. In this hypothetical situation the parties would choose the two principles of justice, argues Rawls, as the principles to govern the basic structure of society.
- Critics have questioned many different aspects of Rawls's theory. For example, the role economic incentives play in his so-called 'egalitarian' theory, whom he defines as the least advantaged and why distributive principles only apply at the domestic level.
- Since the publication of *A Theory of Justice* Rawls has modified certain aspects of 'justice as fairness'. He now presents the theory as a political conception of justice that could be the focus of an overlapping consensus.

Notes

1   All references to *A Theory of Justice* are to the revised edition (1999).
2   Rawls distinguishes between two variants of perfectionism. The first version maintains that society should arrange institutions and define duties and obligations so as to maximize the achievement of human excellence in art, science and culture. The second, more moderate version, is one in which the principle of perfection is accepted as one among several in an intuitionist theory. For a detailed discussion of these positions see *A Theory of Justice*, pp. 285–92.
3   See *A Theory of Justice*, pp. 112–18 for full details.
4   See *A Theory of Justice*, pp. 109–12.
5   See Cohen (1992, 1995b, 1997 and 2000).
6   See Kant's *Groundwork of the Metaphysics of Morals* (1998).
7   Rawls claims:

> The public knowledge that we are living in a society in which we can depend upon others to come to our assistance in difficult circumstances is itself of great value. It makes little difference that we never, as things turn out, need this assistance and that occasionally we are called on to give it … The primary value of the principle is not measured by the help we actually receive but rather by the sense of confidence and trust in other men's good intentions and the knowledge that they are there if we need them. Indeed, it is only necessary to imagine what a society would be like if it were publicly known that his duty was rejected. (Rawls, 1999: 298)

8 Some have tried to remedy this deficiency by extending Rawls's theory of justice to the issue of just health care. See, for example, Norman Daniels's *Just Health Care* (1985).

9 See *Political Liberalism* (1993), pp. 181–2.

10 Here I draw from Phillipe Van Parijs's argument in *Real Freedom for All* (1995), pp. 97–8.

11 See, for example, Rawls's *The Law of Peoples* (1999), Beitz's *Political Theory and International Relations* (1979) and Thomas Pogge's 'An Egalitarian Law of Peoples' (1994).

12 See *The Law of Peoples*, pp. 115–18.

13 'A doctrine is comprehensive when it includes conceptions of what is of value in human life, and ideals of personal character, as well as ideals of friendship and of familial and associational relationships, and much else that is to inform our conduct, and in the limit to our life as a whole. A conception is fully comprehensive if it covers all recognized values and virtues within one rather precisely articulated system.' (Rawls, 1993: 13)

14 See Buchanan *Marx and Justice* (1982).

2 Nozick and the Entitlement Theory of Justice

Summary Contents

2.1	Introduction	33
2.2	The state: is it necessary?	35
2.3	Wilt Chamberlain and the entitlement theory	39
2.4	The principle of initial acquisition	41
2.5	The principle of rectification	46
2.6	Conclusion: self-ownership and private property	49

2.1 Introduction

The just society, according to Rawls, is one that protects citizens' basic liberties and arranges socio-economic inequalities so that they are to the greatest benefit of the least advantaged and attached to offices and positions open to all under conditions of fair equality of opportunity. This contrasts with the conception of justice defended by Robert Nozick. Justice, for Nozick, actually rules out the kind of redistribution that Rawls envisions. In *Anarchy, State and Utopia* (1974) Nozick defends the minimal state. The state should be 'limited to the narrow functions of protection against force, theft, fraud, enforcement of contracts and so on' (Nozick, 1974: xi). Any state that extends its functions beyond this narrow range of functions is unjust. So, for example, the requirements of Rawls's fair equality of opportunity principle and the difference principle would be ruled out. Such an extensive state, argues Nozick, violates people's rights.

In this chapter we shall consider Nozick's argument for the minimal state. I have included Nozick in this first part of the book, which examines contemporary liberal theory, but it is perhaps more accurate to refer to Nozick as a *libertarian* rather than as a 'liberal'. There are certain affinities between these two doctrines but libertarians hold that a minimal state is the only justified state.[1] Unlike Rawls's attempt to combine considerations of liberty with those of equality, (right-wing) libertarians are concerned only with the former. Liberty and equality are, argues Nozick, incompatible. If one is truly committed to the value of freedom then any attempt to enforce, through the coercive apparatus of the state, a particular distributive arrangement, be it egalitarian or otherwise, will violate the freedom of individuals and thus be unjust. Nozick's appeal to the primacy of the value of freedom is a sophisticated one and we shall examine and assess the main components of his argument.

Central to Nozick's argument is an appeal to moral *side constraints*. 'Side constraints upon action reflect the underlying Kantian principle that individuals are ends and not merely means, they may not be sacrificed or used for the achieving of other ends without their consent' (Nozick, 1974: 30–1). Individuals are, argues Nozick, inviolable. Recall that this line of argument was also central to Rawls's rejection of utilitarianism. By defining the right as that which maximizes the good utilitarianism fails to take seriously the distinction between persons. Maximizing utility might justify violating individual rights. But justice, argues Rawls, denies that the loss of freedom for some is made right by a greater good shared by others. It would thus appear that Rawls and Nozick share the same starting point. But this is not so. The scope of individual freedom that Nozick appeals to is more expansive than that of Rawls. The central issue that divides Rawls and Nozick is the stance they take on *property rights*. While Rawls does include among the basic liberties of the person the right to hold and have the exclusive use of personal property, he does not include the wider conception of the right that extends this right to include certain rights of acquisition and bequest, as well as the right to own means of production and natural resources (Rawls, 1993: 298). Nozick's libertarian argument is premised on *absolute* property rights: rights of ownership over oneself and over things in the world (Wolff, 1991: 4). It is thus obvious why, for Nozick, freedom and equality are incompatible. If freedom includes absolute property rights then such freedom will be limited by the egalitarian measures of, for example, Rawls's difference principle. The important question is – should we accept this wide conception of property rights? Nozick believes that such a conception of property rights follows from a commitment to the thesis which underlies our commitment to side-constraints – the *thesis of self-ownership*. This thesis states that 'each person is the morally rightful owner of his own person and powers, and, *consequently*, that each is free (morally speaking) to use those powers as he wishes, provided that he does not deploy them aggressively against others' (Cohen, 1995a: 67).

The so-called 'eye lottery' example is usually invoked to illustrate the intuitive appeal of the thesis of self-ownership and how it captures our concern for side constraints.

> Suppose that transplant technology reaches such a pitch of perfection that it becomes possible to transplant eyeballs with a one hundred per cent chance of success. Anyone's eyes may be transplanted into anyone else, without complications. As some people are born with defective eyes, or with no eyes at all, should we redistribute eyes? That is, should we take one eye from

some people with two healthy eyes, and give eyes to the blind? Of course, some people may volunteer their eyes to transplant. But what if there were not enough volunteers? Should we have a national lottery, and force the losers to donate an eye? (Wolff, 1991: 7–8)

The eye lottery example represents a clear case where our commitment to self-ownership trumps considerations of equality. If one is truly convinced by the egalitarian aspiration of Rawls's project, a project that seeks to mitigate morally arbitrary factors, then one should support the policy of an eye lottery, argues Nozick. Nozick claims that 'an application of the principle of maximizing the position of those worst off might well involve forceable redistribution of bodily parts' (Nozick, 1974: 206). Those born with two healthy eyes do not deserve their eyes. If we can mitigate the misfortune of the natural lottery by adopting an eye lottery, would not such a policy be just? The fact that we feel that such a policy is unjust is evidence of our commitment to the thesis of self-ownership. And if we are to take this thesis seriously, argues Nozick, we should also object to the redistributive policies of Rawlsian justice. Such policies, like the eye lottery, violate the thesis of self-ownership. The only institutional arrangement that respects persons as self-owners is the minimal state.

Rawls would, of course, reject the suggestion that his egalitarian theory would permit something as heinous as the eye lottery. The difference principle only applies to the social primary goods and not to body parts. Furthermore, the first principle of justice protects the integrity of the person. Like Nozick, Rawls would support the intuition that considerations of liberty should trump those of equality in the case of the eye lottery. But unlike Nozick, Rawls does not believe that the same can be said in the case of taxation of earned income. Nozick argues that 'taxation of earnings from labor is on a moral par with forced labor' (Nozick, 1974: 169). This necessarily follows, argues Nozick, from a commitment to self-ownership.[2] Self-owners should be free to use their powers as they wish, provided they do not deploy them aggressively against others. The state violates self-ownership when it forces people, be it through forced labour or taxation, to help the least advantaged in society. Nozick is not saying that people should not *voluntarily* give to help the poor. What he objects to is *compulsory* redistribution. Such a policy is incompatible with respecting persons as self-owners. Before we critically assess Nozick's argument that the only legitimate state is the minimal state, let us consider the argument he develops in Part One of *Anarchy, State and Utopia* – that the minimal state itself is morally justified.

2.2 The state: is it necessary?

What, exactly, is a 'state'? Nozick argues that 'formulating sufficient conditions for the existence of the state … turns out to be a difficult and messy task' (Nozick, 1974: 23). Instead of constructing a complete list of the sufficient conditions for the existence of the state Nozick points out two necessary conditions. Firstly, following Max Weber,[3] Nozick argues that a state has a monopoly over the use of force. Secondly, a state offers protection to anyone who resides within its boundaries. Nozick refers to these as the *monopoly element* and the *redistributive element*, respectively. These two features of the state may appear incompatible with Nozick's commitment to individual rights.

According to the natural rights tradition Nozick invokes, individuals have a right to self-defence and to punish those who violate their rights. This appears to conflict with the monopoly element of the state. The second feature of a state is that it offers universal protection to everyone in the territory and this might require some 'redistribution' as some may not be able to afford the taxes required to fund universal protection. This redistributive element also appears to conflict with self-ownership which requires non-interference with one's person or possessions unless one has consented to it or one has violated the rights of another. The aim of the first part of *Anarchy, State and Utopia* is to show that both the monopoly and redistributive elements of the state are morally legitimate and do not violate individual rights.

Given Nozick's strong commitment to individual rights one may wonder why he does not simply endorse anarchism. In order to decide which arrangement would be more conducive to individual rights, the minimal state or anarchy, of course depends on how one characterizes what life would be like without the state. Hobbes, for example, presents a very pessimistic picture of what life would be like in a 'state of nature'. Life would be 'nasty, brutish and short'. If we begin with Hobbes's portrayal of the state of nature it would be pretty easy to justify the state. But Nozick does not try to justify the state in this way. He seeks instead to persuade those who take a more optimistic view of what life would be like in the state of nature, those who believe that in the state of nature people would generally satisfy moral constraints and act as they should. These are the individuals John Locke describes in his account of the state of nature in *Two Treatises of Government*. In a Lockean state of nature individuals are in 'a *State of perfect Freedom* to order their Actions, and dispose of their Possessions, and Persons as they think fit, within the bounds of the Law of Nature, without asking leave, or dependency upon the Will of any other man' (Locke, 1988: 269). The law of nature requires that each person have rights to life, liberty and property, and the right to enforce these rights.

But in such a state of nature problems will arise, even if people do act morally and respect each other's rights. The law of nature does not provide for every contingency. Disputes will arise due to different interpretations of the natural law. Resolving such disputes is made even more difficult by the fact that people are biased in their own favour. Furthermore, individuals will often lack the power to enforce their rights. Faced with these problems, individuals in the state of nature will engage in behaviour which will result in the creation of the minimal state. These individuals will not consciously set out to create a state but this will be the inevitable outcome of their attempts to overcome the problems they face in the state of nature. Nozick calls this his *invisible hand explanation* of the state. The move from the state of nature to the minimal state involves the following stages of development:

1 The creation of mutual protection agencies.
2 The setting up of commercial protection agencies.
3 The creation of a dominant protection agency.
4 The creation of the ultra-minimal state.
5 The creation of the minimal state.

Let us briefly consider each of these steps. In order to overcome the problems they face in the state of nature, individuals will band together to create a *mutual protection agency*. 'All will answer the call of any member for defense or for the enforcement of his rights' (Nozick, 1974: 12). Such an arrangement is mutually advantageous to all because there is strength in numbers. If someone violates your rights you have a much better chance of exacting compensation if you can rely on the assistance of your fellow agency members.

Despite the obvious advantages of mutual protection agencies, they do come with inconveniences. Firstly, everyone is always on call to serve a protective function. This can be very time-consuming. Secondly, difficulties will arise if two different members of the same association are in dispute. In order to overcome these inconveniences it is rational to set up commercial protective agencies. Such agencies could take care of a variety of functions ranging from apprehending transgressors to determining guilt or innocence and carrying out the appropriate punishment. Such an arrangement would allow individuals to resolve the problems they face as members of a mutual protection agency.

But the creation of commercial protective agencies will also create some problems, argues Nozick. Several different protective agencies will offer their services in the same geographical area and this creates a problem when a conflict occurs between clients of different agencies. If the agencies reach different decisions concerning the guilt or innocence of the other client things could get rather messy. It is not in the interests of either agency to do battle over such disputes. What the competing agencies will find it in their interests to do is join forces and create a dominant protection agency. Nozick summarizes how things have developed this far as follows:

We thus have a situation where almost all persons in a geographical territory are under some common system that adjudicates between their disputes and enforces individuals' rights. Out of anarchy, pressed by spontaneous groupings, mutual-protection associations, division of labor, market pressures, economies of scale, and rational self-interest there arises something very much resembling a minimal state or a group of distinct minimal states. (Nozick, 1974: 16–17)

Is the dominant protective association a state? No. Recall Nozick's two necessary criteria for being a state – a monopoly over the use of force and protection to anyone who resides within its boundaries. At this stage the dominant protective agency has not met either of these conditions. While it may be prudent for individuals to purchase the services of the dominant protective agency they are not obligated to do this. Recall that one of the natural rights Locke attributes to individuals in the state of nature is the right to exact punishment personally. Individuals that do not purchase protection from the dominant protection agency are perfectly within their rights to exact punishment on others if their own rights have been violated. These individuals pose a problem for the agency. Individuals who purchase protection from the agency will want protection from all transgressors, including protection from non-clients who might claim compensation for wrongs they feel have been incurred unjustly on them. The dominant protection agency cannot afford to risk the safety of its clients by permitting non-clients to exact their right to punish its members. The agency thus announces that it has a monopoly over all use of force except that necessary in immediate self-defence. It thus excludes, for example, private retaliation against wrongdoers. By doing so it becomes the *ultra-minimal state* and satisfies the first of the two necessary conditions for being a state – a monopoly over the use of force.

This turn of events seems unfair to the individuals who did not purchase protection from the dominant protection agency. They have a natural right to exact punishment and yet this right has been infringed by the dominant protection agency's claim to a monopoly on the use of force. These individuals are now due compensation for this. They have no way of ensuring that their natural rights will not be violated. Compensation is given to these individuals by extending to them the same protection services that clients are given. All are offered protection and thus the second criterion for statehood is met.

This minimal state does appear to be redistributive as the protection of all will be financed from the tax revenues of some. But Nozick is quick to point out that his minimal state is not 'redistributive' in the sense that people commonly associate this term with. The term 'redistributive' applies, claims Nozick, to the types of *reasons* for an arrangement, rather than to an arrangement itself (Nozick, 1974: 27). The welfare state, for example, is redistributive because it attempts to protect the welfare of the vulnerable members of society. But Nozick's minimal state does not endorse these types of reasons. The reason all are given protection has nothing to do with considerations of welfare or equality. This policy is derived in accordance with the natural rights that Nozick holds so dearly – the rights to life, liberty and property, and the right to enforce these rights. Respect for these same rights not only justifies the minimal state, argues Nozick, it also rules out any more extensive state. We shall consider this argument in the next section.

Nozick takes the anarchist challenge seriously and his *invisible hand explanation* of the state is an attempt to refute the anarchist's claim that any state is illegitimate.

- Should we take the anarchist challenge so seriously?
- In what ways does the state both promote and restrict our freedoms?
- How viable is Nozick's invisible hand explanation of the state?

2.3 Wilt Chamberlain and the entitlement theory

Having provided a justification for the existence of the minimal state, Nozick then tackles the more onerous task of justifying his claim that any state that extends its functions beyond this narrow range of minimal functions is unjust. As noted above, the key to Nozick's argument is the thesis of self-ownership. It is only the minimal state, argues Nozick, that respects each person as the morally rightful owner of his or her person and powers. The welfare state, for example, violates the rights of its citizens when it forces them, through taxation laws, to subsidise the extensive social programmes it funds. Respect for individuals as self-owners requires us, argues Nozick, to reject the approach many theorists take to the issue of distributive justice. Many theorists, especially those on the left, adopt what Nozick would call the 'pie-cutting' approach to distributive justice. That is, they approach the issue of distributive justice as if it were a pie-cutting exercise; as if society's resources were 'manna from heaven' in need of some distributive metric that would tell us how the goods could be fairly divided. But this pie-cutting approach fails to see that distributive issues cannot be separated from production issues. 'Things come into the world already attached to people having entitlements over them' (Nozick, 1974: 160). Respect for persons as self-owners requires us to conceive of distributive justice not as a pie-cutting exercise, but as one that adopts a historical entitlement conception of justice in holdings. The answer to the question – Is it just for me to have X, Y and Z? – is not answered by considering whether I *need* X, Y or Z, or if I *deserve* X, Y, and Z – it is properly answered, argues Nozick, when one asks – Am I *entitled* to X, Y and Z? Did I acquire them in a just manner from a just situation? If, for example, I stole them or bought them from someone who stole them, then I am not entitled to them. But if I acquired them through a fully voluntary transfer from a just situation then I am entitled to them. For example, if they were payment for services rendered or a gift. Nozick's entitlement theory of justice states: *whatever arises from a just situation by just steps is itself just* (Nozick, 1974: 151).

Nozick illustrates the intuitive appeal of the entitlement theory of justice with his Wilt Chamberlain example. The example runs like this. Let us suppose that we begin with a just distribution, call it D1. Nozick allows us to characterize D1 in whatever way we want. Let us assume, being egalitarian, one claims that D1 is the equal society. In this just equal society an individual,

Wilt Chamberlain, is in great demand by basketball teams. He is a great gate attraction and utilizes this bargaining advantage to work out the following lucrative deal with the owners of the team. In each home game, 25 cents from the price of each ticket of admission goes to him. The season starts, and the cheerful fans attend his team's games, each time dropping a separate 25 cents of their admission price into a special box with Chamberlain's name on it. By the end of the season one million fans have attended his home games and thus he winds up with $250,000, which makes him much richer than everyone else. We now have a new distribution – D2. D2 is not the egalitarian distribution we started with. We now have an unequal society. Is this new distribution just?

Nozick argues that D2 is just. The entitlement theory of justice tells us that whatever arises from a just distribution by just steps is itself just. D2 satisfies the requirements of the entitlement theory. The initial distribution was just. Recall that Nozick allows us complete freedom in describing what the initial distribution is so the egalitarian cannot complain that D1 itself was unjust. The steps away from D1 are also just. The contract between Chamberlain and the owners was a fully voluntary contract. The fans who paid the separate 25 cents also voluntarily agreed to this arrangement. They could have spent their money on other things such as going to the movies. Thus, having fulfilled the requirements of the entitlement theory of justice, it appears that D2 must be just.

The Wilt Chamberlain example illustrates an important point in Nozick's libertarian argument: *liberty upsets patterns*. If you allow people to be free they will inevitably engage in activities that will upset the pattern the 'pie-cutting' theorist says is just. The only way to maintain a pattern is to violate the rights of individuals – namely, to violate their right to choose what to do with their entitlements. The egalitarian will argue that the state should step in in D2 and tax Chamberlain's new wealth in order to bring things back to an equal distribution. Maintaining a distributional pattern, argues Nozick, is individualism with a vengeance (Nozick, 1974: 167). The only way a distributive pattern can be maintained is by constantly interfering with the fully voluntary transactions of individuals. By doing so we fail to respect the requirements of the thesis of self-ownership.

Critics have raised a number of objections to Nozick's Wilt Chamberlain example. What do you think is the most compelling argument an egalitarian could make to undermine the Wilt Chamberlain example? When thinking about your answer to this question it may be helpful to consider the following three issues:

- Nozick assumes that absolute property rights will exist in D1, hence the reason why he assumes the steps away from D1 to D2 are 'just'. But egalitarians will reject this claim. Can Nozick give them a convincing reason why D1 should recognize absolute property rights?

- Third parties who did not 'voluntarily' agree to D2 could claim that this new distribution was unjust. Future generations, for example, will ask why the society they live in is one where gross inequalities exist. Is the answer that your grandparents wanted to see Wilt Chamberlain play basketball and thus agreed to give up equality for the chance to see him play grounds for a claim of injustice?
- Even if D2 was the result of 'fully voluntary' transactions does that necessarily make it just? What if the fans were insufficiently reflective and did not think through the full consequences of what they were doing? Do you think the fans would agree to the transactions if they knew that it would result in creating an unequal society and all the disadvantages that come with that?

Further reading

G.A. Cohen, *Self-Ownership, Freedom and Equality* (Cambridge: Cambridge University Press, 1995).

Eric Mack, 'Self-Ownership, Marxism and Egalitarianism: Part 1: Challenges to Historical Entitlement', *Politics, Philosophy and Economics*, 1 (1), 2002: 75–108.

Eric Mack, 'Self-Ownership, Marxism, and Egalitarianism: Part II: Challenges to the Self-ownership Thesis', *Politics, Philosophy and Economics*, 1 (2), 2002: 237–76.

2.4 The principle of initial acquisition

The entitlement theory of justice tells us that whatever arises from a just situation by just steps is itself just. As the Wilt Chamberlain example illustrates, Nozick assumes that 'just steps' are those transactions that are fully voluntary on the part of all the transacting agents. Nozick explains what makes a person's action voluntary as follows:

Whether a person's actions are voluntary depends on what it is that limits his alternatives. If facts of nature do so, the actions are voluntary. (I may voluntarily walk to some place I would prefer to fly to unaided.) Other people's actions place limits on one's available opportunities. Whether this makes one's resulting action non-voluntary depends upon whether these others had the right to act as they did. (Nozick, 1974: 262)

Two conditions must be fulfilled in order for an action to count as non-voluntary for Nozick. Firstly, our options must be restricted by other people. Secondly, their constraining actions must themselves violate rights (Wolff, 1991: 84).

Let us now consider the issue of what Nozick's entitlement theory says about the initial acquisition of property. In order for current distributions to be just they must have been brought about via just steps from a situation which was itself just. If we push this argument back far enough it must be the case that there was an initial just situation if current distributions are to be deemed just by the entitlement theory. Nozick does not, as we shall soon see, maintain that existing distributions actually fulfil this requirement, hence the need for a principle of rectification. But he does maintain that, in principle, it is possible for persons to justly appropriate unowned objects. In order to develop this aspect of his entitlement theory he once again invokes the social contract argument of John Locke.

In the *Second Treatise* Locke puts forward a sophisticated argument for private appropriation. The argument runs like this (modified from Christman, 1986: 160):

1   'Every man has a property in his own person'.
2   Therefore, every man has also a property right 'in the labor of his body and the work of his hands'.
So,
3   If he removes some object out its natural state by mixing his labor with it.
                                        AND
4   There is 'enough and as good left in common for others'.
                                        AND
5   The object or objects do not exceed '[a]s much as anyone can make use of … before it spoils'.
Then,
6   A person has thereby 'fixed [a] property in them'.

Nozick does not endorse this robust justification of initial acquisition but instead focuses exclusively on one of the necessary conditions Locke invokes, the 'enough and as good' proviso. Nozick's strategy is to present a slightly modified version of this necessary condition as a necessary and sufficient condition for the appropriation of property. Let us first consider why Nozick wants to modify the 'enough and as good' proviso.

The proviso needs to be modified, argues Nozick, because it is susceptible to the following regress argument.

[T]here appears to be an argument for the conclusion that if the proviso no longer holds, then it cannot ever have held so as to yield permanent and inheritable property rights. Consider the first person Z for whom there is not enough and as good left to appropriate. The last person Y to appropriate left Z without his previous liberty to act on an object, and so worsened Z's situation. So Y's appropriation is not allowed under Locke's proviso. Therefore the next to last person X to appropriate left Y in a worse position, for X's act ended permissible appropriation. Therefore X's appropriation wasn't permissible. But then the appropriator two from last, W, ended permissible appropriation and so, since it worsened X's position, W's appropriation wasn't permissible. And so on back to the first person A to appropriate a permanent property right. (Nozick, 1974: 176)

If the 'enough and as good' proviso yields the conclusion that appropriating a scarce resource like land is ruled out then it is obvious why Nozick wants to modify it. 'Nozick wants to establish natural, unlimited, rights to property, even in the face of scarcity, and so it is imperative for him to reply to the "zipping back" argument' (Wolff, 1991: 107–8). What Nozick does is distinguish between a stringent and weaker form of the 'enough and as good' proviso. The stronger form maintains that there must be enough and as good left for people to appropriate, hence the problem raised by the regress argument. But the weaker form maintains that there must be enough and as good left for other people to *use*, although not necessarily enough left to appropriate.

But even on this weaker form of the proviso it may appear that appropriating land can be ruled out when such a resource is scarce. So Nozick modifies this weaker form of the proviso to capture what he thinks is the intuitive appeal of the proviso. Namely that it rules out appropriation when such actions *worsen the situation of others*. If my appropriating a plot of unowned land (object X) worsens your situation then I have violated Nozick's modified Lockean proviso. But the fact that my appropriation means that others can no longer appropriate it or use it does not *necessarily* mean that I have worsened their situation. Nozick believes that a system of private property actually brings benefits to all.

Is the situation of persons who are unable to appropriate (there being no more accessible and useful unowned objects) worsened by a system allowing appropriation and permanent property? Here enter the various familiar social considerations favoring private property: it increases the social product by putting means of production in the hands of those who can use them most efficiently (profitably); experimentation is encouraged, because with separate persons controlling resources, there is no one person or small group whom someone with a new idea must convince to try it out; private property enables people to decide on the pattern and types of risks they wish to bear, leading to specialized types of risk bearing; private property protects future persons by leading some of them to hold back resources from current consumption for future markets; it provides alternate sources of employment for unpopular persons who don't have to convince any one person or small group to hire them, and so on. (Nozick, 1974: 177)

Nozick's modified Lockean proviso requires us to weigh the new opportunities my appropriation of object X creates for others against the loss in opportunities others incur. If, on balance, I have not worsened their situation compared to how they were before my appropriation, that is, when object X was in general use, then my appropriation of object X is legitimate.

Cohen provides the following example to illustrate how Nozick's proviso could be satisfied:

> I enclose a beach, which has been common land, declare it my own, and announce a price of one dollar per person per day for the use of it (or, if you think there could not be dollars in what sounds like a state of nature situation, then imagine that my price is a certain amount of massage of my bad back). But I so enhance the recreational value of the beach (perhaps by dyeing the sand different attractive colours, or just by picking up the litter every night) that all would-be users of it regard a dollar (or a massage) for a day's use of it as a dollar well spent: they prefer a day at the beach as it now is at the cost of a dollar to a free day at the beach as it was and as it would have remained had no one appropriated it. (Cohen, 1995a: 76)

This example suggests that Nozick's proviso on acquisition does appear to rule out any plausible grievance others could have to private appropriation. But Cohen is quick to point out that this appearance is only an illusion. There are in fact many possible grounds for rejecting Nozick's proviso. I shall briefly consider two that have been utilized by egalitarians like Cohen to show that Nozick's proviso is not as viable as he suggests. I will do so by illustrating how they could be used in the example Cohen makes above with appropriating a beach.

One line of criticism is to critically assess the conception of welfare employed by the clause 'worsening the situation of others'. There are many ways my appropriation of object X could worsen the situation of others. It may leave you materially worse off. That is, object X may have provided you with your primary source of sustenance and thus my appropriating X means that you are materially worse off. In this case the proviso would require me to compensate you before I can legitimately appropriate object X. If by appropriating object X I create new opportunities that allow you attain at least the same level of material prosperity that you could have attained when object X was in general use then the proviso is satisfied. By what if my appropriation of object X worsens your situation *non-materially*? Suppose that object X was a vital source of your mental well-being. Perhaps it brought you peace of mind or spiritual fulfilment. If my appropriation of object X worsens your situation non-materially what does Nozick's proviso require of me in terms of compensating you? Nothing. As is clear from the passage noted above, Nozick's emphasis on 'efficiency' and 'increasing the social product' means that his proviso invokes a narrow conception of human welfare. One that makes material prosperity *the* fundamental issue for determining whether someone's situation has been worsened by appropriation. This may lead one to reject the proviso on the grounds that there may be non-material reasons for objecting to appropriation and that such reasons are legitimate grounds for a grievance.

One might argue that Nozick's proviso could be modified to recognize a more expansive conception of human welfare, one that recognizes both our material and non-material well-being. But such a strategy would undermine the purpose of Nozick's principle of initial acquisition. Recall that Nozick wants to argue that it is rather easy, in principle, for people to acquire ownership rights over unowned goods. But if we stipulate that the proviso dictates that appropriation must not worsen others materially and non-materially, then the requirements for private appropriation become very stringent. So stringent that they would undermine Nozick's libertarian argument which is premised on the belief that individuals have an extensive natural right to private property. Consider once again Cohen's example of appropriating the beach. In this example it appears that appropriating the beach is justified if my doing so increases the recreational value of the beach to the extent that all would-be users would prefer to pay one dollar for a day at that beach to a free day at the beach as it was before. But this example only satisfies the proviso because everyone places the same value on the beach – namely, a recreational value. But what if the beach has spiritual value for some people. It may be a place where some come to find tranquillity and be at one with nature. Others may value the beach because of its occupational value. That is, it may be the only place where one can make a living fishing, an occupation that one holds dearly. These individuals can complain that they have been worsened by the appropriation of the beach. If we reject the narrow conception of human interests that Nozick assumes (that is, only material considerations matter) then it appears that appropriating land will be very difficult.

A second problem for Nozick's proviso concerns the baseline of comparison it invokes. When determining if my appropriation of object X worsens the situation of others Nozick's proviso requires us to compare how individuals fare in the situation of general use of object X with how they fare in the situation where I have appropriated object X. But why is the comparison only between these two possible scenarios? As Cohen points out, there are a number of different counterfactual situations that might have come into existence. Consider once again the beach example. Nozick only requires us to compare how individuals fare prior to my appropriation of the beach (that is, when it is unowned) with how they fare after I own it. If by appropriating the beach I increase its recreation value, assuming for the sake of argument that is the only relevant value, then I have not worsened the situation of others by appropriating it. But even if my appropriating the beach has improved the situation of all it might not be the *best possible* arrangement. If another individual, call him Bob, had appropriated the beach he would have increased its recreational value even more than I have. Being very efficient and creative, Bob would have created the best beach in the world. On top of that, he could run this better beach on a lower budget than mine and would thus only charge people 50 cents per day, half of my admission price. But according to Nozick's lax proviso everyone has to make do with my suboptimal beach simply because I appropriated the beach first. This is unsatisfactory. The motto 'first come, first served!' should not govern the distribution of goods that are so important to the life prospects of all. By stipulating that the baseline comparison holds exclusively between the situation where I appropriate the beach and no one owns the beach Nozick ignores other possible situations that could give rise to legitimate grievances.

Another relevant baseline that Nozick ignores is the situation of *common ownership*. Why should we assume, as Nozick does, that the world is initially unowned? John Exdell (1977) argues that we should assume instead that land and resources are communal property. If we started with the assumption that the world's resources are commonly owned then the requirements of Nozick's proviso would be much more stringent. My appropriation of the beach would only be justified if I did not worsen the situation of others in a position of common ownership. As noted above, people will have very different interests and will thus place diverse and even incompatible values on the beach. Some will value its recreational value and others its spiritual or occupational value. If all jointly owned the beach then collective decisions would determine how these diverse interests could be accommodated. Perhaps everyone would agree to divide the beach into different areas, with one end of the beach being designated a 'quiet' area, another section being designated for those who wish to fish and yet another area for those who simply wish to use the beach for other recreational purposes (such as swimming). In a situation of common ownership individuals have a say over how the resource is used. If private appropriation is to satisfy the requirement of not worsening the situation of others it would have to leave all at least as well off as they would be in a situation of common ownership. This more stringent interpretation of Nozick's proviso would make private appropriation of land and resources much more difficult.

2.5 The principle of rectification

So far we have examined the first two principles of Nozick's entitlement theory – the principle of transfer and the principle of just initial acquisition. These principles help us to determine when one is entitled to a good or holding. But of course people do not always abide by the requirements of these two principles. Human history is not one of just initial acquisition nor just transfers. It is a history of slavery, conquest, theft and fraud. To remedy such injustices the entitlement theory must invoke a principle of rectification. This principle is 'an essential part [of Nozick's entitlement theory]; for, without it, owing to the inductive nature of the definition of entitlement, if there has been a single injustice in the history of the state, no matter how far back, the state will not be able to achieve a just distribution of goods in the present' (Davis, 1982: 348). Given the actual history of human acquisition and transfers, it is surprising that Nozick's historical theory does not make the principle of rectification more central to *Anarchy, State and Utopia*. The topic 'rectification' appears only five times in the index and totals a meagre seven pages in a book that exceeds three hundred and fifty pages. Thus we are not given a great deal of information as to how the rectification principle could be applied to remedy past injustices. Let us consider what Nozick does tell us before we critically assess his account.

Nozick recognizes that the principle of rectification raises many complex questions for his entitlement theory of justice:

> If past injustice has shaped present holdings in various ways, some identifiable and some not, what now, if anything, ought to be done to rectify these injustices? What obligations do the performers of injustice have toward those whose position is worse than it would have been had the injustice not been done? Or, that it would have been had compensation been paid promptly? How, if at all, do things change if the beneficiaries and those made worse off are not the direct parties in an act of injustice, but, for example, their descendants? How far back must one go in wiping clean the historical slate of injustices? What may victims of injustice permissibly do in order to rectify the injustices being done to them, including the many injustices done by persons acting through their government? (Nozick, 1974: 152)

Given the tough questions raised by the issue of rectification one can perhaps understand why Nozick chooses to say very little about the issue. But if his theory cannot adequately resolve these complicated issues then that casts further doubt on the viability of his entitlement theory. Let us identify some of the distinct issues raised by the principle of rectification.

It is useful to begin by distinguishing between *intragenerational* rectification and *intergenerational* rectification. The former refers to compensation for victims who are alive to collect rectification awards while the latter encompasses all injustices and, in theory, ensures that the present distribution of entitlements be that which would have obtained had only the principles in acquisition and justice in transfer been observed throughout history (Litan, 1977: 234). The issue of intergenerational rectification is by far the more difficult issue and poses perhaps the biggest problem for Nozick's theory. Idealizing greatly, Nozick describes how a principle of rectification could be produced.

> This principle uses historical information about previous situations and injustice done in them (as defined by the first two principles of justice and rights against interference), and information about the actual course of events that flowed from these injustices, until the present, and it yields a description (or descriptions) of holdings in the society. The principle of rectification presumably will make use of its best estimate of subjunctive information about what would have occurred (or a probability distribution over what might have occurred, using the expected value) if the injustice had not taken place. If the actual description of holdings turns out not to be one of the descriptions yielded by the principle, then one of the descriptions yielded must be realized. (Nozick, 1974: 152–3)

In this passage we see that an ideal application of the principle of rectification requires a number of different sorts of information. Firstly, we need information about past injustices. We need to know who the victims and perpetrators of an unjust acquisition or transfer are and/or their descendants. Secondly, in order to determine what the appropriate compensation is we need to know the distribution of holdings *that would have* obtained had the injustice not taken place. Gregory Kavka (1982) calls the compensation requirement of Nozick's rectification principle the *No Net Harm Criterion*. This criterion maintains that victims of injustice are sufficiently compensated if they are no worse off (having received compensation) than they would have been had the injustice not taken place.

There are a number of issues which complicate the implementation of the rectification principle. Firstly, how far do we go back in time? One hundred years, three hundred years, a thousand years? The further we go back the less likely we are to have any information, let alone reliable information, concerning the victims and perpetrators of injustice. Secondly, the task of gathering the subjunctive information necessary to calculate the compensation due to a victim is extremely difficult if not impossible. How could we determine what the life prospects of the current ancestors of, for example, those once enslaved in America would be if slavery had never occurred?[4] This raises a third problem – how do we define what counts as being 'worse off' in this respect? Are we concerned only with material welfare or with other things? Suppose that the ancestors of aboriginal peoples in North American that were treated unjustly by European settlers are not worse off materially, but are in other ways, would they still have legitimate grounds for demanding rectification? Aboriginal peoples might argue that non-material aspects of their lives are worse than they would have been if the injustices committed by European settlers had not happened. They would have had more of a say over how the land was used and thus a better chance of preserving important aspects of their cultural identity that they value. Finally, we have a fourth problem of deciding who should pay to compensate victims of past injustices. Should the descendants of slave-owners compensate the descendants of slaves for the injustices committed against slaves? Should non-aboriginals pay for the injustices committed against aboriginals? Should the developed countries pay for the injustices committed against the developing countries? All of these and other important questions must be addressed if the principle of rectification is to be taken seriously.

Instead of tackling these complex issues Nozick suggests that the best way to resolve the issue of rectification might be to adopt one of the patterned principles of distributive justice which he earlier criticized.

> Perhaps it is best to view some patterned principles of distributive justice as rough rules of thumb meant to approximate the general results of applying the principle of rectification of injustice. For example, lacking much historical information, and assuming (1) that victims of injustice generally do worse than they otherwise would and (2) that those from the least well-off group in the society have the highest probabilities of being the (descendants of) victims of the most serious injustice who are owed compensation by those

who benefited from the injustices (assumed to be those better off, though sometimes the perpetrators will be others in the worst-off group), then a *rough* rule of thumb for rectifying injustices might seem to be the following: organize society so as to maximize the position of whatever group ends up least well-off in society. (Nozick, 1974: 231)

Given the importance the issue of rectification has on Nozick's entitlement theory one is bound to wonder why Nozick does not make this issue more central to *Anarchy, State and Utopia*. Nozick now adds a very important qualification to his argument for the minimal state. To his original declaration that 'taxation is on a moral par with forced labour' we must add: *if and only if no considerations of injustice could apply to justify such taxation.* The minimal state is only justified provided all past injustices have been rectified. What society can claim to have satisfied such a requirement? Once we extend the issue to a global context the issue of rectification becomes even more complicated. Which of the developed countries can truthfully say that they acquired their current level of prosperity from just transfers and just initial acquisitions?

If one is to develop Nozick's principle of rectification then some account of the obligations it imposes on citizens of an unjust society must also be provided. As we saw in the chapter on Rawls, he imposes on citizens a duty to bring about just institutions and a duty to oppose injustices. If rectification is to be taken seriously then similar duties must also be imposed on citizens by Nozick's entitlement theory. Nozick suggests that something like Rawls's difference principle would be necessary in the short run. If one is committed to Nozick's entitlement theory then the current generation, assuming the requirements of rectification have not been satisfied, should support redistributive policies that rectify past injustices. Nozick assumes that such policies will only be necessary in the 'short run', but given the extent of past injustices, at both the national and global levels, one could argue that it is unlikely that such injustices could be rectified quickly, and certainly not in one generation. So Nozick's argument cannot be utilized to undermine redistributive policies in a society that has not rectified past injustices. Nozick should have made the issue of rectification much more central to *Anarchy, State and Utopia* so that commentators would not misinterpret his critique of patterned principles as an objection, in principle, to any state that exceeded the minimal functions of 'protection against force, theft, fraud, enforcement of contracts and so on'. Indeed, one could actually utilize Nozick's argument to justify a number of egalitarian measures given the injustices that have taken place in human history.

2.6 Conclusion: self-ownership and private property

Let us conclude by returning to the issue of self-ownership and consider the implications it has for the right to private property. Recall the analogy Nozick would like to make between the eye lottery and taxation of earnings.

Both policies are unjust for they both violate the thesis of self-ownership. By taxing the earnings of an individual's income (assuming such taxation exceeded that needed to fund defence, the police and the administration of justice) the state violates an individual's right to use his or her powers as they wish. Wilt Chamberlain and the owners of his team are free to enter into whatever contract they wish. This right is entailed by the right to self-ownership. The same is true of the people with two healthy eyes. They have exclusive ownership rights over their body and thus the state cannot force individuals to give an eye to the blind without violating the demands of self-ownership.

The fact that most people react differently to the issues of taxing the rich and taking someone's eye suggests that Nozick employs the thesis of self-ownership in a way that glosses over a number of important issues. Namely, the distinction between owning one's body and owning external objects. Let us bring these more particular issues into focus by distinguishing between the following, increasingly more stringent, interpretations of self-ownership:

S1: Self-owners are the morally rightful owners of their own body and powers.
S2: Self-owners are the morally rightful owners of their own body and powers and have a right to have and hold their personal property.
S3: Self-owners are the morally rightful owners of their own body and powers and thus are imbued with rights of acquisition and bequest over not only their personal property but also over means of production and natural resources (such as factories, land, etc.).

Someone who is committed to either S1 or S2 could reject the eye lottery policy but support taxation of earnings. Nozick assumes that our commitment to moral side constraints is premised on S3 and thus we must reject both the eye lottery and the redistribution of income. But why must we accept S3? Rawls argues in favour of S2 and claims that the liberties it gives to individuals allows 'a sufficient material basis for a sense of personal independence and self-respect, both of which are essential for the development and exercise of the moral powers' (Rawls, 1993: 298). The same could not be said of the liberties entailed by S3. A right to ownership of the means of production and external resources are not *necessary* for a sense of personal independence and self-respect. In fact, Rawls believes that such rights would actually undermine the personal independence and self-respect of many people. This is why such an extensive right is not included in the first principle of justice. To do so would be to permit a minority to control the economy, and indirectly, political life as well (Rawls, 2001: 139). Rawls seeks to ensure that all citizens are put 'in a position to manage their own affairs on a footing of a suitable degree of social and economic equality' (Rawls, 2001: 139). The absolute property rights entailed in S3 would undermine this aspiration.

Rawls provides some grounds for endorsing something like S2 over S3, but what argument does Nozick provide us in favour of S3 over S2? Nozick clearly states in *Anarchy, State and Utopia* that he does not intend to give these rights a foundation:

> The completely accurate statement of the moral background, including the precise statement of the moral theory and its underlying basis, would require a full-scale presentation and is a task for another time. (A lifetime?) That task is so crucial, the gap left without its accomplishment so yawning, that it is only a minor comfort to note that we here are following the respectable tradition of Locke, who does not provide anything remotely resembling a satisfactory explanation of the status and basis of the law of nature in his *Second Treatise*. (Nozick, 1974: 9)

Nozick's failure to provide a basis for the absolute property rights entailed by his commitment to self-ownership has led some to describe his position as 'libertarianism without foundations' (Nagel, 1982). If there is no foundation for Nozick's theory then one can justifiably ask why they should accept it. Why favour a theory that accords so much weight to private property, especially when such a right will result in extensive socio-economic inequalities? Egalitarian liberals like Rawls endorse S2 because it takes seriously considerations of both liberty and equality. When Rawls claims that 'justice denies that the loss of freedom for some is made right by a greater good shared by others' he does not mean the freedom that is entailed in S3.

The concern for providing a clear and convincing foundation for a theory of justice is the primary concern of the next liberal theorist we examine – David Gauthier. Unlike Rawls and Nozick, who appeal to our moral sensibilities of fairness, impartiality and the importance of side constraints, Gauthier constructs a theory of justice that is founded on *non-moral* premises. We consider his contractarian argument in the next chapter.

SUMMARY

- Nozick defends the minimal state which limits the functions of the state to protection against force, theft, fraud, enforcement of contracts and so on. Like Rawls, Nozick believes that justice denies that the loss of freedom for some is made right by a greater good shared by others. However, Nozick believes that the redistributive policies of Rawls's second principle of justice violate this dictum.
- At the heart of Nozick's libertarianism is the thesis of self-ownership. Respect for persons as self-owners requires us to abandon the 'pie-cutting' mentality of justice theorists like Rawls and endorse instead *the entitlement theory of justice*. The entitlement theory maintains that whatever arises from a just situation by just steps is itself just. Nozick utilizes the Wilt Chamberlain example to illustrate the point that liberty upsets patterns.
- An important component of Nozick's entitlement theory of justice is the principle of rectification. Given that human history is one rife with unjust acquisitions and

transfers it is surprising that Nozick spends so little time on this part of his theory. Nozick does propose temporarily implementing a redistributive principle like Rawls's difference principle as a rough rule of thumb for rectifying injustices.

Notes

1   Libertarianism, like liberalism, is a varied political theory and there are many distinct versions of libertarianism. For another version of right-wing libertarianism see Jan Narveson's *The Libertarian Idea* (1988) and for left-wing versions of libertarianism see Hillel Steiner's *An Essay on Rights* (1994) and Michael Otsuka's *Libertarianism Without Inequality* (2003).
2   The only exceptions to this are taxes that are necessary in order to defend rights to person and property.
3   See Max Weber, 'Politics as a Vocation' (1970).
4   One issue which threatens to unravel the plausibility and appeal of the rectification principle is what is called the *existence problem*. The rectification principle requires us to consider how the ancestors of those who were treated unjustly would have fared if the past injustices did not occur. But in many cases the current generation would never have been born if these past injustices did not occur. For example, if African slaves were never brought to America then these individuals would have made very different life choices which would have resulted in them having different children than they actually had. Thus the current generation cannot complain that they would have been better off without slavery as they would not even exist! For a detailed discussion of this issue and the problems it poses for Nozick see Kavka (1982).

3 Gauthier and Justice as Mutual Advantage

Summary Contents

3.1	Introduction	53
3.2	Hobbes and the state of nature	54
3.3	Gauthier and the compliance problem	57
3.4	What is a rational bargain?	63
3.5	The limits of justice as mutual advantage	67

3.1 Introduction

In the first two chapters we examined two competing conceptions of justice – Rawls's theory of justice as fairness and Nozick's entitlement theory of justice. Despite how radically different their theories are, Rawls and Nozick both share some important common ground, namely the methodology they invoke when constructing and defending their theories. Both theories appeal to the moral sensibilities we have concerning what is just. By characterizing his original position as the 'appropriate initial status quo' Rawls appeals to our moral sensibilities of fairness, equality and impartiality. Nozick's entitlement theory of justice appeals to the weight we place on the thesis of self-ownership and the importance of moral side constraints.

This approach to political theory is rejected by those who opt for what Arthur Ripstein calls *foundationalism*.

> Foundationalist political theories attempt to justify political institutions without presupposing any political considerations. In a foundationalist theory, some set of considerations is held to support a particular form of political order, without itself depending on any substantive assumptions about the legitimacy of particular forms of human interaction. Hence the metaphor of a foundation, which holds up an edifice without itself being supported by anything else. (Ripstein, 1987: 115)

The main proponent of foundationalism is Thomas Hobbes (1588–1679). In *Leviathan* Hobbes attempts to justify an absolute sovereign by showing that it would be rational for people to agree to accept this arrangement. The last two decades have witnessed renewed interest in Hobbes's argument.[1] While rejecting, for obvious reasons, Hobbes's conclusion (that is, that an absolute sovereign is justified), contemporary authors have been inspired by the foundationalism of the Hobbesian project. This is most evident in the contractarian theory of David Gauthier, whose theory will be the central focus of this chapter. Like Rawls, Gauthier appeals to the idea of a social contract, as is evident in the title of his influential book *Morals by Agreement*. But unlike Rawls, Gauthier rejects the idea that a theory of justice can be justified by appealing to our moral *intuitions*. On the contrary, justice must be based on *non-moral premises*. To base justice on moral premises is simply to assume what one is trying to justify in the first place. The non-moral premises on which Gauthier founds his moral theory are the premises of rational choice. Gauthier argues that 'the rational principles for making choices, or decisions among possible actions, include some that constrain the actor pursuing his own interest in an impartial way. These we identify as moral principles' (Gauthier, 1986: 3).

We have already briefly encountered rational choice theory in Rawls's discussion of choice behind a veil of ignorance. The two principles of justice are, claims Rawls, the rational choice because they guarantee the highest minimum pay-off. But Rawls has, in his later writings, downplayed the role he places on rational choice theory. In his article 'Justice as Fairness: Political Not Metaphysical' Rawls argues that the reasonable is prior to the rational[2] and he claims that it was an error to describe a theory of justice as part of the theory of rational choice (Rawls, 1985: 237 footnote 20). But Gauthier wants to make exactly that argument. Moral duties, he claims, are rationally grounded (Gauthier, 1986: 2).

Gauthier's argument is a complex one and we could not possibly cover all of the main elements of his theory in this one chapter. In the next section we shall consider Hobbes's account of life in the state of nature and how the Prisoner's Dilemma has been invoked to illustrate the point that moral constraints can be rational. We then examine how Gauthier proposes to answer Hobbes's Foole who questions why we should accept moral constraints. This is what is known as the compliance problem. Thirdly, we consider the details of what constitutes a rational agreement. And finally in the last section of this chapter we consider some of the shortcomings of Gauthier's contractarianism; in particular its failure to provide an inclusive account of who counts as a member of the moral community.

3.2 Hobbes and the state of nature

In *Leviathan* Hobbes describes what life would be like in the absence of state power or any form of society at all. Such a scenario is described as the *state of nature*. Hobbes's vision of human life in this state of nature is very pessimistic, as is evident in the following famous passage from *Leviathan*:

In such condition, there is no place for Industry; because the fruit thereof is uncertain: and consequently no Culture on the Earth; no Navigation, nor use of the commodities that may be imported by the Sea; no commodious Building; no Instruments of moving, and removing such things as require much force; no Knowledge of the face of the Earth; no account of Time; no Arts; no Letters; no Society; and which is worst of all, continuall feare, and danger of violent death; And the life of man, solitary, nasty, brutish and short. (Hobbes, 1996: 89)

Commentators have put forward various accounts of what, according to Hobbes, causes human existence to be so bleak in the state of nature.[3] A central feature of what Jean Hampton (1986) calls *the rationality account of conflict* is that Hobbes held that the dominant passion in human beings is self-preservation. Our desire for self-preservation means that we must, continuously throughout the course of our lifetime, acquire goods to satisfy our needs. Once one adds to this the fact that goods are scarce and that people are roughly equal in physical and mental powers, and thus not capable of simply enslaving others so as to satisfy their own needs, we get a recipe for war. We have to compete with others for these scarce goods. This brings conflict:

And therefore if any two men desire the same thing, which nevertheless they cannot both enjoy, they become enemies; and in the way to their End, (which is principally their owne conservation, and sometimes their delectation only), endeavour to destroy, or subdue one an other. And from hence it comes to passe, that where an Invader hath no more to feare, than an other man's single power, if one plant, sow, build or possesse a convenient Seat, others may probably be expected to come prepared with forces united, to dispossesse, and deprive him, not only of the fruit of his labour, but also of his life, or liberty. And the Invader again is in the like danger of another. (Hobbes, 1996: 87)

This competition for goods gives rise to a second source of conflict – *diffidence*. Individuals in the state of nature do not trust one another. If you cannot trust others then the rational thing to do, if you want to survive, is make a preemptive strike. The best defence is a good offence. To make matters worse, Hobbes claims that our desire for glory gives rise to a third cause of conflict.

In this state of nature, where life is 'nasty, brutish and short', there is no right or wrong, no justice and injustice. Under such conditions Hobbes claims that individuals have a right to every thing, even to someone else's body (Hobbes, 1996: 91). Such a right is rational as you have no guarantee that others will not violate your person in order to satisfy their desire for self-preservation. The result of this state of war is that no one enjoys the benefits that come with social cooperation.

Contemporary commentators have described the dilemma people face in the Hobbesian state of nature as that which individuals face in what is called

	B	
A	**Not invade**	**Invade**
Not invade	(2,2)	(4,1)
Invade	(1,4)	(3,3)

FIGURE 3.1

the *Prisoner's Dilemma*.[4] In the Prisoner's Dilemma the rational course of action is to be non-cooperative yet such a strategy does not yield the optimal outcome. Imagine that you encounter another individual in this Hobbesian state of nature. Should you invade them or not? What is the rational course of action? Hampton describes the situation of the two individuals and their preferences in the payoff matrix (Figure 3.1) as follows:

> Each person has seized a number of goods, wants more, and hungrily eyes the goods seized by the other. Each has the choice of invading in order to seize the goods or refraining from doing so … Each person has a choice of performing one of two actions, and the numbers in the quadrants of the matrix correspond to their preference orderings (4 is lowest, 1 is highest) for the state of affairs represented by the quadrant. A's preference orderings are on the left; B's preference orderings are on the right. (Hampton, 1986: 62)

The most preferred option for each person is to decide to invade and have the other decide not to invade. This brings with it the biggest pay-off as you will get to exploit the other and reap the rewards that come with that. The worst situation is to be the person who gets exploited, that is, to decide not to invade when the other decides to invade. Each person reasons that the rational thing to do is to invade. This option gives you the chance of realizing the best scenario (if the other person defects) and it also guards against the worse possible scenario (you being exploited). The result then is mutual invasion and both end up in a situation that was their second lowest preference. But this outcome is not the optimal outcome. Both persons would have been better off if they both chose not to invade. The Prisoner's Dilemma illustrates how constraints on individual utility-maximizing choice could be rational. Those who find themselves in the Prisoner's Dilemma have a reason to be moral. This reason has nothing to do with moral intuitions. It simply appeals to the interests of the individuals concerned, whatever those interests may be.

Hobbes puts forward a number of laws of nature, or 'theorems', which direct individuals in the state of nature towards a peaceful existence. These include the following:

First law: That every man, ought to endeavour peace, as far as he has hope of obtaining it; and when he cannot obtain it, that he may seek, and use, all helps, and advantages of war.

Second law: That a man be willing, when others are so too, as far-forth, as for
   peace, and defence of himself he shall think it necessary, to lay down this
   right to all things; and be contented with so much liberty against other
   men, as he would allow other men against himself.
Third law: That men perform their covenants made.

The 'laws of nature are to be understood as hypothetical imperatives, with
a rider attached to each of them specifying the conditions under which doing
x is rational' (Hampton, 1986: 90). Given the situation of each individual in
the state of nature, it is not rational to accept the dictates of the laws of nature
if you do not have a guarantee that others will also comply with them. The
way to achieve this is to institute an absolute sovereign who will punish
those who break their covenants.

There are several aspects of Hobbes's argument for an absolute sovereign
that could be questioned. Even if one accepts Hobbes's pessimistic account
of what life would be like in the state of nature, contemporary critics would
claim that an absolute sovereign is unjustified as it is not *necessary* for securing self-preservation. Self-preservation could be secured by a number of
different institutional arrangements. So why settle for an absolute sovereign
if one could also secure, and better secure, self-preservation under a form of
limited government? This relates to a second objection to Hobbes – that his
account of human interests is too narrow. While it is true that we all have an
interest in self-preservation we also have interests which expand beyond
this. We have an interest in certain freedoms (for example, freedom of
religion, occupation, etc.) which could be threatened by instituting an
absolute sovereign. Thirdly, one could question how, given the pessimistic
account of life in the state of nature Hobbes describes, individuals could
come together to create a sovereign in the first place. If there is no sovereign
in place then individuals have no way of knowing for sure that others will
fulfil their end of the bargain when they agree to institute a sovereign. In
order to institute a form of government there must be a certain minimal level
of trust among people. Hobbesian individuals do not possess this minimal
level of trust and thus it seems that they are destined to remain in the state
of war forever.

3.3 Gauthier and the compliance problem

The most influential contemporary proponent of Hobbesian contractarianism is David Gauthier. Gauthier is not, for obvious reasons, attracted to the
conclusions of Hobbes's political philosophy, but he is attracted to Hobbes's
moral methodology. That is, to the aim of justifying moral constraints by
appealing to non-moral premises. Gauthier also endorses Hobbes's *rough
equality* clause. The just society is, for Gauthier, a cooperative venture for
mutual advantage. Those who lack the physical and/or mental powers to
make a contribution to the cooperative enterprise are excluded from the

moral realm. We shall, in Section 3.5, consider the implications of Gauthier's endorsement of Hobbes's rough equality clause.

We shall first examine Gauthier's argument for the rationality of complying with an agreement. We also need to look at what constitutes a rational agreement but let us assume for now that one has agreed to comply with an agreement that will benefit all of the contracting parties. Why should I comply with this agreement if I could personally benefit from breaking the agreement? This is what is called *the compliance problem*. The compliance problem is an important problem for foundationalist theories like Gauthier's because such theories are founded on non-moral premises. Hobbesian contractarianism cannot solve the compliance problem by simply asserting that 'breaking one's covenants is morally wrong' because Hobbesian contractarianism does not rely on moral intuitions. The only response open to Hobbesians is that complying with a rational agreement is in one's own self-interest.

This questioning of the rationality of complying with the demands of morality was first advanced by Glaucon in his challenge to Socrates in Plato's *Republic*. Glaucon argues that if one possessed a magic ring that would make the wearer invisible, even the just man would commit injustices.

> Now suppose there were two such magic rings, and one were given to the just man, the other to the unjust. No one, it is commonly believed, would have such iron strength of mind as to stand fast in doing right or keep his hands off other men's goods, when he could go to the market-place and fearlessly help himself to anything he wanted, enter houses and sleep with any woman he chose, set prisoners free and kill men at his pleasure, and in a word go about among men with the powers of a god. He would behave no better than the other; both would take the same course. (Plato, 1967: 45)

Glaucon's argument appears to be consistent with the methodological assumptions of Gauthier's contractarian project. If rationality consists in maximizing our expected utility, then the rational thing to do would be to break promises and agreements when we can expect that deception would bring us greater benefits than compliance. Hobbes considers this challenge when he addresses the objection raised by the Foole. 'The Foole hath sayd in his heart, there is no such thing as Justice' (Hobbes, 1996: 101). The Foole represents the egoist and challenges Hobbes's third law, that requiring compliance.

Hobbes's solution to the challenge raised by the Foole is the political solution of citing the disutilities that come with breaking your agreement when the sovereign exists. If you are truly rational you should consider the consequences of your actions should you get caught. The state will punish such actions and thus you have a reason, grounded in self-interest, for keeping your agreements. But this political solution is unsatisfactory. The Foole can simply reply that he has no reason to keep his agreement in cases where he thinks he will not be detected, or where the probability of being caught and punished is very small. In such cases the rational choice is to perform the action which will maximize one's expected utility.

Gauthier rejects the political solution which Hobbes proposes as a reply to the Foole in favour of a moral constraint. That is, a constraint that is internal, that operates in the decision making of the agent and is not forced upon her by an external force. In order for Hobbes to formulate an adequate response to the Foole he must break the direct connection between reason and benefit.

> Hobbes needs to say that it is rational to perform one's covenant even when performance is not directly to one's benefit, provided it is to one's benefit to be disposed to perform. But this he never says. And as long as the Foole is allowed to relate reason directly to benefit in performance, rather than to benefit in the disposition to perform, he can escape refutation. (Gauthier, 1986: 162)

Gauthier's solution to the Foole is to revise Hobbes's conception of rationality. This involves moving from the appraisal of one's choices to the appraisal of one's dispositions to choose. Gauthier introduces two possible dispositions rational parties could adopt – straightforward maximization (SM) and constrained maximization (CM). The Foole represents an SM, that is, a person 'who seeks to maximize her utility given the strategies of those with whom she interacts' (Gauthier, 1986: 167). An SM will be on the look-out for trustworthy people she can exploit. If she is able to benefit from breaking her agreement with such individuals she will. This is contrasted with the disposition of a constrained maximizer. A CM is 'a person who seeks in some situations to maximize her utility, given not the strategies but the utilities of those with whom she interacts' (Gauthier, 1986: 167).

Given the choice between opting for the disposition of the straightforward maximizer or the constrained maximizer, what is the rational choice to make? Which will bring you the most utility? The Foole claims that the rational choice is straightforward maximization. You should cooperate if – and only if – cooperating will maximize your expected utility. Should the opportunity arise where you could do better by breaking an agreement then the rational thing to do is break the agreement. But an important issue which the Foole fails to consider is that of how *detectable* our true disposition is. Consider, for example, the game of poker. Some people have a bad poker face. This means that the other players are able to tell whether that person has a good or bad poker hand. If you have a bad poker face you will not be able to win any money at poker. Every time you have a good hand the other players will be able to detect your joy and will fold before you get the chance to win their money. If you have a bad hand and try to bluff by betting a lot of money in the hopes that others will fold everyone else will see that you are sweating and know that you do not have good cards. People with bad poker faces should not play poker, at least not for money.

Gauthier thus raises the question of how good our poker faces are. He considers three different possibilities: that we are transparent, opaque and translucent. Transparency means that we have very bad poker faces. Everyone is able to tell the true disposition of everyone else. If we are transparent, then the choice of the disposition of SM would be irrational. Everyone would know that you are untrustworthy and they would not include you in their cooperative enterprises. Robbed of the opportunity to deceive and cooperate with others, an SM would fare very poorly.

The assumption of opacity is the opposite of transparency. If persons are opaque then they are like professional poker players. No one can tell what their true disposition is. If persons are opaque then the only solution to the problem of natural interaction would be something like the political solution Hobbes envisions. If you could never tell what someone's true disposition was then it would be irrational to trust others without the peace of mind that comes from knowing that defection will be punished by the state.

Between the extremes of transparency and opacity Gauthier claims that there is a more realistic assumption – translucency. To say that people are translucent means that they are 'neither transparent nor opaque, so that their dispositions to co-operate or not may be ascertained by others, not with certainty, but as more than mere guesswork' (Gauthier, 1986: 174). Gauthier accepts the assumption of translucency as the most realistic of the three and then argues that this fact must figure in our calculations when deciding whether to be an SM or CM.

Is it rational to adopt the disposition of an SM in a world full of translucent people? Gauthier claims it is not. Let us return to the Prisoner's Dilemma to illustrate how Gauthier develops his argument for CM. Instead of our individuals having a choice between the two strategies of cooperation or defection they must choose between the dispositions which yield different behaviour. That is, they must choose to be an SM or a CM. There are four possible pay-offs, which are, in hierarchical order:

Defection: 1
Cooperation: u'' (less than 1)
Non-cooperation: u' (less than u'')
Exploitation: 0 (less than u')

In order to calculate what the expected pay-offs will be for both SMs and CMs we must consider a number of relevant probabilities. Gauthier introduces the following three probabilities:

The probability that CMs will recognize each other (and thus cooperate): p
The probability that CMs will fail to recognize SMs but will themselves be recognized (so that defection and exploitation will result): q
The probability that a randomly selected person is a CM: r

With this information to hand, we can now calculate what the expected utilities for SMs and CMs will be. The average expected utility of an SM will be equal to one's expected benefits from non-cooperative interactions (u'), plus one's expected benefits from successful exploitation. The latter will depend on the probability of her interacting with a CM, r, and that she recognizes her but is not herself recognized as an SM, q. In this case an SM gains $(1 - u')$ over her non-cooperative expectation (u'). Gauthier thus presents the expected utililty of an SM as: $u' + [rq(1 - u')]$

A CM expects u' unless she can successfully cooperate with other CMs or she is exploited by an SM. The probability of cooperation is arrived at by multiplying the probability that she interacts with a CM, r, by the probability that they will recognize each other as CMs, p. In this case a CM will gain the difference between cooperation and non-cooperation over her non-cooperation expectation (that is, $u''-u'$). The utility increase a CM can expect from cooperation is thus represented as $[rp(u''-u')]$. The probability of her being exploited is arrived at by multiplying the probability that she interacts with an SM $(1-r)$ with the probability that she fails to recognize her but is herself recognized by him q, thus giving us $(1-r)q$. In the situation of exploitation a CM receives a pay-off of 0 and so loses her non-cooperative expectation (u'). Exploitation thus reduces a CM's utility expectation by a value of $[(1-r)qu']$. Bringing the various possibilities for a CM together, Gauthier produces the following formulation of their expected utility: $\{u' + [rp(u''-u')]-(1-r)qu'\}$

A determination of who can expect the highest pay-off, an SM or a CM, will depend on the probabilities that Gauthier introduces. Gauthier argues that these probabilities tip things in favour of CMs as persons improve their ability to detect the dispositions of those with whom they interact.

> Both CMs and SMs must expect to benefit from increasing their ability to detect the dispositions of others. But if both endeavor to maximize their abilities (or the expected utility, net of costs, of so doing), then CMs may expect to improve their position in relation to SMs. For the benefits gained by SMs, by being better able to detect potential victims, must be on the whole offset by the losses they suffer as the CMs become better able to detect them as potential exploiters … .Those who believe rationality and morality to be at loggerheads may have failed to recognize the importance of cultivating their ability to distinguish sincere co-operators from insincere ones. (Gauthier, 1986: 181)

There are a number of different objections which have been raised against this aspect of Gauthier's argument. Firstly, we could challenge his claim that people are translucent. Gauthier simply assumes this without offering any argument for it. Geoffrey Sayre-McCord (1989) claims that people are often 'trans-opaque'. That is, they deliberately send people misleading signals to the effect that they are trustworthy even though they are not. Many people, argues Sayre-McCord, 'develop winning smiles, travel with a glowing reputation, and cultivate an honest manner' (Sayre-McCord, 1989: 118). These people seem to be very successful at deceiving others. He gives the example of a car salesperson. 'They suffer a horrendous general reputation but still manage to convince almost every customer that, this time, the customer is getting honest treatment and a fair deal on that rare used car too good to pass up' (Sayre-McCord, 1989: 121, note 19). Without providing evidence to back up his assumption of translucency, Gauthier's solution to the compliance problem is unconvincing.

Critics have also questioned the empirical plausibility of Gauthier's assumption that we are capable of developing the dispositions of SMs and CMs. The decision to be a CM, for example, means that one will bind oneself in all future endeavours. We must ask whether this notion of being able to bind oneself is psychologically possible.

> Internalizing the disposition to cooperate entails binding oneself to comply strongly enough to overcome the inclination to straightforwardly maximize. In the absence of rope, mast, and sturdy sailors at one's command, the bonds must originate in one's own psyche. We must work ourselves into a state in which we *automatically* exclude the option of noncompliance when the particular circumstances would make noncompliance the utility-maximizing choice. (Nelson, 1988: 157)

We all make promises to ourselves which we wish to honour at a future time but fail to when temptation proves too strong. If it were possible for us to bind ourselves to the disposition to cooperate would we not also bind ourselves to dispositions that ensure we would always eat a healthy diet and exercise on a regular basis? We all make New Year's Resolutions which we fail to keep. This suggests that Gauthier's introduction of SM and CM is empirically suspect and this further weakens his solution to the compliance problem.

Even if it were possible for us to adopt dispositions in the way Gauthier presupposes, we could also question whether the disposition of a CM is truly the most rational disposition. If we are interested in maximizing our utility then the rational thing to do would be to feign the disposition of a CM or to develop a disposition to cooperate but also to form along with it an ability to inhibit the exercise of the disposition in those circumstances in which inhibiting it would be to one's advantage (Buchanan, 1990: 240).

The compliance problem is a problem for foundationalists like Gauthier because he seeks to reduce morality to a motive (self-interest) which we commonly think of as contrary to, or in conflict with, morality. His theory must be able to persuade the egoist, like Hobbes's Foole, that it is prudent to accept moral constraints. If it cannot, then it appears that the cooperative enterprise itself is in jeopardy unless one appeals to something like Hobbes's political solution.

Consider the following questions:

- How viable is Gauthier's argument for constrained maximization?
- Consider the issue of how detectable our true dispositions are. Do you think Gauthier's assumption of translucency is a reasonable one?
- Do you agree with Glaucon when he claims that even the just man would be unjust if he had a ring that made him invisible?

Further reading

Geoffrey Sayre-McCord, 'Deceptions and Reasons to be Moral', *American Philosophical Quarterly*, 26, 1989: 113–22.

David Copp, 'Contractarianism and Moral Scepticism', in Peter Vallentyne (ed.), *Contractarianism and Rational Choice* (Cambridge: Cambridge University Press, 1991).

Holly Smith, 'Deriving Morality from Rationality', in Peter Vallentyne (ed.), *Contractarianism and Rational Choice* (Cambridge: Cambridge University Press, 1991).

3.4 What is a rational bargain?

In the previous section we considered Gauthier's answer to the compliance problem but we still have to consider what he thinks constitutes a rational agreement. Only by considering this can we see what justice as mutual advantage amounts to. Gauthier's treatment of what constitutes a rational agreement consists of two steps and we will consider and assess these in turn. The first step is to establish an *initial bargaining position*. The second step is to choose, on the basis of the initial bargaining position, a set of options that it is rational to accept. Let us consider first the initial bargaining position.

The initial bargaining position represents what each individual brings to the bargaining table. If cooperation is to be mutually advantageous then it must improve the prospects of all as compared to how they would fare if they opted for non-cooperation. There are many possible interpretations of the initial bargaining position. Hobbes, for example, interprets the initial bargaining position as the non-cooperative outcome of war-against-all. But Gauthier rejects this interpretation. He formulates a different interpretation by beginning with a brief tale about a society of masters and slaves. In this society the masters rule over the slaves through the effective use of power (for example, threat of whips and chains, etc.). After reflecting on how costly it is to maintain the obedience of the slaves one of the young masters, who had recently returned from university where he studied rational choice theory, makes a bold suggestion as to how all members of the society (masters and slaves) could improve their situations. If a bargain were struck between the slaves and masters, one in which they all stood to benefit, then surely, as rational agents, such a deal would be viable. So the young master writes up the terms of such a bargain, called the Bargain of Mutual Benefit. Under this agreement the masters will free the slaves and dismantle their coercive apparatus. In return for their freedom the slaves will voluntarily be the masters' servants. All stand to benefit from such an arrangement. The masters will save money by doing away with coercion and the servants will receive wages that are better than the living allowance they are given as slaves.

The young master manages to persuade the majority of masters that such a deal is viable and they agree to dismantle the institutions of slavery and enshrine the Bargain of Mutual Benefit in their constitution. So, do the ex-slaves agree to fulfil their end of the bargain once the institutions of slavery are dismantled? No. It is not rational to become willing slaves. The slaves agreed to comply with the initial agreement because it did seem rational at the time. But once the institutions of slavery were dismantled the slaves realized that they had no reason to voluntarily comply with an arrangement that was premised on a coercive initial bargaining position. It is only rational, argues Gauthier, to act cooperatively if the initial bargaining position is non-coercive.

All effects of taking advantage must be removed from the initial bargaining position, claims Gauthier, before it is rational for utility-maximizers to accept a bargain. But what kind of behaviour constitutes 'taking advantage' of another and must be removed from the initial bargaining position? To answer this question Gauthier introduces what he calls the *Lockean proviso*. We have already encountered this proviso in Chapter 2 when we examined Robert Nozick's libertarian argument. The Lockean proviso moralizes the Hobbesian state of nature. The Hobbesian non-agreement point is the situation of war-against-all, where everyone has a right to everything. But individuals in the Lockean state of nature respect each other's rights and do not better their situation through interaction that worsens the situation of another. The Lockean proviso thus rules out the kind of predatory behaviour which the masters were engaged in. Gauthier's initial bargaining position is thus the hypothetical result of how individuals would fare in the situation of non-cooperation constrained by the Lockean proviso. That is, how everyone would fare if they were given exclusive right to the use of their body and its powers and did not worsen the situation of others.

It is important to note that Gauthier does not think the proviso says anything about equalizing. As he says: 'the rich man may feast on caviar and champagne, while the poor woman starves at his gate. And she may not even take the crumbs from his table, if that would deprive him of his pleasure in feeding them to his birds' (Gauthier, 1986: 218). Gauthier illustrates why this is the case with his example of the sixteen Robinson Crusoes. He imagines a scenario where sixteen Robinson Crusoes each live on a different island. The sixteen Crusoes and sixteen islands are all different in terms of their characteristics and circumstances. 'There is a clever, strong, energetic Crusoe living very comfortably on a well-supplied island. There is a stupid, weak, lazy Crusoe barely surviving on an ill-supplied island. In between are fourteen other Crusoes' (Gauthier, 1986: 218).

Gauthier also imagines that each Crusoe is equipped with a two-way radio so they can communicate with each other and each knows the others' situation. And each is also able to build a small raft, big enough to carry pro-visions, that could be carried by the current from one island to another (but only in a single direction so trade is not possible). The important question that arises is this. If it is possible for the strong, energetic Crusoe on the well-supplied island to send provisions on a raft to the stupid, weak, lazy Crusoe on the ill-supplied island, is he under any obligation to do so? Gauthier's answer to this question is No. 'Any principle other than the one allowing each Crusoe to benefit himself would be unfair and partial, in requiring some to give free rides to others, or to be hosts for their parasitism' (Gauthier, 1986: 219).

Suppose the situation changes. Larger rafts can be made and migration (in the direction of the currents) is possible. Now the Crusoes can migrate and each may use the resources of any island on which he lands. In this situation the proviso requires that one compensate (fully) any other Crusoe if he takes the fruits of the other's labour. But the proviso does not require the talented Crusoes to migrate to islands where they can help less able Crusoes. Such a requirement would be unfair as it would require giving free rides.

It should now be clear what the role of the Lockean proviso is in Gauthier's theory. It provides an impartial standard from which each bar-gainer's initial position can be assessed. The proviso removes the effects of taking advantage from the initial position. Rights, argues Gauthier, 'provide the starting point for, and not the outcome of, agreement. They are what each person brings to the bargaining table, not what she takes from it' (Gauthier, 1986: 222).

Gauthier's introduction and application of the Lockean proviso is likely to raise some eyebrows and so it should. So far Gauthier has argued that moral-ity can be reduced to the principles of rational choice and that moral intui-tions have no legitimate foundational role to play. That is what makes his project neo-Hobbesian. But Gauthier's commitment to the Lockean proviso seems to contradict these claims and threatens his foundationalism. Why should the initial bargaining position be the moralized Lockean state of nature instead of the Hobbesian position of war-against-all? Other mutual advantage theorists adopt the coercive non-agreement point[5] and it seems that such a position is more consistent with Gauthier's aspiration to develop a theory which appeals not to our moral sensibilities but to the concern for utility-maximization. Peter Danielson (1988) argues that rational agents would treat property rights not as something already built into their initial bargaining positions, but as something which would have to be settled by the bargain. Gauthier's invocation of the Lockean proviso makes his con-tractarian theory more appealing as it allows room for recognizing the importance of individual rights. But by doing this Gauthier has introduced moral premises into his argument and thus compromised his foundationalism.

The second stage of Gauthier's bargaining solution is for the rational agents to examine all possible outcomes of the bargain and agree on how the benefits of cooperation are to be divided. The most anyone could claim from a joint venture would be all of the product minus the value of what the other contributors have made. In order for a cooperative enterprise to be mutually advantageous all parties must receive at least the value of what they contribute. Once the costs of everyone's contributions have been covered the remaining product constitutes the *cooperative surplus*. This is what the rational agents must agree to divide. How should they divide it? Of course all rational parties will make the maximum claim (that is, all of the cooperative surplus) and it would not be possible to satisfy these demands as they would total more than what has been produced. An egalitarian might claim that the cooperative surplus should be divided evenly but remember that Gauthier rejects any such appeal to moral intuitions. The division of the cooperative surplus must be rational. Such a division is rational, argues Gauthier, when, in the case where just two parties are involved, people make *equal relative concessions*. When more than two parties are involved equality of relative concessions may not be possible and thus Gauthier argues that the rational division is the outcome where 'the greatest or *maximimum* relative concession it requires, is as small as possible, or a *minimum*, that is, is no greater than the maximum relative concession required by every other outcome' (Gauthier, 1986: 137).

This is the principle of *minimax relative concession* (MRC). The just person, argues Gauthier, 'is disposed to comply with the principle of minimax relative concession in interacting with those of his fellows whom he believes to be similarly disposed' (Gauthier, 1986: 157). Gauthier provides the following formula for calculating relative concessions:

> The *relative magnitude* of any concession may be expressed as the proportion its absolute magnitude bears to the absolute magnitude of a complete concession. If the initial bargaining position affords some person a utility u^*, and he claims an outcome affording him a utility $u\#$, then if he concedes an outcome affording him a utility u, the absolute magnitude of his concession is $(u\# - u)$, of complete concession $(u\# - u^*)$, and so the relative magnitude of his concession is $[(u\# - u)/(u\# - u^*)]$. (Gauthier, 1986: 136)

Gauthier's derivation of MRC is complex and thus it is difficult to see exactly why MRC is the rational principle to invoke. He provides a number of two-person examples to explain and justify MRC.[6] But even if one agrees with Gauthier that MRC is the rational division in the examples he uses,[7] political theorists will want to know what the political upshot of MRC is. Gauthier does not adequately develop this aspect of his argument. MRC might sound like a plausible principle when applied to simple two-person cooperative ventures, but how could this principle be applied to large cooperative enterprises like modern societies which exist in an era of rapid globalization where millions of people contribute to the cooperative surplus and it is not possible to know what someone's contribution is? Gauthier does believe that, in most cases, the market is the appropriate distributive tool in society.[8] But I think one is justified in remaining puzzled as to how anyone could determine what socio-economic arrangements MRC requires. David Braybrooke is correct when he claims that attempts to place Gauthier's theory in the real world of politics will fail because the theory deprives itself of any possibility of effective application. 'Its demands for information are fantastic – too fantastic ever to be met or even to allow the theory to be used as a guide to improvements within the reach of present social policy' (Braybrooke, 1987: 751).

In Chapter VIII of *Morals by Agreement* Gauthier attempts to strengthen his arguments for the Lockean proviso and MRC by claiming that they express not only the concerns of the rational agent but also those of an ideal impartial actor. Gauthier invokes the ideal of an Archimedean point, an ideal that Rawls also utilizes in his construction of the original position. 'In moral theory, the Archimedean point is that position one must occupy, if one's own decisions are to possess the moral force needed to govern the moral realm' (Gauthier, 1986: 233). But Gauthier does not think the impartial choice would be Rawls's difference principle. On the contrary, 'Archimedean choice must select individual expected utility-maximization, constrained by the proviso and minimax relative concession' (Gauthier, 1986: 235). Those things that would emerge in rational bargaining are the same things that would be chosen by an ideal impartial actor. Morality and rationality, argues Gauthier, are in harmony. But of course Gauthier's conception of morality is different from what most people would associate that term with. In the next section we shall assess some of the counterintuitive consequences of justice as mutual advantage.

3.5 The limits of justice as mutual advantage

Our analysis of Gauthier's contractarian theory has raised a number of internal objections or concerns relating to the viability of justice as mutual advantage. For example, how it can resolve the compliance problem and how it can incorporate the moral constraints of the Lockean proviso and yet remain faithful to its claim of providing a foundation that is independent of moral premises. But the most common objections raised against justice as mutual advantage are not these nor other internal objections, but *external* objections. That is, objections that can be raised even if one assumes that Gauthier's arguments for constrained maximization, the Lockean proviso and MRC, are valid. Critics who develop this line of argument will point to the counterintuitive consequences of justice as mutual advantage and argue that these are more than sufficient grounds for rejecting it as a viable account of social justice. These concerns can be brought to the fore by considering the implications of the rough equality clause which Gauthier endorses. Justice, for Gauthier, only arises among parties who are roughly equal in physical and mental capacities.

> Only beings whose physical and mental capacities are either roughly equal or mutually complementary can expect to find co-operation beneficial to all. Humans benefit from their interaction with horses, but they do not co-operate with horses and may not benefit them. Among unequals, one party may benefit most by coercing the other, and on our theory would have no reason to refrain. We may condemn all coercive relationships, but only within the context of mutual benefit can our condemnation appeal to a rationally grounded morality. (Gauthier, 1986: 17)

Gauthier's version of contractarianism raises important questions about the scope of justice. If justice only applies to those who are roughly equal in physical and mental powers, then what about people who do not satisfy this condition (for example, the young, old, infirm and unborn) or animals? Critics of Gauthier's contractarianism point to these cases as the most effective way of illustrating the shortcomings of justice as mutual advantage.

Allen Buchanan argues that Gauthier's type of project, which Buchanan calls 'justice as self-interested reciprocity' (Buchanan, 1990: 229), gives rise to what he calls *the reciprocity thesis*. The reciprocity thesis states that only those who do (or at least can) make a contribution to the cooperative surplus have rights to social resources (Buchanan, 1990: 230). One might find that the reciprocity thesis does cohere with some of our intuitions about what is fair. For example, that free-riders who *choose* not to contribute should not expect to receive something back from society. But the reciprocity thesis rules out entitlements for *all* free-riders, those that have chosen to free-ride and those who, for reasons beyond their control, must free-ride if they are to survive or live meaningful lives. This second category of free-riders would include people who are born with handicaps so severe that they would never be able to contribute. These individuals would not, according to justice as mutual advantage, be entitled to provisions such as publicly funded health care services for such a policy would violate the reciprocity thesis by permitting these individuals to free-ride off those who contribute and pay the taxes for such programmes. As Buchanan points out, the implications of Gauthier's theory might be even more radical than denying non-contributors rights of distributive justice:

> If justice as reciprocity is extended to all rights, not just rights of distributive justice, it is even more radical and, one is tempted to say, even more inhumane. If, as Gauthier believes, all moral rights, including the so-called negative rights to refrain from injuring and killing, are rationally ascribable only to potential contributors to social wealth, then we violate no rights if we choose to use noncontributors in experiments on the nature of pain or for military research on the performance of various designs of bullets when

they strike human tissue, slaughter them for food, or bronze them to make lifelike statues. (Buchanan, 1990: 232)

Buchanan argues that justice as mutual advantage fails to recognize 'that questions of justice arise not only with respect to relations among contributors but also at the deeper level of what sort of cooperative institutions we ought to have, insofar as the character of these institutions will determine in part who can contribute' (Buchanan, 1990: 238). Buchanan's point can be illustrated by reflecting on how our own society has evolved over time and with it who counts as a contributor. Many people who have physical or mental handicaps can contribute in our present society due to changes in, for example, technology. Consider the case of Stephen Hawking, the eminent physicist. No one would dispute the fact that he has made a very important contribution to our society. But two hundred years ago someone with Lou Gehrig's disease would not have had the opportunity to make such a contribution. Changes in technology bring changes in who counts as a contributor. Something as basic as making buildings more accessible (wheelchair accessible, for example) influences the capacity with which some will be able to contribute.

Even the basic skills necessary for qualifying as a contributor have changed over the course of the past century. One's level of physical strength was more of an asset in an agrarian society, but in the complex information age of the modern world an ever increasing number of occupations require skills such as reading, writing and computer literacy. Given the fact that the capacity to be a contributor is socially determined, Buchanan argues that Gauthier's version of contractarianism is incomplete and thus defective because it does not consider the question of whether the scheme of cooperation unjustly excludes some persons from participating.

Gauthier's invocation of the rough equality clause also raises concerns about the status of children, the elderly, future generations and animals. Justice as mutual advantage only extends membership in the moral community to those with whom it is beneficial to cooperate. Gauthier does argue that moral relationships can be extended to include the young, old and future generations. The young represent future contributors and the old past contributors. Concern for future generations can also be accommodated, argues Gauthier, by viewing society 'as a bargain in which the terms remain constant over time, so that each generation offers its successor the same agreement that it accepted from its predecessor' (Gauthier, 1986: 305). But questions can be raised concerning how persuasive this aspect of Gauthier's argument is. Why should utility-maximizers be concerned with the old as they can no longer expect to benefit from them nor will they ever benefit from future generations that will be born long after they have died.

While many contractarians agree with Gauthier that animals are excluded from the moral community, critics charge that such a conclusion discriminates on the basis of species. Advocates of the animal rights movement claim that all animals, humans and non-humans, are equal. Justice as mutual advantage, they argue, is premised on the unsubstantiated assumption that not only do human interests matter more than the interests of non-human animals, but that the interests of the latter do not matter at all. Many people believe that acts of cruelty towards animals are unjust and the fact that justice as mutual advantage remains silent about such heinous acts is further evidence of its shortcomings as a viable account of morality.

Proponents of justice as mutual advantage will not be moved by many of the objections we have just raised. Claims about the rights of the disabled or animals are premised on moral intuitions and thus cannot be backed up by non-moral premises. The mutual advantage theorist rejects the methodological assumptions of striving for a reflective equilibrium. It is counterproductive, they argue, to construct a theory which coheres to our moral sensibilities as it is an open question as to whether or not these sensibilities are themselves justified. In order to be justified they must, argues Gauthier, reflect what rational individuals would agree to in a mutually advantageous bargain. The debate between those contractarians partial to Rawls's approach and those partial to Gauthier's is thus a difficult one to assess as the proponents disagree on the criteria by which a theory should be assessed. Those who defend the appeal to our moral sensibilities claim that Gauthier's theory is so counterintuitive that it should not even be called a theory of justice. Those who are attracted to Gauthier's project will claim that such an objection is merely question-begging. It presupposes that one already knows what is moral or just.

But even if we put this methodological dispute to the side, there are pressing concerns that can be raised against Gauthier's theory by those who share his commitment to foundationalism. Gauthier's arguments for constrained maximization, the Lockean proviso and minimax relative concession are so ambitious that it is not surprising that critics have remained unconvinced about their viability. To substantiate the claim that it is rational to abide by moral constraints is a much debated topic in moral philosophy and could be a book in itself. To tackle that issue as well as specify what the content of a rational bargain would be is truly ambitious and perhaps part of the allure many find in *Morals by Agreement*.

Discuss the following statements:

1   Animals, like human beings, can feel pain and pleasure. Therefore any plausible moral theory must take their interests into account. But Gauthier's theory does not do so because he reduces justice to rational self-interest. Gauthier's account of morality is unfairly biased in favour of human beings.

2   The social structure of our society may impede the ability of some to contribute. So if we believe that it is important that people 'contribute' to society surely it is equally important that society take reasonable measures to ensure that the widest possible range of potential contributors have the

opportunity to fulfil this obligation. We also need to take seriously the question of what constitutes 'contributing' to society.

3 Those who criticize Gauthier's theory for failing to take seriously the concerns of the infirm, animals or future generations, etc. are relying on 'moral intuitions' that cannot be defended. Thus these objections are not pressing. Gauthier's project requires us to radically reform our conception of morality, so simply appealing to unsubstantiated intuitions is counterproductive for it is exactly those intuitions that Gauthier's methodology rules out.

SUMMARY

- Gauthier rejects the appeal to moral intuitions and argues that moral duties are rationally grounded. By doing so, Gauthier's theory must tackle the compliance problem because he cannot assume that people will fulfil their agreements simply because it is moral to do so. Central to Gauthier's resolution of the compliance problem is his assumption that our true dispositions are translucent, hence rational persons would be constrained maximizers.

- In order to determine what the content of a rational agreement is one must first establish an initial bargaining position (the Lockean proviso) and then a set of feasible options that it is rational to choose. The latter is determined by the principle of minimax relative concession. The political upshot of Gauthier's argument is difficult to ascertain but he does embrace (with a few qualifications) the free market. He rejects Rawls's egalitarian liberalism on the grounds that, by treating talents as a common asset, Rawls's theory demands the giving of free rides.

- Critics point to the counterintuitive consequences of Gauthier's theory to reveal how deficient an account of justice it is. The implications of the theory for the treatment of the disabled, the unborn and animals have led many to conclude that Gauthier's theory should not even be described as a theory of justice.

Notes

1 See, for example, David Gauthier (1986), Jean Hampton (1986), Gregory Kavka (1986) and Quentin Skinner (1996).
2 For a discussion of the reasonable and the rational see Rawls (1993), pp. 48–54.
3 Hampton (1986) distinguishes between the following three accounts: the rationality account of conflict, the passions account and the shortsightedness account. See her discussion of these distinct accounts in Chapters 2 and 3 of *Hobbes and the Social Contract*.
4 For a discussion of how this story relates to a prisoner (hence its being called the 'Prisoner's Dilemma') see Gauthier (1986), pp. 79–80.
5 See James Buchanan (1975).
6 See *Morals By Agreement*, pp. 137–41.
7 For challenges to this see Russell Hardin (1988) and Jean Hampton (1988).
8 Gauthier does have reservations about relying on the market in the real world. See, for example, his discussion of taxing inheritance in Chapter IX of *Morals by Agreement*.

4   Dworkin on Equality

Summary Contents

4.1 Introduction   73
4.2 Dworkin on equality of resources   75
4.3 Welfare reform and the basic income proposal   80
4.4 Political equality and democracy   85
4.5 Against luck egalitarianism   89

4.1 Introduction

Our discussion of the various versions of contemporary liberal theory should make it apparent that liberty is one of the core values that liberals cherish. Rawls and Nozick, for example, reject utilitarianism because they believe that a public philosophy that permits the loss of freedom for some in the interests of the greater overall good is a deficient theory. Despite Gauthier's attempt to construct a contractarian theory that is devoid of moral premises even he appeals to the value of liberty when he invokes the Lockean proviso. But what about the value of equality? Is this not also a fundamental value for liberals? Much depends on which version of liberalism one is talking about as well as what one means by equality. Nozick, for example, believes that liberty and equality are incompatible values if by equality one means that some patterned distributive principle should be established and maintained. Gauthier rejects any appeal to the notion of *moral equality* hence he does not find the consequences of the reciprocity thesis problematic. But Rawls's egalitarian liberalism has inspired contemporary liberals to take more seriously the project of reconciling the values of liberty and equality. In this chapter we shall consider one of the main theorists who has made equality more central to liberalism – Ronald Dworkin. Liberty, argues Dworkin, is an aspect of equality rather than an independent political ideal potentially in conflict with it. Dworkin's argument for equality of resources has sparked much debate among liberals and egalitarians and considering this theory will prove useful in helping to see how egalitarian liberals have developed their position beyond Rawls's theory as well as illustrate the different practical issues egalitarian liberalism can be applied to.

To set the stage for Dworkin's argument it is worth recalling two of the main concerns expressed in the first chapter with respect to the way Rawls defined the least advantaged. Firstly, Rawls stipulates that he constructs a theory of justice for the simpler case of a society of 'normal, fully cooperating members'. But this tactic makes Rawls's theory less attractive to those who believe that inequalities in the natural lottery of life should be a central concern for a theory of justice. By excluding the severely handicapped from the category of the least advantaged Rawls's theory does not take seriously the egalitarian intuition that inequalities in our natural endowments should be compensated. Secondly, critics have argued that Rawls includes many of the undeserving poor in the category of 'least advantaged' and the idea of maximising the prospects of those who choose to be non-productive does not cohere with our moral sensibilities. There is a difference between someone who is less advantaged as a result of circumstances beyond their control (for example, being born with a severe handicap) and someone who is less advantaged as a result of their own choice (for example, choosing to live off welfare payments instead of working). A concern for these two issues has given rise to the position Elizabeth Anderson (1999) calls 'luck egalitarianism'.[1] Luck egalitarians construct their theories around what is called the choice/chance (or choice/circumstances) distinction. 'People's fates are determined by their choices and their circumstances' (Dworkin, 2000: 322) and this must remain, argue luck egalitarians, a fundamental insight when considering what constitutes a just distribution. Luck egalitarians disagree on exactly what should be equalized (for example, resources, opportunity for welfare, etc.) but they believe that inequalities in the advantages that people enjoy are just if they derive from the choices people have voluntarily made, but that inequalities deriving from unchosen features of people's circumstances are unjust.

Ronald Dworkin is one of the main advocates of luck egalitarianism and his theory will be the focus of this chapter. Dworkin begins *Sovereign Virtue* by declaring:

> No government is legitimate that does not show equal concern for the fate of all those citizens over whom it claims dominion and from whom it claims allegiance. Equal concern is the sovereign virtue of political community – without it government is only tyranny – and when a nation's wealth is very unequally distributed, as the wealth of even very prosperous nations now is, then its equal concern is suspect. For the distribution of wealth is the product of a legal order: a citizen's wealth massively depends on which laws his community has enacted – not only its laws governing ownership, theft, contract, and tort, but its welfare law, tax law, labor law, civil rights law, environmental regulation law, and laws of practically everything else. (Dworkin, 2000: 1)

Like Rawls, Dworkin believes that the basic structure of society should be publicly justified to all citizens. But unlike Rawls, Dworkin does not believe that this can be accomplished by emphasizing a version of 'political liberalism' that does not invoke ethical assumptions and controversies about the good life. On the contrary, Dworkin appeals to a diverse array of general ethical values. His version of 'comprehensive liberalism' rests on two fundamental principles of ethical individualism – the principle of equal importance and the principle of special responsibility. These principles maintain the following:

Principle of Equal Importance: It is important, from an objective point of view, that human lives be successful rather than wasted, and this is equally important, from an objective point of view, for each human life.

Principle of Special Responsibility: though we must all recognize the equal objective importance of the success of a human life, one person has a special and final responsibility for that success – the person whose life it is. (Dworkin, 2000: 5)

These two principles make different demands on government. The principle of equal importance requires 'government to adopt laws and policies that ensure that its citizens' fates are, so far as government can achieve this, insensitive to who they otherwise are – their economic background, gender, race, or particular set of skills and handicaps' (Dworkin, 2000: 6). The principle of special responsibility 'demands that the government work, again as far as it can achieve this, to make their fates sensitive to the choices they have made' (Dworkin, 2000: 6). Over the course of *Sovereign Virtue* Dworkin elaborates on what the content of these twin demands is by considering a number of theoretical issues and political controversies. In the next section we shall consider some of the theoretical issues by focusing on Dworkin's argument for equality of resources.

4.2 Dworkin on equality of resources

When someone declares themselves to be an 'egalitarian' we commonly assume that they hold particular beliefs concerning what might be called *distributional equality*. They might, for example, believe that everyone should have equal incomes or be equally happy. Distributional equality concerns the index of goods an egalitarian believes should be equally distributed. Dworkin's main concern is with distributional equality and he considers two general theories – equality of welfare and equality of resources. Formulated as theories that treat people as equals they state the following:

Equality of Welfare: A distributional scheme treats people as equals when it distributes or transfers resources among them until no further transfer would leave them more equal in welfare.

Equality of Resources: A distributional scheme treats people as equals when it distributes or transfers so that no further transfer would leave their shares of the total resources more equal. (Dworkin, 2000: 12)

Utilitarianism is the main tradition that adopts a welfarist metric when assessing the merits of actions and policies/laws and its proponents include Jeremy Bentham (1748–1832) and John Stuart Mill (1806–1873). Utilitarians defend the 'greatest happiness principle' which holds that actions are right in proportion as they tend to promote happiness; wrong as they tend to produce the reverse of happiness. This is the guiding principle of utilitarianism. But utilitarians endorse different accounts of what constitutes human happiness. Bentham defends a hedonistic account of human welfare. He argues that 'nature has placed man under the governance of two sovereign masters, pain and pleasure. It is for them alone to point to what we ought to do, as well as to determine what we shall do' (Bentham, 1996: 585). According to Bentham's hedonism, welfare is equated with the experience or sensation of pleasure. Bentham held that all pleasures were equal, thus 'pushpin is as good as poetry' if we receive the same intensity and duration of pleasure from both activities.

One of the main objections raised against 'conscious-state theories' like Bentham's is that put forth by Robert Nozick in *Anarchy, State and Utopia*. Nozick asks us to consider the following scenario.

> Suppose there were an experience machine that would give you any experience you desired. Superduper neuropsychologists could stimulate your brain so that you would think and feel you were writing a great novel, or making a friend, or reading an interesting book. All the time you would be floating in a tank, with electrodes attached to your brain. Should you plug into this machine for life, preprogramming your life's experiences? (Nozick, 1974: 42)

Nozick believes that most of us would not agree to be hooked for life to this machine. Why not? Because we value something else besides merely experiencing the sensations of pleasure. We want to *actually* write a great novel or make friends or read an interesting book and not just experience the mental sensations that accompany these things.

Those who are dissatisfied with the prospect of equating human welfare with mental states might find the 'preference-satisfaction' account of utility more attractive. According to this view, our welfare depends not on experiencing certain mental states but in having our preferences satisfied. The experience machine does not satisfy our preferences as our preferences are more extensive than merely experiencing certain mental sensations. Dworkin calls this version of welfarism 'success theories of welfare' as they 'suppose that a person's welfare is a matter of his success in fulfilling his preferences, goals, and ambitions, and so equality of success, as a conception of equality of welfare, recommends distribution and transfer of resources until no further transfer can decrease the extent to which people differ in such success' (Dworkin, 2000: 17).

If we adopt a success theory of welfare we must distinguish between a number of different kinds of preferences that we will deem illegitimate.

Take, for example, those uniformed preferences which may undermine our welfare. Suppose I have a preference for drinking the contents of the cup on my desk. That preference is based upon my belief that the cup contains some cool, refreshing water. But that belief could be mistaken. Perhaps a disgruntled colleague snuck into my office and poisoned my water! If this is the case then satisfying my preference for drinking the contents of the cup will harm my welfare. This type of consideration might lead us to add the qualifier that our welfare involves the satisfying of *informed* or *rational* preferences. But then how do we stipulate what makes a preference 'informed' or 'rational'? These are difficult questions which those who defend success theories of welfare must address.

Dworkin introduces three distinctions which success theories must also consider. These are: political preferences, impersonal preferences, and personal preferences. Political preferences are preferences 'about how the goods, resources, and opportunities of the community should be distributed by others' (Dworkin, 2000: 17). An example of a political preference would be one's desire for a certain political regime (democracy, for example). Impersonal preferences are preferences about things other than my own or anyone else's life, such as the preference that a certain species of plant or animal should not become extinct. Personal preferences are preferences about our own lives, such as my preference for being healthy. Some of the preferences from each of these three categories must be eliminated, argues Dworkin, from the equalizing calculation if equality of welfare is to be viable. Suppose, for example, that everyone in our society has a political preference for a harmonious multicultural society, everyone except Bob. Bob is a racist and has a political preference for living in a segregated society. If our society is a harmonious multicultural society then Bob's welfare, with respect to his political preferences, is less than that of the rest of us. If equality of welfare is the goal then we should compensate Bob for this inequality by giving him some extra goods. Such a requirement is perverse and equality of welfare will only be an attractive account of distributional equality if it can rule out counterintuitive cases like this.

Dworkin's analysis of the different versions of welfarism is quite detailed but we need not pursue these points further here. But there are two points which are worth emphasizing with respect to the appeal of equality of welfare and its shortcomings. Firstly, its appeal. The ideal of equality of welfare is appealing in that it coheres with the first of the two principles of ethical individualism Dworkin emphasizes – the principle of equal importance. Consider, for example, how people with handicaps would be treated in this society. Their welfare is just as important as the welfare of those who do not have handicaps. Thus those whose welfare is impeded by such burdens will receive extra resources so that they can enjoy the same level of welfare as others. Equality of welfare thus fares well with respect to the principle of equal importance because it requires that the needy receive more resources.

But equality of welfare fails to accommodate the second principle which Dworkin takes to be fundamental, the principle of special responsibility. If equality of welfare is the goal then it cannot provide sufficient room for the idea that we have special and final responsibility for the success of our lives. My welfare might be impeded not because of factors beyond my control (such as a handicap) but because of factors that I can be personally responsible for (expensive tastes, for example). Perhaps I have cultivated expensive tastes and thus need extra resources in order for me to achieve the same level of welfare that others (with less expensive tastes) have.[2] According to equality of welfare my demand for extra resources, like those of the person with a handicap, is legitimate. Equality of welfare fails as a distributive ideal because it does not afford enough room for considerations of personal responsibility. Like Rawls's difference principle, equality of welfare fails to distinguish between the deserving and undeserving poor. Dworkin puts forward his account of equality of resources as an alternative distributive ideal that incorporates both the principle of equal importance *and* the principle of special responsibility.

   Dworkin's argument for equality of resources is a rich and sophisticated one and we can only briefly consider some of its main components. Dworkin's attempt to merge the two fundamental principles of ethical individualism are most stark in his hypothetical tale of shipwrecked survivors who are washed up on a desert island that has abundant resources. Let us assume for the moment that everyone has the same natural talents. The immigrants agree to divide the resources of the island equally among them. Each person is given 100 clam shells to bid on the various resources. These people will obviously have different preferences and this will be reflected in what they spend their clam shells on. If the majority of immigrants have a preference for sun tanning on the beach then those parts of the beach will be very costly. If the majority have a preference for living as farmers then those parts of the island conducive to agriculture will be very costly, etc. The distribution that would result from such an auction would be 'ambition sensitive'. That is, the bundle of goods people end up with would reflect only the choices they made. No one could complain that someone else received preferential treatment as all started with 100 clam shells and were free to bid on those resources they wanted. Of course some resources will be more expensive than others but this is not grounds for a complaint as this stems from your own personal preferences and those of the other immigrants. You could change your preferences so that you could appropriate more of the less expensive resources. Such an auction will treat all as equals if it satisfies what Dworkin calls the 'envy test'. The envy test maintains that 'no division of resources is an equal division if, once the distribution is complete, any immigrant would prefer someone else's bundle of resources to his own bundle' (Dworkin, 2000: 67).

   The first part of Dworkin's hypothetical story captures the concern for the special responsibility principle. The initial bundle of goods the immigrants have are the result of their own ambitions, tastes, etc. But what happens once the auction is completed and the immigrants begin to produce things? Let us now drop the initial assumption that all have equal natural talents. Given the fact that some immigrants will be more skilful, others will fall sick, etc. it will not be long before the conditions of the envy test will fail to be met. These events thus threaten to undermine the first fundamental principle of ethical individualism – the principle of equal importance. This principle maintains that it is important that human lives be successful rather than wasted. But a 'starting-gate' theory that holds that justice requires equal initial resources and *laissez-faire* thereafter will undermine the requirements of this principle. Dworkin argues that we must not allow the distribution of resources to be endowment-sensitive, that is, 'to be affected by differences in ability of the sort that produce income differences in a *laissez-faire* economy among people with the same ambitions' (Dworkin, 2000: 89).

Dworkin introduces the *hypothetical insurance scheme* to alleviate the concerns about abandoning the ideal of an endowment-insensitive distribution. He modifies the auction story by declaring that, prior to the auction, the immigrants are denied information about their natural endowments and are given the opportunity to purchase insurance against handicaps and unequal skills. Under these conditions of uncertainty people would be willing to part with some of their 100 clam shells to guard against having disabilities or lacking skills. Those who fare poorly in these respects will receive compensation in the form of extra resources paid out by these insurance schemes. Such schemes will be funded by those who are fortunate not to have to make an insurance claim but will have to pay an insurance premium.

The hypothetical auction Dworkin invokes is likely to cause some confusion in terms of understanding how it relates to the real world, where we don't begin with equal resources nor do we have insurance schemes in place for things like skill. Dworkin attempts to make the link between the theory and the real world by tackling a number of applied topics in Part II of *Sovereign Virtue*, including health care, welfare programmes, electoral reform and affirmative action. In the real world, for example, there is a need for taxation and redistribution. Income tax is a device society can use to neutralize the effects of handicaps and differential talents. But a tax system can only roughly approximate the results of the insurance scheme and will not achieve a truly ambition-sensitive/endowment-insensitive distribution. Nor is there one simple solution which will do justice to the demands of the two fundamental principles of ethical individualism. Dworkin endorses, for example, a decent minimum of medical care for all citizens and the option to buy private health insurance. But his endorsement of universal health coverage is not founded on the rescue principle, which instructs us to spend all we can on health care 'until the next dollar would buy no gain in health and life expectancy at all' (Dworkin, 2000: 309). Equal concern for all does not necessarily entail that we spend exorbitant amounts of public funds trying to save the lives of those who have little chance of surviving for long. Society must make tough decisions regarding which medical tests and procedures should be deemed 'necessary and appropriate' for coverage under the publicly funded health care system and also allow individuals to choose for themselves how much more they wish to spend to insure themselves against other possible misfortunes. Such an arrangement is a just compromise between the demands of equal importance and special responsibility.

Dworkin further elaborates on the practical implications of equality of resources in his discussion of welfare and electoral reform and we now turn to these two issues in the following two sections.

Dworkin invokes the example of making one's will to reveal the different considerations which the two theories of equality will bring to the fore. Considering this example will help bring out some of the potential problems with equality of welfare. Suppose your children have roughly equal wealth already and, being a political philosopher, you wish to design your will so as to achieve equality of welfare among your children. You have five children with different talents and ambitions. Dworkin provides the following information on the children:

One is blind.
One is a playboy with expensive tastes.
One is a prospective politician with expensive ambitions.
One is a poet with humble needs.
One is a sculptor who works in expensive material.

If equality of welfare is your goal, how would you divide the inheritance? In order to answer that question you must consider how you would define 'welfare' and which of the children would need the largest portion of the inheritance in order to bring their welfare up to the level of the other children. After considering this example, debate what you think are the strengths and weaknesses of the ideal of equality of welfare.

4.3 Welfare reform and the basic income proposal

As we noted above, Dworkin believes that the hypothetical insurance scheme can be used to justify limited universal health coverage. The principle of universal concern states that it is important that human lives be successful rather than wasted and a community committed to limited universal health coverage expresses its commitment to this principle by taking reasonable steps to help compensate individuals for the misfortune of the natural lottery of life. But handicaps are only one example of the misfortune brute luck can bring us. There are also other natural inequalities (for example, in native talents) and social inequalities (such as the wealth of the family you are born into). How does Dworkin propose we tackle these issues? Like the case of handicaps, Dworkin invokes the hypothetical insurance scheme to deal with differential talents. In fact, Dworkin sees the difference between handicaps and talents as one of degree and thus believes the insurance model is appropriate for both cases. 'Though skills are different from handicaps, the difference can be understood as one of degree: we may say that someone who cannot play basketball like Wilt Chamberlain, paint like Piero, or make money like Geneen, suffers from an (especially common) handicap' (Dworkin, 2000: 92).

Dworkin's hypothetical unemployment insurance scheme does not provide a definitive answer to the question of what welfare programme real societies should adopt but it does 'bracket a range of welfare programs that a reasonable person or legislature might think required by the twin principles that people's lives are of equal importance and that each person has a responsibility to take control of his own life' (Dworkin, 2000: 340). In particular, Dworkin believes that 'a welfare scheme with no cutoff, that either may or must provide training and job assistance, and that conditions compensation on good-faith endeavor to find employment, is preferable either to a more severe or a more generous program' (Dworkin, 2000: 340).

It might strike some as contradictory for Dworkin to say that equality of resources takes seriously the principle of special responsibility and yet precludes cutting off welfare benefits. How do we show a commitment to the principle that people have a special and final responsibility for the success of their life if we permit individuals to receive welfare benefits after long-term unemployment? Bill Clinton's 1996 Welfare Reform Act, for example, placed limits on the benefits the unemployed could receive. Many Americans believed that such a measure was necessary for breaking the dependency the unemployed had on welfare benefits. The only way to make people take responsibility for their life, they could argue in reply to Dworkin, is to cut off welfare benefits. So such a programme could be justified by appealing to the fundamental principles Dworkin endorses. Such reform sought to make lives be successful rather than wasted and to ensure that people take responsibility for their lives.

Dworkin anticipates this kind of response and argues that conservatives who maintain that long-term unemployment is the result of work-aversion or other negative traits such as laziness overestimate the extent to which personality accounts for these things. The disagreement between Dworkin and conservatives centres on the way they conceive of what Dworkin calls the *strategic problem*. The strategic problem concerns how we should draw the line between those influences on a person's life prospects which he or she must take responsibility for and those whose influence the community has a responsibility to mitigate. Conservatives want to place responsibility for employment in the hands of the individual. This argument, claims Dworkin, rests on three points. Firstly, it relies on the factual claim that most welfare recipients are scroungers as opposed to the genuinely needy. Secondly, it relies on predictive judgements about the motivational and behavioural consequences of welfare. Namely, that welfare perpetuates a culture of dependency. This implies these people would apply themselves if they had to. Thirdly, the conservative argument relies on the controversial morality that it is acceptable to deny welfare to those who really need it in order to coerce those who do not to work.

Rather than substantiating that the factual and predicative judgements of the conservative argument are false, Dworkin simply claims that his competing welfare strategy does not get entangled in these controversial psychological presumptions. But this response to the conservative argument is not satisfactory because Dworkin's hypothetical unemployment insurance tale is bound to get just as entangled in these issues. Consider, for example, the following passage in which Dworkin asks us to imagine what unemployment insurance people in contemporary America would be willing to buy.

> But we might nevertheless capitalize on the imaginary [unemployment insurance] exercise by asking what unemployment insurance people with a representative mixture of the tastes and ambitions most Americans have … would buy if they had the wealth that is average among us and were acting prudently. There is no single right answer, I agree, to hypothetical questions like that one. Which insurance opportunities people would be offered, and which of these they would take up, would depend on hosts of contingencies and market and personal decisions that we can sensibly imagine in different ways. But if we could construct a narrow range of unemployment insurance policies such that it is plausible to assume that almost every American who was acting rationally would buy a policy within that range, whatever other insurance he added to it, we could design the core structure of an eminently defensible welfare program based on that information. (Dworkin, 2000: 333)

But if many Americans believe, as those who supported Clinton's welfare reforms did, that long-term unemployment is mostly a case of individual choice and not circumstances beyond their control, then why should we believe Dworkin's claim that the insurance scheme would produce a narrow range of unemployment policies that precluded those that cut benefits off after a few years of receiving benefits? Whether or not it would be prudent to opt for policies that have no limit on welfare benefits will depend on what we think of the controversial psychological presumptions Dworkin thinks his approach can avoid. Without providing a more conclusive argument as to why we should not ascribe more personal responsibility to the issue of unemployment Dworkin's criticisms of the Welfare Reform Act are unpersuasive.

Conservatives are not the only ones who are likely to find Dworkin's defence of the welfare state unpersuasive; many egalitarians sympathetic to equality of resources reject Dworkin's conclusions. The Belgian political philosopher Phillipe Van Parijs, for example, appeals to equality of resources to justify a citizen's unconditional basic income. Such an income would be paid to each full member of society (1) even if she is not willing to work, (2) irrespective of her being rich or poor, (3) whoever she lives with, and (4) no matter which part of the country she lives in. This basic income would provide citizens with what Van Parijs calls 'real freedom'. Real freedom is the freedom to choose among the various lives we might wish to live.

Van Parijs's argument for this unconditional basic income is complex but the central contention for it can be stated as follows:

1   Each person should have equal opportunity to pursue a conception of the good life.
2   Each person is entitled to an equal share of available external wealth.
3   Each person is entitled to an unconditional income equal to the value of a per capita share of available external wealth.
4   In the circumstances of at least some of the advanced capitalist countries today, an income equal to the per capita share of external wealth will be a substantial income (i.e., one that is at, or close to, a level sufficient to cover a standard set of basic needs).
Therefore,
5   In at least some advanced capitalist countries today, each citizen is entitled to an unconditional basic income set at or close to a level sufficient to cover a standard set of basic needs. (White, 1997: 313–14)

A vital component of Van Parijs's argument is his appeal to Dworkin's equality of resources. This underlies, for example, the second premise in the argument noted above. But the obvious difference between Dworkin's position and Van Parijs's is the stance they take on making benefits conditional. Dworkin believes that the principle of special responsibility entails that welfare recipients should have to make a good faith endeavour to find a job. But under Van Parijs's proposal everyone receives a basic income, both the employed and the unemployed. Van Parijs argues that liberals like Rawls and Dworkin are violating a central tenet of liberalism when they make willingness to work a precondition of receiving benefit. This central tenet is the liberal doctrine of neutrality. It states that the government should not favour certain conceptions of the good life over others.[3] Ironically, Rawls and Dworkin are the main proponents of this doctrine but Van Parijs believes that neutrality is violated when a theory gives preferential treatment to those who prefer to work.

In order for a theory of distributive justice to be truly neutral, argues Van Parijs, it must make the basic income *unconditional*. But how would this basic income be funded? Van Parijs claims that the tax base for the basic income would come from natural resources, transfers of non-natural wealth (for example, inheritances, etc.) and employment rents. The latter is a novel suggestion and crucial for Van Parijs's claim that the income would be substantial. Jobs are one of the resources that should be equalized. That does not mean that we provide conditions of employment for everyone. That would be very costly and not everyone wants to work so it would be unfair to spend public funds on such a programme. But what society can do is charge employment rents on those who work and use these taxes to fund the unconditional basic income which everyone, the employed and unemployed, will receive. The more income you make from your job the higher your employment rent.

The main objection critics have made to Van Parijs's argument is that it permits the voluntarily unemployed to free-ride off the those who work.[4] Van Parijs replies to this objection by asking us to recognize the realities of the labour market.

> People fail to realize that much of the income that goes to labour in fact derives from our common inheritance of resources. Most of the income that is generated by labour in our society is generated in the context of jobs. Now jobs are very unequally accessible to people and even if everyone had a job there would still be many jobs that are restricted to a small number of people because many people do not have the talents that are required in order to perform them ... So what I ask people who make this free-rider objection to realise is how large this background of 'gifts' that we receive in all sorts of forms, actually is. These 'gifts' are appropriated to a very unequal and unfair extent by the people who happen to be able to 'contribute' by having the best paid and most attractive jobs. (Van Parijs, 1997: 14–15)

The principle of equal concern, for Van Parijs, entails that all have not only a right to do what one might want to do, but that each person should have the greatest possible opportunity to do whatever he or she might want to do. This is achieved when society implements the highest sustainable unconditional basic income. Liberals like Rawls who maintain that Malibu surfers[5] should not be entitled to public funds are violating neutrality, argues Van Parijs, because they are giving preferential treatment to those who prefer to work. Malibu surfers are entitled to their fair share of society's resources. The charge that the voluntarily unemployed are taking an unfair share of society's resources is misguided, argues Van Parijs. '[T]hose who take an unfair share of society's resources are not those who opt for such a low-production, low-consumption lifestyle. They are people like myself and most of my readers, who, thanks to the attractive job they were given, appropriate a huge employment rent' (Van Parijs, 1991: 130).

Critically assess Dworkin's argument for the welfare state and Van Parijs's basic income proposal.

- To what extent do you think the welfare state is compatible with the principle of special responsibility?
- Do you agree with Dworkin's criticisms of the 1996 Welfare Reform Act?
- Van Parijs claims that everyone should be entitled to a basic income, even those who are not willing to work. What do you think of this radical suggestion?
- Should jobs be included among the resources to be equalized, as Van Parijs suggests?

Further reading

David Schmidtz and Robert Goodin, *Social Welfare and Individual Responsibility: For and Against* (Cambridge: Cambridge University Press, 1998).
Robert Goodin, *Reasons for Welfare* (Princeton, NJ: Princeton University Press, 1988).
Stuart White, *The Civic Minimum* (Oxford: Oxford University Press, 2003).

4.4 Political equality and democracy

Moving beyond the more specific question of distributional equality, Dworkin also considers what the implications of the principle of equal concern are for the distribution of political power in society. What political institutions and procedures should an egalitarian society adopt? The principle of equal concern makes democracy the obvious political regime. A monarchy or dictatorship will fail to take seriously both of the fundamental principles of ethical individualism. The unlimited authority which a monarch or dictator can wield threatens both the principle of equal importance and the principle of special responsibility. A democracy's commitment to universal suffrage and other fundamental liberties (for example, freedom of speech and expression) makes it the best political arrangement for securing equal concern. But democracies can vary widely in terms of the institutions and procedures they adopt. The abstract principle of equal concern does not provide us with definitive answers as to the precise details of which democratic model an egalitarian community should adopt.[6] Instead, it can help us construct an ideal by which we can assess the existing democratic procedures of our own particular political community. This is Dworkin's aim. One of the issues that he thinks is of fundamental importance in American politics is limits on campaign spending. American politics, claims Dworkin, 'are a disgrace, and money is the root of the problem' (Dworkin, 2000: 351).

According to the Federal Election Commission,[7] the total amount of campaign contributions the 2000 American Presidential candidates George Bush and Al Gore received was, respectively, $94,466,341 and $49,202,745. Running an effective political campaign, whether it be a national or local campaign, requires vast amounts of wealth and this reliance on rich contributors, argues Dworkin, is the root of the problem with American politics. 'The more money politicians need to be elected, the more they need rich contributors, and the more influence such contributors then have over their political decisions once elected' (Dworkin, 2000: 351).

American federal law does limit how much individual citizens and groups can give to political campaigns but a 'soft money' loop-hole exists that permits donors to make unlimited donations to political parties and campaigns for funds that are used on 'issue advocacy' media campaigns that do not explicitly urge voters to vote for or against any candidate. Many other democratic countries place a cap on campaign expenditures but similar limits have been struck down as unconstitutional by the American Supreme Court. In *Buckley* v. *Valeo* (1976),

> the Supreme Court ruled that expenditure limits are unconstitutional because they violate the First Amendment of the United States Constitution, which provides that Congress shall 'make no law' abridging the freedom of speech or association. Prohibiting a politician or anyone else from spending as much money as he wishes to press his political convictions and policies, the Court said, is restricting his freedom of speech. (Dworkin, 2000: 352)

Support for the ruling in *Buckley* comes from a popular strategic assumption about the best way to realize and protect democracy. Dworkin calls this the *democratic wager*. The democratic wager holds 'that democracy is best protected by a principle that forbids government to limit or control political speech in any way for the purpose of protecting democracy' (Dworkin, 2000: 353). This is so because democracy is understood as a political arrangement designed to enforce the will of the majority. According to this 'majoritarian' conception of democracy, 'the democratic ideal lies in a match between political decision and the will of the majority or plurality of opinion' (Dworkin, 2000: 357). Free speech is thus paramount for majoritarians and hence why they believe that the decision in *Buckley* was correct. The best way of ensuring that citizens have the opportunity to inform themselves as fully as possible and to deliberate about their choices is 'to permit anyone who wishes to address the public to do so, in whatever way and at whatever length he wishes, no matter how unpopular or unworthy the government or other citizens deem his message to be' (Dworkin, 2000: 359).

Rejecting the proposal for limits on campaign expenditures is necessary, argue majoritarians, because the existing arrangement provides a fuller opportunity for information and reflection. Allowing the government to limit what citizens hear limits that opportunity and thus limits democracy. But this argument will only be persuasive if one assumes that unlimited expenditures create the fullest opportunity for information and reflection. But the ballooning of political expenditures has also brought a rise in 'smear' campaigns, political jingles and sound-bites. How much information and reflection do these communications convey? Limits on campaign spending might force political parties to focus more on solving society's problems and less on fundraising. With only limited funds available political parties might take a more responsible approach to campaigning so that they focus more on making a persuasive argument for their main platforms rather than on negative campaigning and sound-bites.

In place of the majoritarian conception of democracy Dworkin defends the *partnership conception*. The partnership conception of democracy has three dimensions. These are:

1   *Popular sovereignty*. This sovereignty is defined as a relation between the public as a whole and the various officials who make up its government. Partnership democracy demands that the people, and not officials, be masters.
2   *Equality*. Citizen equality demands that they participate as equals.
3   *Democratic discourse*. Citizens must deliberate together as individuals before they act collectively and this deliberation must focus on the reasons for and against that collective action. (Dworkin, 2000: 363–4)

Unlike the democratic wager strategy invoked by majoritarians, which rules out limitations or regulations of political speech for the purpose of protecting democracy, Dworkin's ideal of partnership adopts a more discriminating approach to free speech. Take, for example, laws forbidding political canvassing on election day within a stipulated distance from polling places. Why are such laws a good idea? The majoritarian conception of democracy cannot provide a persuasive answer to this question. But the partnership conception of democracy can. Dworkin argues that 'it is fairer to citizens as participants not to allow any candidate or group the special and unseemly advantage of a last-second appeal at the crucial moment of voting, and it improves democratic deliberation to allow citizens a space for final reflection, free from importuning, before they vote – to allow them freedom from *politics* when that freedom is most important' (Dworkin, 2000: 378). Dworkin believes that such laws are also consistent with the First Amendment[8] because they do not violate principles of political impartiality or any other aspect of popular sovereignty.

Money can be, and is, argues Dworkin, an impediment to the partnership conception of democracy in America. When the rich are the only real players in the political contest political equality is nothing but an illusion. Equal suffrage is a necessary but not sufficient condition of true citizen equality. Citizens must also participate as equals. They cannot do this when wealth plays such a vital role in determining the contours of the political agenda. Nor can citizens reason together about the common good when political campaigning is reduced to negative advertisements, slogans and sound bites. By adopting limits on campaign spending America would be more in line with the other democracies and would create conditions more congenial to the partnership conception of democracy.

One aspect of Dworkin's work in legal theory which seems to conflict with his partnership conception of democracy is his commitment to constitutionalism and judicial review. Constitutionalism, argues Dworkin, means 'a system that establishes individual legal rights that the dominant legislature does not have the power to override or compromise' (Dworkin, 1995: 2). Dworkin believes that judicial review is a way of ensuring that majority rule is *legitimate* majority rule. It is quite easy to see how one might think that the practice of judicial review undermines the partnership model of democracy that Dworkin defends. Partnership democracy demands, claims Dworkin, that the people, and not officials, be masters. But the power judges wield in

America raises doubts about how much control the people actually have. Judges are not elected by the people nor are they accountable to them and yet they have the power to override legislation that has been passed by democratically elected officials. One of Dworkin's most competent critics who criticizes his stance on this issue is Jeremy Waldron. Waldron points out, for example, that between 1885 and 1930 American state and federal courts struck down some 150 pieces of legislation concerning labour relations, labour conditions and working hours (Waldron, 1998: 337–8). When unelected officials have so much power how can Dworkin remain faithful to both judicial review and the partnership conception of democracy?

Those who defend constitutionalism and judicial review argue that it is necessary to limit majority rule in this way. The constitution guarantees all citizens those rights we believe are fundamental and thus even a democratically elected majority are not justified in violating them. So those who defend judicial review believe that it makes society more just. They point, for example, to cases such as *Brown* v. *Board of Education* (1954) in which the Supreme Court ruled unanimously to end racial segregation in public schools. But even if we acknowledge that judicial review can serve a positive role does it not *necessarily* conflict with the democratic ideal that Dworkin appeals to? Dworkin believes it does not. In *Freedom's Law: The Moral Reading of the American Constitution* Dworkin argues that in some circumstances judicial review does not conflict with democracy but it actually enhances it. Recall that one of the important dimensions of the partnership conception of democracy is democratic discourse. Citizens must deliberate together as individuals. Dworkin believes that constitutional adjudication actually improves the quality of public debate on important issues.

> When an issue is seen as constitutional … and as one that will ultimately be resolved by courts applying general constitutional principles, the quality of public argument is often improved, because the argument concentrates from the start on questions of public morality … When a constitutional issue has been decided by the Supreme Court, and is important enough so that it can be expected to be elaborated, expanded, contracted, or even reversed by future decisions, a sustained national debate begins, in newspapers and other media, in law schools and classrooms, in public meetings and around dinner tables. (Dworkin, 1996: 345)

Waldron rejects Dworkin's argument and appeals to empirical evidence to substantiate this. If Dworkin is correct, argues Waldron, then we would expect to find national debates about issues that are not constitutionalized in other countries to be less robust and well-informed. But this is not so. In fact, the quality of public debate on issues like abortion might be even better in countries like the United Kingdom and New Zealand where such issues are not constitutionalized. Such debates do not have to be framed around how to interpret a document that is over two hundred years old. Waldron also points to the issue of capital punishment. The public does not need this issue to be an interpretative debate about the constitution before it can become a moral debate. Reducing it to the former results in excluding important considerations relating to the broader aims of penal policy (Waldron, 1998: 339).

Dworkin's commitment to judicial review seems to be in tension with all three dimensions of his partnership conception of democracy. When judges make the final decisions on fundamental moral and political questions the officials, and not citizens, are masters. So judicial review appears to threaten popular sovereignty. Citizen equality demands that citizens participate as equals but the important role Dworkin ascribes to the courts threatens this equality. Citizens may be equals in the democratic process but if this process is subordinate to the decisions of unelected and unaccountable officials citizens may feel that the political process offers little hope of lasting and effective change. Finally, when judges are given the final say on resolving important moral and political controversies this may detract, not enhance, the quality of public debate. The important issue becomes 'is X constitutional?' and thus other important issues may be ignored.

Discuss the following statements:

1   Limits on campaign expenditure are essential for ensuring the integrity of the democratic process. Without such measures in place the democratic process is driven by money and this is unjust. When political parties must rely on rich contributors these contributors are given a lot of power and this power imbalance perverts the democratic process.

2   Dworkin's defence of judicial review is unconvincing. The fact that judges are not elected is sufficient for us to declare that judicial review is undemocratic and therefore unjust. We should not give these officials the power to override legislation that has been passed by democratically elected officials.

3   I think it is ironic that a liberal like Dworkin would advocate limits on campaign spending. I thought liberals believed that rights are 'trumps' that cannot be violated. If so, then surely they must defend an individual's right to political speech, including that individual's right to spend money on promoting the political party he or she wants to promote. But yet Dworkin supports limiting this right in the name of 'protecting democracy'. I think the best way to protect democracy is by protecting the fundamental rights of its citizens and thus I oppose limits on campaign expenditure.

4.5 Against luck egalitarianism

Dworkin's theory of equality of resources is premised on the choice/chance distinction. The ideal distributive arrangement is one that is 'ambition-sensitive' and 'endowment-insensitive'. An unequal society is just if this inequality reflects the choices people make but not their circumstances that they are not responsible for. This is the central tenet of 'luck egalitarianism'. The two fundamental principles of ethical individualism Dworkin invokes are utilized by him to help reinforce the intuition that the choice/chance distinction should remain the fundamental insight when considering the issue of distributional equality. We shall now consider one of the most forceful arguments against luck egalitarianism. In 'What is the Point of Equality?' Elizabeth Anderson criticizes theorists like Dworkin and Van Parijs for making beach bums and the lazy and irresponsible the main focus of debates about egalitarianism. The aim of equality, she argues, is not to eliminate the impact of brute luck from human affairs but to end oppression.

Anderson argues that luck egalitarianism fails the most fundamental test any egalitarian theory must meet: that its principles express equal respect and concern for all citizens (Anderson, 1999: 289). It fails this test in the following three ways:

1   It excludes some citizens from enjoying the social conditions of freedom on the spurious ground that it's their fault for losing them.
2   It makes the basis for citizens' claims on one another the fact that some are inferior to others in the worth of their lives, talents and personal qualities.
3   In attempting to ensure that people take responsibility for their choices, luck egalitarianism makes demeaning and intrusive judgements about people's capacities to exercise responsibility and effectively dictates to them the appropriate uses of the freedom. (Anderson, 1999: 289)

Let us address these three points in turn, focusing in particular on how they relate to Dworkin's theory. Recall Dworkin's insurance analogy. Dworkin argues that justice demands that the state compensate everyone for whatever risks of bad brute luck they would have insured themselves against if all were equally likely to suffer from the risk. But a problem arises with respect to what Dworkin calls 'option luck'. Brute luck concerns risks that are not the result of deliberate gambles (such as being born with a severe mental handicap). Option luck concerns risks that are the result of our choices (for example, investing all your money in a company that goes bankrupt). Dworkin's principle of equal concern requires us to compensate people for the misfortunes of bad brute luck. We do this by providing, for example, minimum universal health coverage and welfare programmes. But the principle of special responsibility tells us that individuals have special and final responsibility for the success of their lives and thus we are not collectively responsible for the misfortune people suffer from their option luck. Taking this line seriously, argues Anderson, has some counterintuitive results.

She considers a number of cases to illustrate this point. Consider, for example, the uninsured driver who negligently makes an illegal turn and causes an accident with someone else. This driver deliberately took a number of risks. He chose not be to insured and he chose to disobey traffic regulations. Should we provide him with medical assistance when he shows up at the hospital needing life-saving surgery? Should we provide the assistance he will need to live a successful life with the disability he received from the accident he was responsible for? What about people who voluntarily choose dangerous occupations, like police officers and firefighters? The risks they expose themselves to are ones of their own doing. Should we thus hold these people responsible for the medical costs of the treatment they might need when injured on the job? Denying that we have a collective responsibility to provide medical assistance to negligent drivers, police officers, etc. is perfectly consistent with the central tenet of luck egalitarianism. This, argues Anderson, is wrong. We have a collective moral responsibility to victims of both bad brute luck and bad option luck.

Anderson's second objection concerns the way victims of bad brute luck are treated by luck egalitarians. Dworkin's principle of equal concern requires us to compensate those who have handicaps and little native (or non-marketable) talents. But this compensation is premised on pity, argues Anderson, not on equal respect and concern. This compensation is given because the worst off are viewed as being inferior to others. Anderson asks us to image what a letter from the State Equality Board to the worst off would look like if it was crafted by a luck egalitarian. It would say something like the following, which effectively illustrates her point that the reasons luck egalitarians give for granting aid is disrespectful to the worst off.

> To the disabled: Your defective native endowments or current disabilities, alas, make your life less worth living than the lives of normal people. To compensate for this misfortune, we, the able ones, will give you extra resources ...

> To the stupid and untalented: Unfortunately, other people don't value what little you have to offer in the system of production. Your talents are too meagre to command much market value. Because of the misfortune that you were born so poorly endowed with talents, we productive ones will make it up to you: we'll let you share in the bounty of what we have produced with our vastly superior and highly valued abilities. (Anderson, 1999: 305)

This relates to the third and final objection Anderson raises against Dworkin, that luck egalitarianism makes demeaning and intrusive judgements of people's capacities. It makes private judgements about the value of its citizens' worth as workers publicly recognized opinions and thus 'disparages the internally disadvantaged and raises private disdain to the status of officially recognised truths' (Anderson, 1999: 306). As such it runs counter to the true spirit of equality which seeks to 'promote institutional arrangements that enable the diversity of people's talents, aspirations, roles, and cultures to benefit everyone and to be recognised as mutually beneficial' (Anderson, 1999: 308). Anderson favours what she calls *democratic equality* over luck egalitarianism. Democratic equality seeks to abolish socially created oppression. Unlike Dworkin's emphasis on distributional equality, democratic equality views equality as a social relationship instead of a pattern of distribution.

In fairness to Dworkin we should note that he also acknowledges the importance of the more central issue of political equality, as became apparent in the discussion of the partnership conception of democracy above. Dworkin also addresses, for example, the issue of affirmative action.[9] So, like Anderson, Dworkin is also concerned with the broader issue of oppression. But Dworkin's discussion of these applied topics is often detached from the ethical principles he makes so central in the early theoretical chapters of *Sovereign Virtue*. The principles of equal concern and special responsibility are invoked by Dworkin in his discussion of health care and welfare, for example, but do not play a key role in his discussion of campaign spending, abortion and affirmative action. These are issues that do not really bring the choice/chance distinction into play. And that is exactly the point Anderson makes. The main concern for egalitarians should be with ending oppression and not eliminating the impact of brute luck from human affairs. Dworkin's twin principles of ethical individualism are ill-equipped to tackle the more general and pressing issue of oppression.

SUMMARY

- Dworkin endorses a version of comprehensive liberalism which is premised on two fundamental principles of ethical individualism – the principle of equal importance and the principle of special responsibility. Dworkin favours equality of resources over equality of welfare as the latter fails to accommodate the principle of special responsibility. Equality of welfare cannot deal with the problem of expensive tastes.
- Dworkin's argument for equality of resources is one of the most developed accounts of what is known as *luck egalitarianism* – the view that inequalities in the advantages people enjoy are just if they derive from the choices people have voluntarily made, but that inequalities deriving from unchosen features of people's circumstances are unjust. Dworkin invokes the hypothetical tale of shipwrecked survivors on an island in order to show that equality of resources justifies a system of taxation and redistribution.
- A number of applied topics are addressed by Dworkin in *Sovereign Virtue*, ranging from health care and welfare provision to electoral reform. Critics of Dworkin have taken issue with both the central tenets of luck egalitarianism and Dworkin's stance on issues like judicial review.

Notes

1 Those who endorse this position include, among others, Ronald Dworkin (2000), Richard Arneson (1989), G.A. Cohen (1989) and Philippe Van Parijs (1995).
2 For example, I might claim that I must have a bigger home and more cars than the average person if I am to attain the same level of welfare others have.
3 The issue of state neutrality will be a central focus of the communitarian critique examined in Chapter 5.
4 See Elster (1986), White (1997) and Farrelly (1999).
5 See *Political Liberalism*, pp. 181–2, note 9.
6 It should be noted, however, that Dworkin is also an eminent legal scholar and has extensively argued in favour of American constitutionalism and believes that the United Kingdom should adopt the American-style arrangement of judicial review. See Ronald Dworkin, *A Bill of Rights for Britain* (1990).
7 Available on the Web at http://www.fec.gov/finance_reports.html.
8 The First Amendment states: Congress shall make no law respecting an establishment of religion, or prohibiting the free exercise thereof; or abridging the freedom of speech, or of the press; or the right of the people peaceably to assemble, and to petition the Government for a redress of grievances.
9 See Chapters 11 and 12 of *Sovereign Virtue*.

Part Two:
Alternative Traditions

5 Communitarianism

Summary Contents

5.1 Introduction   97
5.2 Deontological liberalism and the unencumbered self   99
5.3 State neutrality   102
5.4 Walzer and complex equality   106
5.5 Miller on nationalism   110
5.6 Conclusion   115

5.1 Introduction

Stuart Hampshire succinctly captures one of the core commitments of liberals when he claims that 'the essence of a liberal morality is the rejection of any final and exclusive authority, natural or supernatural, and of the accompanying compulsion and censorship' (Hampshire, 2000: 35). Central to the liberal morality is the belief that individual rights should be given a high priority. The emphasis liberals place on individual rights has given rise to a distinct criticism which dominated many of the debates in political theory in the 1980s and 1990s – communitarianism. The 'liberal–communitarian' debate covers a varied range of issues and theorists and there is no simple contrast between liberalism and communitarianism. In this chapter we shall focus on two prominent communitarian critics – Michael Sandel and Michael Walzer.[1] These two theorists challenge distinct aspects of liberalism and they effectively illustrate the practical significance of the liberal–communitarian debate. Michael Sandel's two influential books *Liberalism and the Limits of Justice*[2] and *Democracy's Discontent* examine the conception of the self implicit in contemporary liberalism. Sandel calls this conception of the self the *unencumbered* (or *voluntarist*) *conception of the self*. This vision of the self, argues Sandel, informs the public philosophy of contemporary American politics. Sandel labels this public philosophy *the procedural republic*. He claims:

> The political philosophy by which we live is a certain version of liberal political theory. Its central idea is that government should be neutral toward the moral and religious views its citizens espouse. Since people disagree

about the best way to live, government should not affirm in law any particular
vision of the good life. Instead, it should provide a framework of rights that
respects persons as free and independent selves, capable of choosing their
own values and ends. Since this liberalism asserts the priority of fair procedures over particular ends, the public life it informs might be called the procedural republic. (Sandel, 1996: 4)

The procedural republic is ill-equipped, argues Sandel, to deal with the two
fears that define the anxiety of contemporary American politics – the fear of
losing control of the forces that govern our lives and the fear that the moral
fabric of community is eroding. In the following two sections we examine
the two prongs of Sandel's communitarian critique. Firstly, that liberalism is
premised on the unencumbered conception of the self. And secondly, that
this conception of the self gives rise to a public philosophy that has the costly
consequences Sandel claims it has.

Michael Walzer's communitarian critique also focuses on American politics but Walzer's concern is not with the conception of the self liberalism
invokes. Walzer takes issue with the methodology many contemporary
liberals invoke when constructing a theory of justice. His argument is radically pluralistic and he rejects the universalist aspirations of liberals who
seek to construct a theory of justice that can be applied universally to all
cultures. Justice, argues Walzer, is a human construction and thus we cannot
arrive at answers to the difficult questions justice raises if we conceive of justice
in a way that ignores the particularist claims that are bound to arise when
one considers the history, culture and membership of different societies. We
cannot derive principles of justice from an abstract thought experiment
which asks what principles rational persons would choose if they knew
nothing of their situation except that they desired an abstract set of primary
goods. Each community creates its own social goods and thus what each
community thinks should be justly distributed will vary from culture to
culture. What members of hierarchies and caste societies value is very
different from what members of liberal democratic societies value.
Furthermore, even within one community there will be a plurality of principles to regulate the plurality of goods. There aren't one or two fundamental
principles that govern the regulation of all social goods. The principle that is
appropriate for these different goods is determined by the social meaning of
the good in question. How we should distribute health care or education, for
example, will depend on what we take these goods to mean. We do not begin
with abstract principles and then simply apply them to these goods. In addition to criticizing the universalist aspirations of liberalism, Walzer puts forth
his own positive theory of distributive justice – what he calls *complex equality*.
We shall examine the details of that account and some of the concerns that
have been raised against Walzer's theory.

In section 5.5 we shall consider how the particularist approach advocated
by Walzer has been applied to the issue of nationalism by David Miller (1995).
If, as communitarians argue, we are *social* beings and this fact should inform

our account of the demands of justice, then what are the implications of this view for international justice? Does the fact that we inherit distinct national identities justify our giving a priority to the interests of our compatriots over those of non-nationals? If national boundaries do have ethical significance what duties do we have to non-nationals and what justifies those duties? Examining Miller's argument will thus further illustrate the practical significance of the issues at stake in the liberal–communitarian debate.

5.2 Deontological liberalism and the unencumbered self

Sandel's communitarian critique takes issue with 'rights-oriented' liberalism. Sandel does not reject the liberal's claim that rights are important but rather he questions the claim that rights can be identified and justified in a way that does not presuppose any particular conception of the good life. Rawls, for example, claims that the right is prior to the good. The assertion that the right is prior to the good is characteristic of deontological theories and can be understood in two different but related ways: in a moral sense and in a foundational sense. Following Sandel's characterization of these two senses, I will label these D1 and D2, respectively. They are defined as follows:

D1:   Justice is primary in that the demands of justice outweigh other moral and political interests.

D2:   The primacy of justice describes not only a moral priority but also a privileged form of justification; the right is prior to the good not only in that its claims take precedence, but also in that *its principles are independently derived*. (Sandel, 1998: 2)

Liberals like Mill and Locke, claims Sandel, are committed to D1. Rawls is also committed to D1. His critique of utilitarianism captures the moral sense in which Rawls argues for the priority of justice. But Rawls is also committed, argues Sandel, to D2. This is what makes his version of liberalism, like Kant's moral philosophy, deontological. The priority of the right over the good is, according to Sandel's interpretation of deontology, an *epistemological* and not merely moral claim. It claims that we can know what the right is independently of the good.

If Rawls's theory of justice is derived independently of the good then one must ask what his theory is premised on. Sandel claims that it is premised on a particular conception of the self.

For justice to be the first virtue, certain things must be true of us. We must be creatures of a certain kind, related to human circumstance in a certain way. We must stand at a certain distance from our circumstance, whether as transcendental subject in the case of Kant, or as essentially unencumbered subject of possession in the case of Rawls. (Sandel, 1998: 175)

Sandel points to two key aspects of Rawls's theory to support his claim that Rawls relies on this unencumbered conception of the self: the original position and Rawls's direct argument for the second principle of justice. In the original position the parties are mutually disinterested. The assumption of mutual disinterest is not just a psychological assumption, argues Sandel, it is also an epistemological claim. 'A claim about the forms of self-knowledge of which we are capable' (Sandel, 1998: 54). Sandel points to the following passage from *A Theory of Justice* as evidence of this epistemological claim:

> ...I make no restrictive assumptions about the parties' conceptions of the good except that they are rational long-term plans. While these plans determine the aims and interests *of a self*, the aims and interests are not presumed to be egoistic or selfish. Whether this is the case depends upon the kinds of ends which a person pursues. If wealth, position, and influence, and the accolades of social prestige are a person's final purposes, then surely his conception of the good is egoistic. His dominant interests are *in himself*, not merely, as they must always be, interests *of a self*. (Rawls, 1999: 111, emphasis added by Sandel)

The claim that interests are interests *of* a self, argues Sandel, shows that Rawls conceives of the self as a subject of possession.

> In so far as I possess something, I am at once related to it and distanced from it. To say that I possess a certain trait or desire or ambition is to say that I am related to it in a certain way – it is mine rather than yours – and also that I am distanced from it in a certain way – that it is mine rather than me. (Sandel, 1998: 55)

What the liberal conception of the self cannot make sense of, argues Sandel, is that some of our ends are *constitutive* ends, ends that we are bound to even though we might not have voluntarily chosen them. He provides the example of Robert E. Lee to illustrate this.[3] On the eve of the American Civil War Lee found himself in a dilemma as he was a Virginian and yet, as an officer in the Union army, regarded secession as treason. When the Civil War broke out he thus found his devotions pulled him in two directions. The moral ties he felt to his native State were not ones he voluntarily chose, but he felt bound by them nonetheless. His decision to fight for the South reflects a quality we often admire in people. That quality is

> the disposition to see and bear one's life circumstance as a reflectively situated being – claimed by the history that implicates me in a particular life, but self-conscious of its particularity, and so alive to other ways, wider horizons. But this is precisely the quality that is lacking in those who would think of themselves as unencumbered selves, bound only by the obligations they choose to incur. (Sandel, 1996: 16)

This conception of the unencumbered self is not only evident in Rawls's original position, with its veil of ignorance, but it is also evident, argues Sandel, in Rawls's direct argument for the second principle of justice. Recall that in Chapter 2 of *A Theory of Justice* Rawls rejects the systems of natural liberty and liberal equality because they do not go far enough in mitigating the morally arbitrary factors of the social and natural lotteries of life. Sandel claims that this argument is premised on Rawls's 'notion of the self as a pure, unadulterated, "essentially unencumbered" subject of possession' (Sandel, 1998: 92). Sandel describes Rawls's argument from the systems of natural liberty to democratic equality as stages in the dispossession of the person. 'With each transition, a substantive self, thick with particular traits, is progressively shorn of characteristics once taken to be essential to its identity; as more of its features are seen to be arbitrarily given, they are relegated from presumed constituents to mere attributes of the self' (Sandel, 1998: 93). Under the principle of natural liberty the self is still conceived as a 'thickly constituted self, burdened by the accidents of social and cultural contingency' (Sandel, 1998: 93). This thickly constituted self is stripped of these properties in the system of liberal equality. 'But even the principle of fair opportunity, in rewarding individual effort, conceives the province of the self too expansively' (Sandel, 1998: 93). And so in the third and final interpretation, democratic equality, the self is stripped of all contingently given attributes.

Sandel's characterization of the liberal view of the self has been criticized by liberals.[4] In *Liberalism, Community and Culture* Kymlicka argues that Sandel misconstrues what liberals like Rawls claim we can distance ourselves from.

> What is central to the liberal view is not that we can *perceive* a self prior to its ends, but that we understand our selves to be prior to our ends, *in the sense that no end or goal is exempt from possible re-examination*. For re-examination to be meaningfully conducted I must be able to envisage my self encumbered with different motivations than I now have, in order that I have some reason to choose one over another as more valuable for me. My self is, in this sense, perceived prior to its ends, i.e. I can always envisage my self without its *present* ends. But this doesn't require that I can ever perceive a self totally unencumbered by any ends – the process of ethical reasoning is always one of comparing one 'encumbered' potential self with another 'encumbered' potential self. There must always be some ends given with the self when we engage in such reasoning, but it doesn't follow that any *particular* ends must always be taken as given with the self. (Kymlicka, 1989a: 52–3)

One might argue that Sandel misconstrues both the original position and the argument from arbitrariness in order to support his interpretation of deontological liberalism and there is some validity to this charge. Far from being an argument about the dispossession of the self, the main issue that the argument from arbitrariness addresses is how economic institutions are to be arranged and assessed. The system of natural liberty, for example, is objectionable not because it treats citizens as thickly constituted selfs but because such an arrangement cannot be publicly justified. In particular it cannot be justified to those citizens who fare poorly in the natural and social lotteries of life. It is the unfairness of such a system, and not its conception of the self, that leads Rawls to reject it. Furthermore, Sandel's claim that the original position invokes controversial claims about the self stems from his failure to see it as a heuristic device designed to clarify what the fair terms of social cooperation are. Rawls argues that the claim that the original position presupposes a particular metaphysical conception of the person is

> an illusion caused by not seeing the original position as a device of representation. The veil of ignorance, to mention one prominent feature of that position, has no specific metaphysical implications concerning the nature of the self; it does not imply that the self is ontologically prior to the facts about persons that the parties are excluded from knowing … We must keep in mind that we are trying to show how the ideal of society as a fair system of social cooperation can be unfolded so as to find principles specifying the basic rights and liberties and the forms of equality most appropriate to those cooperating, once they are regarded as citizens, as free and equal persons. (Rawls, 1993: 27)

The confusion concerning the role the 'unencumbered self' plays in Rawls's liberalism stems from the fact that Rawls actually posits diverse justifications for his two principles of justice. Recall that Buchanan (1982) distinguishes between the *principles matching justification, the conditions matching argument* and the *Kantian interpretation*.[5] The first two justifications would only appeal to embedded persons, those who have the moral sensibilities that justice as fairness invokes. But the third justification supports Sandel's position. One might argue that this justification is not central to Rawls's position but Rawls's recent shift to a political conception of justice suggests that even Rawls himself believes that his early theory relies on the Kantian conception of the self.

Debates about the textual accuracy of Sandel's interpretation of Rawlsian liberalism should not detract one from the practical significance of Sandel's communitarian critique. In his second book, *Democracy's Discontent*, Sandel argues that this vision of the unencumbered self informs public debate in contemporary America and that this has costly consequences. If American constitutional law and debates about the political economy do appeal to the unencumbered conception of the self and this undermines self-government and community, as Sandel maintains, then liberals must take seriously his communitarian critique.

5.3 State neutrality

What matters most for the liberal self, argues Sandel, 'is not the ends we choose but our capacity to choose them' (Sandel, 1996: 12). In their quest to respect persons as autonomous, unencumbered selves liberals endorse the ideal of state neutrality.[6] The government must remain neutral about questions of the good life because only a neutral stance respects persons as free and independent selves who are capable of choosing for themselves their values and ends. This respect would be violated if, for example, the government required (or even just encouraged) citizens to adhere to a particular religious faith.

Sandel criticizes the neutral aspiration of liberals. Firstly, there are many cases where the state simply cannot remain neutral. Sandel gives the example of abortion, an issue which deeply divides many Americans. Whatever decision the government makes regarding abortion it cannot be neutral with respect to the underlying moral and religious controversy. If, for example, the government grants women the right to abortion then the government is making a judgement about the claim made by many religious people that abortion is morally tantamount to murder. The judgement in this case is that the belief that life begins at conception is wrong. This is what happened in *Roe* v. *Wade* (1973) when the American Supreme Court struck down a Texas law against abortion. Despite the Court's attempt to take a neutral stance on the contentious issue of when life begins its decision to strike down the Texas law meant that it took a stance on exactly that issue: namely, it supported the judgement that life does not begin at conception. The government simply cannot resolve an issue like abortion without engaging in moral and religious controversy.

In addition to its not always being possible, Sandel also argues that state neutrality has costly consequences. The aspiration for neutrality is one that has emerged over the past fifty years in American constitutional law and this is evident in a number of judicial decisions ranging from the separation of church and school to restrictions on hate speech and pornography. Sandel points to the failed attempts to prevent the harm of group defamation as evidence of how prevalent the unencumbered conception of the self is in contemporary American constitutional law. The court's handling of the Skokie controversy of 1977–8 illustrates this point. The controversy concerned the freedom of a neo-Nazi group to march through Skokie, Illinois, a predominately Jewish community. The municipal ordinances which prohibited the dissemination of materials inciting hatred based on race, national origin or religion were declared unconstitutional. Part of the rationale for rejecting such restrictions, claims Sandel, stems from the court's acceptance of the liberal view of the self:

> ... on the liberal conception of the person, the highest respect is the self-respect of a self independent of its aims and attachments. However much I prize the esteem of others, the respect that counts cannot conceivably be injured by a slur against the racial or religious groups to which I happen to belong. For the unencumbered self, the grounds of self-respect are antecedent to any particular ties or attachments, and so beyond the reach of an insult to 'my people'. (Sandel, 1996: 82)

The controversy over Indianapolis's anti-pornography law also illustrates this point. The 1984 Indianapolis ordinance sought to restrict pornography on the grounds that it degraded women and undermined civic equality and the ordinance was invalidated by the courts. A central justification behind the law, articulated by feminists like Catharine MacKinnon, was that pornography is an intrinsic harm because it shapes our understanding of the relations between the sexes. But this emphasis on the social nature of communication is at odds with the liberal conception of the self. Persons are, according to the liberal view, autonomous agents and choose their own identity. Autonomous agents who choose their own ends and values are not susceptible to the intrinsic harms that underlie the justification of the Indianapolis ordinance.

When the doctrine of state neutrality is utilized to protect racists, neo-Nazis or violent pornographic depictions, as it has in decisions in American constitutional law, it neglects the realities of many situated selves who are members of historically subordinated groups. Furthermore, it also prevents political communities from acting democratically to realize important goods. This is why Sandel claims that it gives rise to a public philosophy that has costly consequences.

It is difficult to assess the validity of Sandel's critique of neutrality because the ideal of neutrality has been characterized in many different ways. This makes it difficult to determine which laws or policies actually violate neutrality and which are consistent with it. Rawls, for example, distinguishes between procedural neutrality, neutrality of effect and neutrality of aim (Rawls, 1993: 191–5). He argues in favour of the latter. Does neutrality of aim necessarily rule out the kinds of measures Sandel thinks are reasonable? Much will depend on how stringently one conceives of neutrality of aim. Neutralist liberals like Rawls recognize that the state should not be neutral between all conceptions of the good, but only between permissible conceptions of the good (Rawls, 1993: 193). Which conceptions of the good are permissible and which are impermissible? Obviously those that harm others are impermissible but the concept of harm itself is subject to many different interpretations. The examples Sandel provides, such as the municipal ordinances limiting hate speech and pornography, could be justified on the grounds that these expressions harm others but the courts did not accept these arguments because the courts subscribe to the unencumbered conception of the self and thus believe that autonomous agents choose their own ends and values. Such agents are not easily manipulated by racist or sexist expressions and thus the alleged harms done by these expressions are sufficiently low enough to warrant treating such expressions as 'permissible conceptions of the good'. If the American courts adopted a different conception of the self, one which emphasized our social nature, they might have come to different conclusions.

The political economy

The public philosophy of the procedural republic not only dominates American constitutional debates, argues Sandel, it also permeates political discourse generally. Debates about the political economy, for example, are dominated by two considerations: prosperity and fairness. But the limited parameters of contemporary debates neglect a concern that was central to republican political theory.[7] Namely, the concern for economic arrangements that are most hospitable to self-government. Self-government means 'deliberating with fellow citizens about the common good and helping to shape the destiny of the political community' (Sandel, 1996: 5). This cannot be accomplished if the government does not play a formative role in helping to cultivate the moral and civic character of its citizens. Robbed of its formative role, the government, like most things in the age of consumerism, treats citizens as consumers. The function of government is to satisfy the existing preferences of the citizenry, not to shape what these preferences are let alone judge some as more worthy than others.

The sharp increase in economic inequality America has experienced from the late 1970s, argues Sandel, has undermined the spirit of friendship self-government requires. The bigger the gap between the rich and poor the less the sense that they share the same fate. The rich no longer care about the quality of public services when they have the option of buying quality private education and can pay private security services to patrol their residential communities. Affluent Americans are evacuating public spaces, retreating to privatized communities. Sandel claims:

> As affluent Americans increasingly buy their way out of reliance on public services, the formative, civic resources of American life diminish. The deterioration of urban public schools is perhaps the most conspicuous and damaging instance of this trend. Another is the growing reliance on private security services, one of the fastest-growing occupational categories in the 1980s. So great was the demand for security personnel in shopping malls, airports, retail stores, and residential communities that by 1990 the number of private security guards nationwide exceeded the number of public police officers. (Sandel, 1996: 332)

With the decline of community has come a decline in concern for the common good. Politics, argues Sandel, needs to be concerned with restoring *civic spaces*, places where people can engage in debate about the common good, such as churches, schools and community centres. But this formative ambition runs counter to the dictates of state neutrality. The neutral state is not concerned with cultivating civic virtues. Respect for persons requires respecting them as independent selves, unencumbered by moral or civic ties they have not chosen. Thus contemporary liberalism cannot inspire a public philosophy that can remedy the discontents of American politics.

Consider the issue of state neutrality:

- Do you think the state can and should be neutral?
- What about contentious policy issues like censoring hate speech and pornography or publicly funding the Arts?
- Do you agree with Sandel's claim that self-government requires that citizens possess, or come to acquire, certain qualities of character? What are these qualities of character and how could we cultivate them?

Further reading

George Sher, *Beyond Neutrality: Perfectionism and Politics* (Cambridge: Cambridge University Press, 1997).
Harry Brighouse, 'Neutrality, Publicity, and State Funding of the Arts,' *Philosophy and Public Affairs*, 24 (1), 1995: 36–63.
William Galston, *Liberal Purposes: Goods, Virtues and Duties in the Liberal State* (Cambridge: Cambridge University Press, 1991).

5.4 Walzer and complex equality

The second communitarian critic, whom we shall now consider, is Michael Walzer. As we noted above, Walzer takes issue with the methodology liberals employ when approaching the issue of distributive justice. Walzer's approach is *particularist* instead of universalist. He claims that 'different social goods ought to be distributed for different reasons, in accordance with different procedures, by different agents; and all these differences derive from different understandings of the social goods themselves – the inevitable product of historical and cultural particularism' (Walzer, 1983: 6).

Distributive justice, argues Walzer, should not be conceived of as a unified search for a single distributive criterion to govern a short list of basic goods. Most theorists approach distributive justice as if it were a social process of the following form:

> *People distribute goods to (other) people.*

Such an approach, claims Walzer, is too simple. Distributive justice concerns a complex social process which is more accurately captured in the following statement:

> *People conceive and create goods, which they then distribute among themselves.*

Like Nozick, Walzer is critical of theorists who treat goods as if they were manna from the heavens.[8] Before goods are distributed they are conceived and created. Walzer wants to 'shift our attention from distribution itself to conception and creation: the naming of the goods, and the giving of meaning, and the collective making' (Walzer, 1983: 7). Each community creates it own social goods and thus the list of goods governed by principles of distributive justice will differ from society to society. Walzer rejects the idea of a single set of 'primary goods' which are applicable across all moral and material worlds. Even something as basic as food can have different meanings in different societies. 'Bread is the staff of life, the body of Christ, the symbol of the Sabbath, the means of hospitality, and so on' (Walzer, 1983: 8).

Walzer devotes whole chapters to a diverse list of goods which most societies value, though the meanings of these goods differ from culture to culture. These goods, in the order in which he addresses them are:

Membership
Security and welfare
Money and commodities
Office (i.e. positions of employment)
Hard work
Free time
Education
Kinship and love
Divine grace
Recognition
Political power.

What distributive principle(s) could cover such a diverse range of goods? By making the theory of goods central to his account of distributive justice Walzer effectively demonstrates his point that there is no single criterion, or a single set of interconnected criteria, for all distributions. It is appropriate to distribute some goods in accordance with the principle of free exchange (e.g. money), others with desert (e.g. punishment and honours) and still others with need (e.g. security and welfare). A determination of which distributive criterion is just for each different good depends, argues Walzer, on the meaning of the social good itself. Take a social good like health care. Walzer notes that, until recent times, the practice of medicine was mostly a matter of free enterprise. Doctors were often attached to noble houses and royal courts and thus the benefits of medical care were limited to an elite minority. But in time our attitudes, and our institutions, changed. In contemporary liberal societies the social understanding of health care prescribes some form of communal care instead of a market regulation of medical care. We believe that care should be provided according to need and not to wealth. Walzer claims that 'among modern citizens, longevity is a socially recognized need; and increasingly every effort is made to see that it is widely and equally distributed, that every citizen has an equal chance at a long and healthy life:

hence doctors and hospitals in every district, regular check-ups, health education for the young, compulsory vaccination, and so on' (Walzer, 1983: 87).

The emphasis and priority Walzer places on the social meaning of goods raises a number of concerns. Firstly, are there any shared social meanings of goods like welfare and security? Dworkin (1985), for example, argues that the good of health care is extremely contentious in a society like America.

> In the United States we sponsor medical research through taxes, and after long political struggles we offer Medicare to the old and Medicaid to the poor, though the latter remains very controversial. Walzer thinks these programs demonstrate that our community assigns medical care to a particular sphere, the sphere of needs that the state must satisfy. But the brutal fact is that we do not provide anything like the same medical care for the poor that the middle classes can provide for themselves, and surely this also counts in deciding what the 'social meaning' of medicine is in our society. Even those who agree that some medical care must be provided for everyone disagree about limits. Is it part of the social meaning of medicine that elective surgery be free? That people 'need' heart transplants? (Dworkin, 1985: 216)

Amy Gutmann (1995) expresses a similar concern when she argues that the social meanings of some goods are multiple and the multiple meanings sometimes conflict. Gutmann considers the example of productive employment in America. One meaning of the good 'productive employment' means careers, and thus the appropriate distributive criterion would be careers open to talent. The relevant consideration that should govern the distribution of careers should be the qualifications of the candidates. But, argues Gutmann, 'people also *need* productive employment in order to live a decent life in our society, where the decency of our lives includes our being respected by our fellow citizens, being treated as equals' (Gutmann, 1995: 103). This need standard competes with the qualification standards. The resolution of these competing distributive principles cannot be solved by deciding what 'jobs' really means in our society. In order to resolve this kind of conflict Gutmann argues that we must bring in moral considerations, considerations that go beyond the social meanings of the good in question.

The concerns expressed by Dworkin and Gutmann raise serious problems for the viability of Walzer's interpretive approach. Another concern critics raise is the relativistic and conservative consequences of Walzer's position. If we are to turn to existing conventions for guidance on what the appropriate distributive criteria are does this not simply legitimize the status quo? On what basis can we even criticize our own conventions let alone those of authoritarian regimes? Justice, argues Dworkin, is our critic and not our mirror and thus 'Walzer's relativism is faithless to the single most important social practice we have: the practice of worrying about what justice is' (Dworkin, 1985: 219). But surprisingly, the main focus of *Spheres of Justice* is actually the development of a radical account of distributive justice called *complex equality*. Let us briefly consider this account as it will reveal the fundamental tension between Walzer's methodology and his normative conclusions.

Complex equality

Despite the obvious relativistic and conservative implications of Walzer's particularist methodology he actually defends a theory of distributive justice that is very radical. He calls this theory complex equality. Each social good represents a distinct sphere of justice and complex equality obtains when

> No citizen's standing in one sphere or with regard to one social good can be undercut by his standing in some other sphere, with regard to some other good. Thus, citizen X may be chosen over citizen Y for political office, and then the two of them will be unequal in the sphere of politics. But they will not be unequal generally so long as X's office gives him no advantages over Y in any other sphere – superior medical care, access to better schools for his children, entrepreneurial opportunities, and so on. (Walzer, 1983: 19)

Complex equality is contrasted with the system of simple equality. The former seeks to equally distribute (or more widely share) some dominant good, like money. But complex equality can permit inequalities in social goods. What complex equality resists is the convertibility of social goods, so that a good like money cannot be converted into better medical care, etc. Complex equality requires the distinct distributive spheres be autonomous. Domination occurs when possession of one social good or set of goods is allowed to be transferred into an advantage in another sphere and thus complex equality is necessary to rule out domination.

The appropriate arrangements for a society like contemporary America, argues Walzer, are those of

> a decentralised democratic socialism; a strong welfare state run, in part at least, by local and amateur officials; a constrained market; an open and demystified civil service; independent public schools; the sharing of hard work and free time; the protection of religious and familial life; a system of public honouring and dishonouring free from all considerations of rank or class; workers' control of companies and factories; a politics of parties, movements, meetings, and public debate. (Walzer, 1983: 318)

Walzer's ideal of complex equality could be utilized to criticize many different aspects of Western democratic societies. Walzer's concern with non-domination, for example, is well suited to feminism which is concerned with male dominance. This issue will be more fully addressed in Chapter 8. But let us briefly consider Walzer's comments on the family for they reveal what is a fundamental tension between Walzer's methodology and his normative conclusions.

The family, argues Walzer, constitutes a significant sphere of justice:

> Important distributions are carried out within the family and through the alliance of families. Dowries, gifts, inheritances, alimony, mutual aid of many different kinds: all these are subject to customs and rules that are conventional in character and reflect deep, but never permanent, understandings. (Walzer, 1983: 227–8)

If we were to apply Walzer's interpretive methodology to the sphere of the family in order to provide some guidance on what the appropriate distributive principle is for the family the results would be antithetical to feminism. The historical record of the family is that of an institution that unjustly favours males over females. Historically, and in many current cultures it still is the case, it was only the male offspring that inherited the family's assets, was encouraged to pursue higher education, a career, or be involved in politics. The place for women was in the home. Thus feminists have, according to Walzer's methodology, no grounds for objecting to what they call the 'injustices' within the family as there is no universal standpoint from which such proclamations can be made. The only standpoint that can be taken is that which appeals to the social meanings of these goods in our own culture.

   This response would be consistent with Walzer's methodology but it is not the response he himself makes. The domination of women is unjust and can be construed as such by the standards of complex equality, argues Walzer. But 'the real domination of women has less to do with their familial place than with their exclusion from all other places. They have been denied the freedom of the city, cut off from distributive processes and social goods outside the sphere of kinship and love' (Walzer, 1983: 240). When inequalities in the sphere of the family are translated into inequalities in other spheres (such as politics) then the requirements of complex equality have been violated. But, as Susan Okin points out, the feminist implications of the ideal of complex equality require 'a radical break not only from prevailing patterns of behaviour but also from widely, though not completely, shared understandings in our society about the social meanings, institutions, and implications of sexual difference' (Okin, 1989: 116). Thus the two strands of Walzer's argument, his appeal to shared social meanings and the ideal of complex equality, appear to be in tension with each other. It is a concern with the potentially conservative implications of communitarianism that has led many theorists to criticize it as a normative political theory. The degree to which such a criticism would be true of Walzer depends on whether one places a greater emphasis on his moral methodology or his ideal of complex equality.

5.5 Miller on nationalism

Communitarians like Sandel and Walzer are critical of the liberal tendency to conceive of justice in purely abstract terms, so that individuals are treated as 'unencumbered selves' and little attention is paid to the fact that social goods have different meanings for different communities. The particularist approach advocated by communitarians has significant implications for not only domestic justice, but also for the way we conceive of global justice. The liberal aspiration for universalism has led some, such as Beitz, to proclaim that the demands of justice should apply globally and thus we are not justi- fied in giving preferential treatment to compatriots. Beitz's argument is a form of *ethical universalism*. Ethical universalism maintains that 'all persons ought to be treated with equal and impartial consideration for their respec- tive goods or interests' (Gewirth, 1988: 283). National boundaries have no significant ethical relevance for ethical univeralists because considerations such as one's nationality are irrelevant to the issue of what we owe to each other. If person X is suffering and will die without my intervention the fact that person X is not a compatriot is irrelevant. They are a *human being*, and that is sufficient for saying that I have a duty to aid them.

Ethical particularists do not deny that we have some duties to non-nationals, but they defend a competing account of the structure of ethical life. As David Miller puts it, ethical particularists hold that 'relations between persons are part of the basic subject-matter of ethics, so that fundamental principles may be attached directly to these relations' (Miller, 1995: 50). Relations such as the fact that person X is my brother or a compatriot play a significant role in determining how much consideration I ought to (and can) place on person X. Ethical particularism, argues Miller, treats agents as already 'encumbered with a variety of ties and commitments to particular other agents, or to groups or collectivities, and they begin their ethical reasoning from those commitments' (Miller, 1995: 50). Miller defends ethical particularism and applies it to the issue of nationalism. Let us consider some of the details of Miller's argument for nationalism as it will further illustrate the practical significance of the communitarian critique of liberalism.

Miller argues that national boundaries are ethically significant. 'The duties we owe to our compatriots may be more extensive than the duties we owe to strangers, simply because they are compatriots' (Miller, 1988: 647). Miller's defence of nationalism rests on three interconnected propositions. These are:

1 It may properly be part of someone's identity that they belong to this or that national grouping.
2 Nations are ethical communities.
3 People who form a national community have a good claim to political self-determination (Miller, 1995: 10–11).

Let us briefly consider each of these in some detail. The first proposition divides into two further propositions, one more contentious than the other. The non-contentious claim is that nations really exist. Miller distinguishes between a nation and a state. These two terms are often used synonymously but it is important to distinguish between them. A 'state' 'is a body that successfully claims a monopoly of legitimate force in a particular territory' (Miller, 1995: 19). But a 'nation' refers to a community of people with an aspiration to be politically self-determining. A nation is a community that is (1) constituted by shared belief and mutual commitment, (2) extended in history, (3) active in character, (4) connected to a particular territory and (5) marked off from other communities by its distinct public culture (Miller, 1995: 27). Thus we can have more than one nation in a state (for example, the former Soviet Union), one nation that is split between two states (for example, Germany before reunification) and people of a single nationality scattered as minorities in a number of different states (for example, Palestinians).

The second, and more contentious, part of Miller's first proposition concerning national identity is that in making our nationality part of our identity we are not doing something that is rationally indefensible. The degree to which this is true depends on the kind of national identification one wishes to defend. Certain forms of national identification certainly are rationally indefensible. The history of humanity is littered with examples of conquest and slaughter in the name of nationalism and Miller does not wish to defend such a version of nationalism. This becomes evident once we turn to the second and third propositions of his account of nationalism. Identifying ourselves with a nation need not lead to the injustices of war. In fact, Miller argues that nationalism serves many important purposes, including promoting many of the values liberals cherish.

The second proposition of Miller's account of nationalism is that nations are ethical communities. This does not mean that we have no duties to people outside our nation, but that the duties we owe to our compatriots are different and more extensive than those we owe to people in other nations. This vision of ethical life is one that places greater emphasis on our natural sentiments than on our capacity for rational reflection. Thus this approach is Humean rather than Kantian. David Hume 'saw that morality had to be understood in relation to natural sentiments, so that the judgements we make about others must reflect their (and our) natural preferences for kinsmen and associates' (Miller, 1995: 58 note 11).[9] A vast array of motives moves us to fulfil other-regarding requirements – love, pride, etc. By narrowing the scope of permissible motives to rational conviction the demands of ethical universalism will fail to motivate us as they do not recognize that we are embedded selves with a variety of ties and commitments.

Miller argues that if one were to take the demands of ethical universalism seriously they would led to counterintuitive consequences. He claims:

> … I believe that ethical universalists who believe in a duty to protect basic rights of the kind I have been discussing – and, even more so, those who believe in a general utilitarian duty to promote the welfare of fellow human beings – ought to take seriously the case of benevolent imperialism. Given that many existing states signally fail to protect the basic rights of their members, and given also that on universalist grounds we can attach no intrinsic value to the obligations of community or to national self-determination,

why not subject the members of these states to benign outside rule? … Why make a fetish of self-government if your basic rights will be better protected by outsiders? (Miller, 1995: 78)

Ethical particularism does not lead to benevolent imperialism, rather it is committed to the principle of *national self-determination*. This is the third proposition of Miller's account of nationalism. National self-determination is valuable from a nationalist perspective for a number of reasons. Miller identifies three main reasons: concerns for social justice, protection of the national culture, and the expression of collective autonomy (Miller, 1995: 83–90). With the right to be nationally self-determining comes the obligation to respect a similar right for others. The principle of national self-determination imposes on states a diverse array of duties. These include:

1 The duty to abstain from materially harming another state.
2 The duty not to exploit states that are one-sidedly vulnerable to your actions.
3 The duty to comply with whatever international agreements have been made, including of course treaties to establish confederal institutions.
4 Obligations of reciprocity arising from practices of mutual aid whereby states come to one anothers' assistance in moments of need.
5 Obligations to ensure the fair distribution of natural resources. (Miller, 1995: 104–5).

Miller notes that the fifth of these is the most problematic so a brief consideration of it would be useful to bring out the differences between Miller and Beitz. This obligation is not a general obligation for the rich states to help poor ones. The duty is entailed by respect for the self-determination of other national communities. This duty arises because 'nations cannot provide for the basic needs of their members and cannot exercise any sort of collective autonomy unless they have a sufficient resource base to be economically viable' (Miller, 1995: 105). Furthermore, once nations have reached this sufficient threshold the richer states are not obligated to continue to redistribute, as is entailed by something like Beitz's global difference principle. Respect for the self-determination of other national communities, argues Miller

involves treating them as responsible for decisions they may make about resource use, economic growth, environmental use and so forth. As a result of these decisions, living standards in different countries may vary substantially, and one cannot then justify redistribution by appeal to egalitarian principles of justice such as the Rawlsian difference principle. (Miller, 1995: 108)

Miller's defence of nationalism brings to the fore the practical significance of the communitarian critique of liberalism. The majority of people, argues Miller, 'are too deeply attached to their inherited national identities to make their obliteration an intelligent goal' (Miller, 1995: 184). Thus the humanitarian sentiment that every human being should matter equally to us is unrealistic. But despite this obvious difference between Miller and Beitz, Miller's ethical particularism does recognize a diverse array of duties that states must fulfil if they are to take the principle of national self-determination seriously. Miller's argument shows that one need not invoke a vision of global citizenship in order to generate international duties. But ethical universalists will charge that these duties are not stringent enough. By permitting us to place greater concern on our compatriots the duties entailed even by the principle of national self-determination can be undermined. If, for example, the obligation to ensure a fair distribution of natural resources means that the richest countries will have to give to the poor countries to such a degree that the quality of life in the richest countries would decline, nationalists can simply ignore this duty by claiming that duties to their compatriots trump those they owe to non-nationals. This is why Beitz criticizes Rawls for limiting the difference principle to the domestic realm. While the difference principle appears to be very egalitarian, by limiting its application to the domestic sphere it has costly consequences for the most disadvantaged in the world. The challenge facing nationalists like Miller is to provide an account of when the redistributive duties entailed by the principle of national self-determination can override the special duties we have to compatriots. Many would argue that the disparity between the standards of living in the richest and poorest countries stems from the fact that members of the rich countries place too much weight on their national identification, to the detriment of those who live in extreme poverty.

Discuss the following statements:

1   Ethical particularism seems like a more plausible account of ethical life than ethical universalism because people do (and should) care more for their compatriots than they do for non-nationals. This is not to say that we shouldn't care about non-nationals, of course we should. But the ties we have to compatriots are much more extensive. I think we are justified in giving a priority to the poor in our own society simply because they are *our* poor.

2   National boundaries do not have any ethical significance, on the contrary, they serve many immoral purposes. National boundaries help ensure that the 'haves' of this world remain the 'haves' and keep the 'have-nots' out of their country. Miller believes that national self-determination promotes concerns of social justice. I think he is wrong. I do not think we shall ever create a just world order as long as we identify (at least primarily) with some national grouping.

3   Reflect on your own national identity and what being 'British' (or 'American', 'Canadian', etc.) consists of. Discuss the pros and cons of nationalism.

5.6 Conclusion

Assessing the liberal–communitarian debate is difficult as liberals and communitarians advance many different claims, some of which are more compatible than others. The invocation of the ideal of *community* can mean different things and thus it can sometimes be used to inspire an emancipatory public philosophy or be used to legitimize repressive customs and traditions. Those attracted to communitarianism see its potential to achieve the former whilst those critical of communitarianism believe it cannot escape the tendency of the latter.

Andrew Mason (2000) makes a number of useful distinctions that are worth bearing in mind when assessing the liberal–communitarian debate. The first distinction is that between a mere association of people and the ordinary concept of community. A mere association 'consists of people who interact with one another primarily on a contractual basis, in order to further their own self-regarding interests' (Mason, 2000: 20). This contrasts with the ordinary concept of community. A community is 'constituted by a group of people who share a range of values, a way of life, identify with the group and its practices and recognize each other as members of that group' (Mason, 2000: 21). Of the different versions of liberalism examined in Part One of this present book, Gauthier's contractarian project relies on a mere association of people and not a community. What binds utility-maximizers to the dictates of minimax relative concession is their concern for their own self-interest, not shared values or a way of life. Nor do these individuals recognize each other as members of a group when they only extend membership in the cooperative enterprise to those who can fulfil the requirements of the reciprocity thesis. Of the different versions of liberalism we have examined Gauthier's is the most susceptible to the charge that it neglects or undermines community.

The charge that the liberalisms of Rawls, Nozick or Dworkin undermine community is arguably harder to establish. This is due to the fact that, as Mason points out, the *moralized concept* of community includes the additional conditions that there be solidarity between its members and no systematic exploitation. These additional conditions are subject to different interpretations. Nozick could argue that his minimal state fulfils these two further conditions of community. The Kantian dictum on which Nozick premises his entitlement theory – 'treat individuals as ends-in-themselves and never as a means only' – requires members to give each others' interests some non-instrumental weight. So citizens who internalize that dictum have a sense of solidarity. Furthermore, Nozick would argue that by ruling out redistributive policies the minimal state ensures that there will be no systematic exploitation. Such exploitation exists when the state forces people, through taxation, to support the policies of, for example, the welfare state.

Many people would challenge Nozick's conception of both solidarity and exploitation and thus argue that his moralized conception of community is illusory.   Solidarity requires more than merely respecting the individual rights of others. Furthermore, the vulnerable members of society are still susceptible to exploitation when their fate rests in the hands of the generosity of philanthropists. Without a more extensive state in place the elimination of exploitation is not possible.

The extent to which the liberal-egalitarianism of Rawls and Dworkin invokes a defensible moralized conception of community is also debatable and further complicates the alleged dichotomy between liberalism and communitarianism. When one considers Rawls's difference principle or Dworkin's partnership conception of democracy then their liberalisms look very communitarian. But their commitment to state neutrality, for example, clearly distinguishes them from communitarians like Sandel. Furthermore, they do not approach to the issue of distributive justice in the particularist manner advocated by Walzer. So there remain substantial disagreements between liberals and communitarians. In this chapter we have examined what the practical significances of these disagreements are. From the issues of censoring hate speech and debates about the political economy, to complex equality and nationalism, the communitarian challenge brings a number of important issues to the fore and has forced liberals to re-cast their theories in a way that takes more seriously the charge that liberalism rests on faulty foundations and gives rise to a public philosophy that has costly consequences.

SUMMARY

- Sandel argues that contemporary liberal theory is premised on the unencumbered conception of the self and that this conception of the self gives rise to a public philosophy that undermines self-government and a sense of community. He cites examples ranging from the regulation of freedom of expression to debates about the political economy to illustrate the costly consequences of state neutrality.
- In *Spheres of Justice* Walzer criticizes the abstract, universalist approach liberals take to the issue of distributive justice. Walzer rejects the idea that there is a single set of 'primary goods' which are applicable across different societies. Despite the obvious relativistic and conservative implications of Walzer's methodology he actually endorses a radical conception of justice entitled *complex equality*.
- Miller defends a version of nationalism that is premised on the communitarian insight that agents are encumbered with a variety of ties and commitments to particular agents or to groups or collectivities. Miller argues, contra ethical univeralists, that national boundaries are ethically significant. This has important ramifications for determining what the demands of international justice are.

Notes

1   Other important communitarians include Charles Taylor (1985, 1990) and Alisdair MacIntyre (1981). There is a vast literature on the liberal–communitarian debate. For a comprehensive examination of the main theorists in this debate see Mulhall and Swift (1992).
2   References to this work are to the second edition published in 1998.
3   See *Democracy's Discontent*, pp. 15–16.
4   See Thomas Pogge's *Realizing Rawls* (1989), Chapter 2, for extensive criticism of Sandel's argument.
5   See section 1.8 in Chapter 1 of this book.
6   George Sher (1997) provides a more expansive account of the reasons why liberals endorse neutrality. These are:

   1   because non-neutral government decisions violate the autonomy of citizens;
   2   because non-neutral government decisions pose unacceptable risks of oppression, instability, or error;
   3   because non-neutral government decisions rest on value-premises that cannot be rationally defended (Sher, 1997: 15).

7   Many political theorists have recently turned to the republican tradition to offer an alternative to contemporary liberalism. See, for example, Pettit (1997) and Dagger (1997).
8   But, as will become apparent shortly, Walzer does not endorse Nozick's libertarianism.
9   See David Hume, *A Treatise of Human Nature* and David Miller (1981).

6 Multiculturalism

Summary Contents

6.1   Introduction: the politics of recognition   119
6.2   Kymlicka and the rights of national minorities   122
6.3   Polyethnic rights   127
6.4   Barry against multiculturalism   131

6.1 Introduction: the politics of recognition

In recent years the liberal–communitarian debate has faded from the prominence it enjoyed in normative political theory during the 1980s and 1990s. But that debate has had a lasting impression on both the issues political theorists now feel should be addressed as well as the way they theorize about these issues. This is most evident in the current debates about one of the most important issues to have evolved out of the liberal–communitarian debate[1] – *multiculturalism*. Multiculturalism covers a wide range of issues and has been defended and criticized by theorists of diverse political traditions. This makes any attempt to present multiculturalism as a unified, coherent theory insincere and so I will not attempt to do that in this chapter. Whilst there is no consensus among multiculturalist theorists concerning the principles, goals and policies they believe best promote multiculturalism, what unites these theorists is their concern that we should resist the wider society's homogenizing or assimilationist thrust and its tendency to assume that there is only one correct, true or normal way to understand and structure the relevant areas of life (Parekh, 2000: 1). This assimilationist thrust is evident in the conception of citizenship endorsed by the liberal theories of justice canvassed in Part One. Despite the differences between the liberalisms of the distributive paradigm, what they share is the belief that justice requires *equal rights* for all citizens. Rawls, Nozick, Gauthier and Dworkin may disagree on what is the foundation of the rights they defend (for example, concerns of impartiality and fairness, self-interest, etc.), but they agree that whatever rights justice does require these rights should apply equally to all citizens, regardless of their gender, religion or ethnicity. It is unjust, for example, to exclude women or Catholics or African-Americans from exercising the rights other citizens enjoy, like freedom of expression and the right to vote. As Will Kymlicka notes, the logical conclusion of liberal principles of justice 'seems to be a "colour-blind" constitution – the removal of all legislation differentiating people in terms of their race or ethnicity (except for temporary measures, like affirmative action, which are believed necessary to reach a colour-blind society)' (Kymlicka, 1989a: 141). But multiculturalists view the aspiration for a colour-blind society as ill-founded for it is not possible to separate the state and ethnicity, for example, and when the liberal state attempts to do this it unfairly privileges certain ways of life over others.

The charge that liberalism privileges certain ways of life over others might sound misplaced given the emphasis liberals like Rawls place on the fact of 'reasonable pluralism'. It is precisely *because* liberals take pluralism seriously, they might retort, that they endorse a neutralist public philosophy that entails equal rights for all citizens. But multiculturalists do not believe that the liberalisms of the distributive paradigm take diversity seriously enough. Parekh argues that Rawls, like many liberals, 'is sensitive to moral but not cultural plurality' and that thus liberals take little account of the cultural aspirations of such communities as the indigenous peoples, national minorities, subnational groups, and the immigrants (Parekh, 2000: 89). Kymlicka argues that liberals like Rawls and Dworkin have falsely assumed that members of a *political community* are members of the same *cultural community*. Kymlicka describes these two kinds of community:

> On the one hand, there is political community, within which individuals exercise the rights and responsibilities entailed by the framework of liberal justice. People who reside within the same political community are fellow citizens. On the other hand, there is the cultural community, within which individuals form and revise their aims and ambitions. People within the same cultural community share a culture, a language and history which defines their cultural membership. (Kymlicka, 1989a: 135)

The liberal theories of justice canvassed in Part One ignore the fact that many modern democratic societies are multinational and/or polyethnic. The former are states that have incorporated previously self-governing cultures such as aboriginal peoples whilst the latter are states where cultural diversity arises from immigration. Canada is an example of a country that is both multinational and polyethnic. It has national minorities (such as aboriginal peoples and the Québécois) as well as a significant immigrant population. The politics of equal citizenship and economic redistribution are not fully equipped, argue multiculturalists, to deal with the diverse concerns which are raised in multinational and polyethnic states. Multiculturalists thus endorse the *politics of recognition* (Taylor, 1993) which inspires a public philosophy premised on the concepts of identify and difference instead of the principle of equal citizenship. The politics of recognition does, like the politics of equal citizenship, have a universal basis but that basis is not that everyone should be treated the same. On the contrary, the politics of recognition requires that '*everyone* should be recognized for his or her unique identity ... The universal demand powers an acknowledgement of specificity' (Taylor, 1993: 38).

'Multiculturalism is not about difference and identity *per se* but about those that are embedded in and sustained by culture; that is, a body of beliefs and practices in terms of which a group of people understand themselves and the world and organize their individual and collective lives' (Parekh, 2000: 2–3). It is useful to see the current debates about multiculturalism as an extension of the liberal/communitarian debate because multiculturalists echo the communitarian's concern that we recognize that we are social beings that are embedded in particular cultures and value different cultural practices. Bhikhu Parekh argues that multiculturalism occupies a middle position between two dominant strands of political theory – naturalism (or monism) and culturalism (or pluralism). The former is espoused by a diverse array of philosophers ranging from Greek and Christian philosophers to Hobbes, Locke and Mill, all of whom 'assumed that human nature was unchanging, unaffected in its essentials by culture and society, and capable of indicating what way of life was the best' (Parekh, 2000: 10). Culturalists, on the other hand, like Vico, Montesquieu, Herder and the German Romantics, argued for the opposite view. They believed that 'human beings were culturally constituted, varied from culture to culture, and share in common only the minimal species-derived properties from which nothing of moral and political significance could be derived' (Parekh, 2000: 10). But both of these positions, argues Parekh, are deeply problematic.

> Neither naturalism nor culturalism gives a coherent account of human life and helps us theorise multicultural societies. One stresses the undeniable fact of shared humanity, but ignores the equally obvious fact that human nature is culturally mediated and reconstituted and cannot by itself provide a transcendental basis for a cross-culturally valid vision of the good life; the other makes the opposite mistake. Neither grasps the two in their relationship and appreciates that human beings are at once both natural and cultural, both alike and unlike, and like in unlike ways. (Parekh, 2000: 11)

So multiculturalists share the conviction that *cultural plurality* must figure prominently in our theorizing about how we ought, collectively as a society, to live together. But contemporary liberalism ignores this plurality when it endorses the assimilationist politics of equal citizenship. Furthermore, because liberals believe that their theory is 'culturally neutral' they are blind to the fact that they unfairly privilege the interests of the cultural majority over the interests of cultural minorities. The practical significance of multiculturalism is most effectively illustrated by separating some of the distinct practical issues at stake in the debates about multiculturalism. In this chapter I intend to cover three distinct issues. Firstly, in the next section we consider Kymlicka's argument for granting national minorities (for example, aboriginal peoples) rights of self-government. These rights permit aboriginal peoples to limit the rights of non-aboriginals (such as their property or voting rights) within aboriginal territorial jurisdictions in order to ensure that national minorities can protect the good of cultural membership. This good, argues Kymlicka, is a primary good and national minorities face burdens members of the cultural majority do not face. This inequality in cultural circumstances is an *unchosen* inequality and thus compensation, in the form of rights of self-government, is required and this can be justified on egalitarian liberal grounds. In section 6.3 we consider polyethnic rights, such as exemptions from motor-cycle helmet laws, humane slaughter regulations and dress codes.[2] In the concluding section we consider some of the liberal criticisms that have been made in reply to the arguments advanced by multiculturalists.

6.2 Kymlicka and the rights of national minorities

One of the staunchest defenders of the rights of national minorities is Will Kymlicka (1989a, 1995a) who argues that egalitarian liberals ought to supplement traditional human rights with minority rights. In this section we shall consider Kymlicka's egalitarian liberal argument for special political and social rights for aboriginal peoples. Doing this will allow us to develop some of the themes canvassed in the first part of the book, thus further illustrating the practical significance of these abstract theoretical debates. Kymlicka argues that the unusual powers and rights that the aboriginal population in Canada and the United States are given are not, contrary to what is commonly assumed, inconsistent with liberal theories of justice. These rights are self-government rights which permit aboriginal communities to restrict the mobility, property and voting rights of non-aboriginal people. Kymlicka's liberal defence of these self-government rights is developed in two stages. Let us consider both of these stages in turn.

The first stage of Kymlicka's argument is to argue that cultural membership has a more important status in liberal thought than is explicitly recognized. Liberals place a great deal of emphasis on the values of autonomy and self-respect; they emphasize the importance of deciding for yourself what life to lead. The government, for example, should not tell individuals what occupation they are best suited for, whom to date, what hobbies to pursue or what religious faith to adhere to. Individuals should be free to choose for themselves what sort of life they wish to lead. But the choice of options that are open to us is not infinite but rather it is determined by our cultural heritage.

> Different ways of life are not simply different patterns of physical movements. The physical movements only have meaning to us because they are identified as having significance by our *culture*, because they fit into some pattern of activities which is culturally recognized as a way of leading one's life. We learn about these patterns of activity through their presence in stories we've heard about the lives, real or imaginary, of others. They become potential models, and define potential roles, that we can adopt as our own.

> From childhood on, we become aware both that we are already participants in certain forms of life (familial, religious, sexual, educational, etc.), and that there are other ways of life which offer alternative models and roles that we may, in time, come to endorse. We decide how to lead our lives by situating ourselves in these cultural narratives, by adopting roles that have struck us as worthwhile ones, as ones worth living (which may, of course, include the roles we were brought up to occupy). (Kymlicka, 1989a: 165)

The cultural structure of our society determines the context of choice that autonomous individuals can chose from when deciding what sort of lives to pursue. The list of occupations that one is free to choose from, for example, will be determined by the cultural characteristics of one's society. For example, making a living being a computer analyst, farmer, cosmetic surgeon or shepherd are only real options in societies that have the requisite cultural characteristics. The option of making a living being a shepherd is not on the list of options open to individuals growing up in the hustle and bustle of urban life in New York City. Because cultural heritage is inextricably linked to our autonomy and self-respect liberals ought to pay greater attention to it, argues Kymlicka. He suggests that cultural membership be treated as one of Rawls's primary goods. Recall that these are goods every rational person is presumed to have an interest in. The rational parties in the original position would have an interest in cultural membership because they have an interest in leading a good life. The ability to lead a good life is impaired when one does not enjoy cultural membership because the options open to one are alien or at least are much more narrow than the options open to individuals who enjoy cultural membership. Imagine how different the life prospects of the parties in the original position would be if, once the veil of ignorance was lifted, it turned out that the dominant culture of their society communicated in a different language and valued ways of life radically different from the ones they had grown up with. Let us expand on this point by turning to the second part of Kymlicka's argument for minority self-government rights.

The second stage of Kymlicka's argument is to establish the point that members of minority cultural communities may face particular kinds of disadvantages (with respect to the good of cultural membership) and that these disadvantages require and justify the provision of minority rights. To make this point Kymlicka suggests we revisit Dworkin's auction tale of the shipwrecked survivors on the desert island. But Kymlicka slightly modifies the example. Instead of survivors from one ship being washed up on a desert island Kymlicka asks us to image two ships, one large and one small, are shipwrecked on the island and the passengers of the two ships proceed with Dworkin's auction without ever leaving their ships.[3] Once all of the island's resources have been bid on, and the conditions of the envy test satisfied, the passengers from the two ships disembark eager to start utilizing the different resources they have acquired. But it turns out that the two ships are from different nationalities. The passengers from the small ship now find themselves in a disadvantaged position.

> The members of the minority culture are now in a very undesirable position. Assuming, as is reasonable, that their resources are distributed evenly across the island, they will now be forced to try to execute their chosen lifestyles in an alien culture – e.g. in their work, and, when the state superstructure is built, in the courts, schools, legislatures, etc. (Kymlicka, 1989a: 188)

In this new scenario we have a distribution of resources in which no one envies the bundle of social resources others possess but the members of the minority culture envy the members of the dominant culture because they are free to utilize their resources within a certain context (that is, their own cultural community). The members of the two cultural groups are thus unequal. Furthermore, this inequality is not the result of the voluntary choices of the members of the minority culture. They do not choose to be the minority culture. This is just how things turned out. Thus, if egalitarian liberals truly want to eliminate or reduce the impact of bad brute luck they should support compensating the members of the minority culture for this unchosen inequality which they face. And it is exactly this kind of inequality which national minorities face in contemporary societies. Kymlicka claims:

> A two-year old Inuit girl who has no project faces this inequality. Without special political protection, like the restrictions on the rights of transient workers, by the time she is eighteen the existence of the cultural community in which she grew up is likely to be undermined by the decisions of people outside the community. That is true no matter what projects she decides to pursue. Conversely, an English-Canadian boy will not face that problem, no matter what choices he makes. The rectification of this inequality is the basis for a liberal defence of aboriginal rights, and of minority rights in general. (Kymlicka, 1989a: 189)

The appropriate compensation for the unchosen inequality which national minorities face, argues Kymlicka, is not money but special political rights such as the rights of self-government. But justice only requires that we give these special rights to national minorities and not to immigrants. Immigrants whose cultural identity is different from the dominant culture of the country they emigrate to will face an inequality perhaps equal to that which members of national minorities face. But Kymlicka argues that the inequality immigrants face can be characterized as a *chosen* inequality and thus justice does not require compensation as it does in the case of national minorities who were forced to incorporate into a larger state. Immigrants chose to leave their own culture when they decided to emigrate to a new country. So the pressure to integrate which immigrants experience is not the result of circumstances beyond their control but of the voluntary choices they have made. The choice to emigrate could thus be characterized as a *culturally expensive taste* and justice does not require that we compensate inequalities that people are responsible for. Immigrants voluntarily sacrifice the good of cultural membership for some other good (for example, economic prosperity).

The case of refugees represents an interesting case for Kymlicka's argument. Unlike immigrants, refugees do not have the option of staying in their original culture (without jeopardizing their safety). So the cultural inequality they experience when they move to a foreign culture stems from circumstances beyond their control. But justice does not require, argues Kymlicka, that refugees be treated as national minorities. Long-term refugees do suffer an injustice but 'this injustice was committed by their home government, and it is not clear that we can realistically ask host governments to redress it' (Kymlicka, 1995a: 99). The best refugees could hope for is to be treated as immigrants.

Both liberals and multiculturalists could raise concerns against Kymlicka's argument for minority rights. As Kymlicka (1989a: ch. 13) notes, apartheid is the most common example used by critics of minority rights. White South Africans could justify limiting the rights of black South Africans on the grounds that this is necessary to protect the culture of white South Africans. Thus talk of 'minority rights' could be used to conceal unjust racist policies. Kymlicka notes that one cannot deny the *prima facie* applicability of minority rights to white South Africans. But he argues that the actual policies of apartheid are not justified by the argument he develops. 'Petty apartheid' (segregation in washrooms, swimming pools, etc.), for example, could not be justified on his account of minority rights as such measures do not aim at cultural security but rather are premised on blatant racism (Kymlicka, 1989a: 246). Furthermore, the land claims of white South Africans (to the majority of land) and the policy of forcing the remaining population into discrete homelands against their will violate both the principles of equal respect and equalizing cultural circumstances that inform Kymlicka's liberal defence of minority rights. Thus Kymlicka believes that endorsing minority rights will not lead to justifying blatantly unjust policies like apartheid.

Liberals may feel uneasy about endorsing self-government rights for national minorities for fears that this will encourage secession and thus threaten the social unity needed to keep society stable. Kymlicka acknowledges that these fears are valid given that 'the sense of being a distinct nation within a larger country is potentially destabilizing' (Kymlicka, 1995a: 192). However, he argues that denying national minorities these rights is also destabilizing and perhaps more likely to lead to secession as national minorities will feel resentful that the dominant culture refused to accommodate their concerns. Thus liberals cannot escape concerns about social unity. The important question is what poses the greatest threat to instability – granting or refusing self-government rights?

Multiculturalists have criticized Kymlicka's liberal defence of minority rights. Parekh, for example, questions Kymlicka's claim that immigrants waive the right to live by their culture when they leave their country of origin. 'Since culture is for Kymlicka a primary good, it is difficult to see how one can abandon one's right to it any more than to one's life or liberty'

(Parekh, 2000: 103). Furthermore, Parekh does not believe that Kymlicka's liberal justification of minority rights is fair to nonliberal cultures because it does not respect them in their 'authentic otherness' (Parekh, 2000: 108). Aboriginal peoples are not the immigrants of the small ship envisioned in the Dworkinian tale and by characterizing the demands of multinationals in this way Parekh believes that Kymlicka's approach to cultural diversity is deficient. Kymlicka's liberal defence of minority rights is an *instrumental* approach to cultural diversity as the real concern behind valuing cultural diversity is the concern for autonomy. But this public philosophy will not express true concern for people of culturally diverse societies, argue Parekh. 'Respect for a person … involves locating him against his cultural background, sympathetically entering into his world of thought, and interpreting his conduct in terms of its system of meaning' (Parekh, 2000: 240–1). Kymlicka's argument does not require this. Respect for minority rights is premised on the modified Dworkinian hypothetical shipwreck tale and the egalitarian liberal's aspiration to achieve an 'ambition-sensitive'/'endowment-insensitive' distribution.[4]

Charles Taylor argues that Kymlicka's argument fails to recapture the actual demands made by the groups concerned, such as aboriginal peoples. Taylor claims:

> Kymlicka's reasoning is valid (perhaps) for *existing* people who find themselves trapped within a culture under pressure, and can flourish within it or not at all. But it doesn't justify measures designed to ensure survival through indefinite future generations. For the populations concerned, however, that is what is at stake. (Taylor, 1993: 41 note 16)

Taylor's criticism seems valid if one considers what Kymlicka says about the children of parents who emigrate. Kymlicka claims that 'it is important that governments should strive to make the children of immigrants feel "at home" in the mainstream culture, to feel that it is "their" culture' (Kymlicka, 1995a: 216 note 19). But one can then ask why should we not support the same policy for the children of national minorities? While *existing*, adult members of these minority groups face the disadvantage of being unequal in cultural circumstances, a policy of assimilating that minority culture would ensure such inequalities are not passed on to future generations. So why should society not pursue a policy of assimilating national minorities if that will eliminate inequality in cultural circumstances in the long term rather than implement *permanent* minority rights for the sake of the existing generation? Concerns about cultural inequality, like those concerning economic inequality, are complicated by considerations of both intragenerational and intergenerational justice and these considerations must be addressed when considering what particular policy we should endorse concerning the efforts to mitigate cultural inequalities.

The discussion of Kymlicka's defence of minority rights in this section has focused only generally on the issue of self-government rights but the category of group-specific measures a society could opt for to accommodate national minorities is wide-ranging. These rights range from territorial autonomy, veto powers and guaranteed representation in central institutions to land claims and language rights. (Kymlicka, 1995a: 109). A determination of how a particular society should mitigate cultural inequality must consider the wide range of options open to it as well as the particular disadvantages its national minorities face. The situation of French-speaking Canadians in Quebec, for example, is very different from the situation of aboriginal peoples in Canada. One cannot determine, in the abstract, which particular rights are appropriate in any given situation. Attention must be given to the particularities of the country in question.

Consider Kymlicka's liberal defence of minority rights:

- Do you agree with his claim that cultural membership is a primary good?
- What advantages/disadvantages do you feel you have in your society, given your cultural identity?
- Do the immigrants of the small ship face an inequality that warrants compensation?
- Are rights of self-government the appropriate form of compensation if compensation is warranted?

6.3 Polyethnic rights

In addition to championing the rights of national minorities, multiculturalists also defend special treatment (such as financial support or legal protection) for members of ethnic or religious groups. Multiculturalists are concerned that, like the aspiration to assimilate national minorities, the aim of assimilating immigrants also unfairly privileges certain ways of life (namely, those valued by the dominant culture) over other ways of life. Consider, for example, public holidays and the structure of the week itself. In Western countries these things reflect Christian beliefs and yet is it fair that a multicultural society reflect the beliefs of just one of the many religions its citizens espouse? The liberal claim to separation of state and ethnicity is a myth, charge multiculturalists, and thus the concepts of equal respect and equal opportunity themselves must be interpreted in a culturally sensitive manner. Let us consider three policy issues as a way of illustrating the concerns multiculturalists have for polyethnic rights. These are the cases of helmet exemptions for turban-wearing Sikhs, humane animal slaughter exemptions for Jews and Muslims, and the 'headscarves affair' that first surfaced in France in 1989.

In the United Kingdom wearing a helmet became a legal requirement for drivers and passengers on motorcycles in the early 1970s. Multicultural critics campaigned against this law claiming that it violated freedom of religion. The charge was that the law was unfair to turban-wearing Sikhs. These individuals had to make a choice that members of other religious groups did not have to make – that between adhering to their religious beliefs (which involve wearing a turban) or travelling by motorcycle. But liberals would deny that such a law is unequal. According to the liberal vision of equal citizenship there is no inequality here as all citizens enjoy the same rights. The helmet law is not discriminatory because it does not explicitly declare that 'Sikhs shall not ride motorcycles'. What 'prevents' a Sikh from riding a motorcycle is his religion and not the law, liberals will retort.[5]

But the helmet law was amended in 1976 and Sikhs were exempted from wearing helmets. Multiculturalists believe this change to the law was the right thing to do. The turban met the appropriate safety standards and thus it was deemed an adequate substitute for the helmet. Since the justification for requiring motorcyclists to wear a helmet was concerns for their safety and wearing a turban also satisfies that aim then there is no reason not to permit turban-wearing Sikhs to be excluded from the law. Such a measure is a way of accommodating cultural diversity; it locates individuals against their cultural background and shows respect for the different beliefs and practices citizens of a pluralistic society have.

Similar concerns arise in the case of humane slaughter regulations. Many countries have passed legislation requiring the humane slaughter of animals for consumption (for example, stunning the animals prior to killing them). Most Western countries have exemptions from humane slaughter regulations so that Jews and Muslims can slaughter animals in accordance with traditional methods that violate the procedures for humane slaughter. Are such exemptions justified? Multiculturalists argue that such exemptions are necessary as they show respect for the importance of the religious practices of Orthodox Jews and observant Muslims. This issue is more complex than the case of exemptions from motorcycle helmets, as granting an exemption in the case of the latter was seen as consistent with the aim of the legislation (safety). But in the case of humane slaughter regulations the aim is to minimize the suffering of animals and permitting ritual slaughters[6] is not consistent with that aim. Unlike the helmet law example, where the aim of public safety could be achieved by having an exemption to the rule, in the case of humane slaughter regulations we have competing aims – minimize the suffering of animals or tolerate religious practices of butchery. Multiculturalists argue that such exemptions are a reasonable compromise between these two aims. Such a measure shows respect for the value some people place on religion. But the difficulty with this position is deciding where to draw the line. If respect for custom can override the aim of protecting animal welfare when it comes to slaughtering them then why not permit something like cockfighting? Furthermore, customs change and if one truly believes that humane slaughter regulations promote an important interest then one will not view exemptions from these regulations as a *reasonable* compromise. As Barry notes, 'it is hard to see why some cows and sheep should have to suffer in ways that are unacceptable generally in order to enable people with certain religious beliefs to eat their carcasses' (Barry, 2001: 43).

Exemptions from humane slaughter regulations is a difficult issue because proponents on both sides of the debate will find it difficult, indeed maybe impossible, to 'sympathetically enter into the world of thought' (Parekh, 2000: 240) of the other. Those who are passionate about animal welfare will not comprehend why some religious groups simply cannot change their customs whilst some religious groups might find the idea of altering valued traditions for the sake of animal welfare to be bewildering. When value systems differ in this way it is not easy to determine what constitutes a fair compromise.

Another issue which highlights what is at stake in the debates about multiculturalism is the headscarves affair, which occurred in France. Parekh succinctly summarizes the details of this affair:

> Three Muslim girls from North Africa, two of them sisters, wore *hijab* (head scarf) to their ethnically mixed school in Creil, some 60 kms north of Paris. In the previous year 20 Jewish students had refused to attend classes on Saturday mornings and autumn Friday afternoons when the Sabbath arrived before the close of the school, and the headmaster, a black Frenchman from the Caribbean, had to give in after initially resisting them. Worried about the trend of events, he objected to the Muslim girls wearing the *hijab* in the classroom on the grounds that it went against the *laïcité* [secularism] of French state schools. Since the girls refused to comply, he barred them from attending the school. As a gesture of solidarity many Muslim girls throughout France began to wear *hijabs* to school and the matter acquired national importance. (Parekh, 2000: 249)

Eventually it was ruled that pupils could wear 'discreet' religious symbols (such as the cross) but not 'ostentatious symbols which in themselves constitute elements of proselytism or discrimination' (cited in Parekh, 2001: 250) and the *hijab* was deemed to fall into this latter category and thus banned. The headscarves affair deeply divided the French, as different positions were taken with respect to the importance of symbolic significance. As Parekh notes, the main opposition to permitting the wearing of the *hijab* was that it went against the principle of secularism, which is part of the French identity. To become French one must integrate, and the school is a central mechanism by which people are assimilated into French culture. But Parekh criticizes the French decision, claiming that the decision to permit the cross and other Christian symbols but not the *hijab* amounted to treating Muslim girls unequally (Parekh, 2000: 253). Furthermore, the belief that the *hijab* symbolizes and reinforces female subordination, which Parekh argues was popular among most secular Frenchmen and feminists, fails to 'appreciate the complex processes of social change and intercultural negotiation [which the *hijab*] symbolized and triggered' (Parekh, 2000: 254). Parekh argues:

> Muslim immigrants in France, Britain and elsewhere are deeply fearful of their girls entering the public world including the school. By wearing the *hijab* their daughters seek to reassure them that they can be culturally

trusted and will not be 'corrupted' by the norms and values of the school. At the same time they also reshape the semi-public world of the school and protect themselves against its pressures and temptations by subtly getting white and Muslim boys to see them differently to the way they eye white girls. The *hijab* puts the girls 'out of bounds' and enables them to dictate how they wish to be treated. Traditional at one level, the *hijab* is transgressive at another, and enables Muslim girls to transform both their parental and public cultures. (Parekh, 2000: 253–4)

Critics of multiculturalism might seize on the headscarves example and use it to argue against polyethnic rights on the grounds that immigrants (and even national minorities) should assimilate into the culture of the society they live in. A strong sense of unity and common belonging, they might argue, is needed to ensure peace and stability and exemptions and similar measures for religious or ethnic groups threaten that sense of unity. But multiculturalists can agree that *some* degree of integration is necessary (and desirable); the difficult questions are how much assimilation is necessary and what is the just way of achieving that assimilation.

Even if one rejects the multiculturalists' claim that minority rights are valuable because they preserve cultural diversity or embody a culturally sensitive interpretation of the principle of equal treatment, some multicultural policies might simply be justified because they help secure peace. Sometimes pursuing assimilation might undermine the very thing we are aiming for (such as peace and stability). In *The Multiculturalism of Fear* Jacob Levy argues that multicultural policies represent a way of keeping the peace, though the version of multiculturalism he envisions is much narrower than that of either Parekh or Kymlicka. Levy's argument builds on Judith Shklar's (1989) argument about the priority of what she calls the 'liberalism of fear' over the 'liberalism of rights'. 'Shklar insists that liberalism is a political doctrine first, and one which must be sensitive to political realities. In particular, it must be responsive to the realities of where cruelty comes from and what form it takes' (Levy, 2000: 23). Applying Shklar's argument to multiculturalism, Levy argues that we should not treat multiculturalism as an end-in-itself but rather as a means of securing peace. He considers, for example, the policy of the Communist government of Bulgaria which required all personal and family names to be in Bulgarian thus preventing the sizeable Turkish minority from using Turkish names. Let us suppose, for the sake of argument, that such a policy could plausibly be characterized as one necessary for assimilating this minority into the dominant culture. What is wrong with this policy? The liberalism of rights will criticize such a policy on the grounds that it violates individual rights (such as freedom of expression, etc.). But, as Levy points out, if that is what is objectionable about the policy then we would have to say that such a policy was on a par with a policy that disallowed name changes like that of the artist formerly known as Prince (to a symbol for androgyny which cannot be pronounced). But if we do not feel that such policies are equally contemptible then something more subtle must be going on, argues Levy. The liberalism of fear helps explain what this something is. The restrictions on Turkish names is historically and intentionally linked with violence and cruelty toward excluded communities. Such a policy represents a much greater threat to peace and justice than the policy which disallows Prince's name change. Levy's point is that it is important to take into consideration the significance people place on their ethnic identities and practices, not because these things should be accorded significant moral weight, but because doing so will help us avoid violence (such as inter-ethnic civil wars), cruelty and political humiliation.

The cases of exemptions from motorcycle helmet laws, humane slaughter regulations and the regulations of dress in both schools and the workplace[8] are a few examples of the difficult cases polyethnic states face. Multiculturalists utilize these examples, and the fact that many state symbols such as flags and anthems reflect a particular ethnic or religious background, to show that the claim that the state and ethnicity are (or can be) separated is a myth. The public philosophy inspired by contemporary liberalism is 'difference-blind' (Taylor, 1993: 62) and thus ill-equipped to resolve the difficulties that arise in multicultural societies. In the following section we conclude our discussion of multiculturalism by considering some of the liberal objections that have been raised against multiculturalism.

6.4 Barry against multiculturalism

In this final section we shall consider one of the most vocal critics of multiculturalism, the egalitarian liberal Brian Barry (2001). Our examination of the distinct multicultural policies examined so far should make it evident that any general critique of multiculturalism is likely to be of limited use as the range of policies defended by multiculturalists is very diverse and it is unlikely that a criticism that might apply to granting self-government rights to national minorities would also apply to, for example, exemptions from humane slaughter regulations. However, it is useful to consider general criticisms, for those who wish to defend multiculturalism as a coherent public philosophy must be able to defend it against such criticisms. By doing so one not only comes to appreciate the complexity of issues at stake in the theoretical debates between liberals and multiculturalists, for example, but such an exercise often helps theorists on both sides of the debate to see that perhaps there is more common ground than they thought there was or they gain a fuller appreciation of the strengths and weaknesses of both their and their opponents' arguments.

In *Culture and Equality* Barry develops a multi-faceted egalitarian critique of multiculturalism. One of Barry's central complaints is that multiculturalists abuse culture (Barry, 2001: ch. 7). They do this when they maintain that it is some sort of defence of a practice to say that it forms an element in the culture of the group whose practice it is. So, for example, when one defends exemptions from humane slaughter regulations on the grounds that it is part of the *culture* of Orthodox Jews and observant Muslims that they butcher animals in a way that contravenes those regulations. But this kind of reasoning provides grounds for justifying unjust historical practices (such as slavery) as well as falsely assuming that human beings do not have a capacity for cultural adaptation. 'Culture is no excuse', argues Barry.

> If there are sound reasons against doing something, these cannot be trumped by saying – even if it is true – that doing it is part of your culture. The fact that you (or your ancestors) have been doing something for a long time does nothing in itself to justify your continuing to do it. … If slave-owners in the South had had access to the currently fashionable vocabulary, they would doubtless have explained that their culture was inextricably linked with the 'peculiar institution' and would have complained that abolitionists failed to accord them 'recognition'. But this simply illustrates that the appeal to 'culture' establishes nothing. Some cultures are admirable, others are vile. Reasons for doing things that can be advanced within the former will tend to be good, and reasons that can be advanced within the latter will tend to be bad. But in neither case is something's being part of the culture itself a reason for doing anything. (Barry, 2001: 258)

While multiculturalists might retort that by utilizing an example like slavery Barry is providing only a caricature of their position, he does provide a more contemporary and compelling example to make his point. This is the example of the marches carried out by the Orange Order in Northern Ireland. The Orange Order parade from Drumcree church in Portadown has had a destabilizing effect on the peace process in Northern Ireland and has caused rioting and public disorder. The traditional parade route of the Orange Order was through areas predominantly occupied by Roman Catholics. 'Members of the Garvaghy Road Residents' Coalition have protested against the parade since they see it as a provocative display of triumphalism that allows the Orange Order to assert the supremacy of Britishness and Protestantism over Irishness and Catholicism' (O'Neill, 2000: 29). When the British government intervened in an attempt to resolve the issue the Orange Order objected on grounds that it was part of their tradition and custom to march down their historical route. But the response 'We've always marched down that route', argues Barry, is not a justification of such a practice. When culture is fetishized, as it is by multiculturalists, then it leads to justifying just about any practice, no matter how reprehensible the practice may be.

Many critics of multiculturalism share Barry's concern that multiculturalism commits us to a public philosophy that will require tolerating unjust practices. But many multicultural theorists also share this concern and build that concern into their defence of multiculturalism. Kymlicka is perhaps the best example of a theorist who does this. Because Kymlicka does not believe that culture itself is *intrinsically*[9] valuable he would agree with Barry that culture itself cannot be a defence of a practice. Cultures are valuable and warrant protection, argues Kymlicka, because they contribute to some more basic human interest. Thus, when cultural practices are in conflict with these basic human interests the justification for protecting these practices is dissolved. Liberal principles, argues Kymlicka, impose two fundamental limitations on minority rights. Firstly, the basic civil or political liberties of all citizens, including members of the minority culture, cannot be compromised. In addition to these 'internal restrictions', 'liberal justice cannot accept any such rights which enable one group to oppress or exploit other groups, as in apartheid' (Kymlicka, 1995a: 152). Thus a minority culture's demands for 'external protections' 'are legitimate only in so far as they promote equality between groups, by rectifying disadvantages or vulnerabilities suffered by the members of a particular group' (Kymlicka, 1995a: 152).

So sophisticated defences of multiculturalism, like Kymlicka's, do not endorse the claim that Barry takes multiculturalists to be committed to. Namely, that it is some sort of defence of a practice to say that it forms an element in the culture of the group whose practice it is. But what of Barry's claim that multiculturalism falsely assumes that human beings do not have a capacity for cultural adaptation? Barry makes such a charge against James Tully's (1995) defence of granting exemptions from fishing bans for Native Americans. Tully claims that 'fishing a specific body of coastal water is constitutive of the cultural identity of the Aboriginal Musqueam nation' (Tully, 1995: 172). Barry charges that multiculturalists like Tully assume that any change to a culture constitutes a change to the group's 'cultural identity'. But such a conclusion is obviously false as all cultures undergo some change whilst still retaining their identity. Underlying this dispute is the issue we already considered in Chapter 5 – the dispute over the conception of the self. Multiculturalists emphasize the fact that we are embedded selves. 'Like communitarians, multiculturalists insist that a person's good is primarily defined by membership and active participation in a (dominant) community of some kind' (Freeman, 2002: 18). Multiculturalists are thus inclined to interpret some changes to a culture as constituting a greater threat to cultural identity than liberals who believe that, whilst we are not necessarily 'unencumbered selves', we are more adaptive than multiculturalists and communitarians presuppose. Thus, liberals would argue, claims about preserving cultural identity are not as urgent or pressing as multiculturalists often portray them. Jeremy Waldron (1995), for example, does not believe that people are connected to their own culture in any deep way but live in a 'kaleidoscope of cultures'.

Another central concern of Barry's is that a politics of recognition undermines the politics of redistribution. The latter relies on a sense of solidarity in which citizens conceive of politics as 'a society-wide conversation about questions of common concern' (Barry, 2001: 302). But the politics of multiculturalism is divisive and thus undermines the commitment to social equality.[10] Multiculturalism wrongly assumes that all group disadvantages must stem from its distinctive cultural attributes.

The consequences of this 'culturalization' of group identities is the systematic neglect of alternative causes of group disadvantage. Thus, the members of a group may suffer not because they have distinctive culturally derived goals but because they do poorly in achieving generally shared objectives such as a good education, desirable and well-paid jobs (or perhaps a job at all), a safe and salubrious neighbourhood in which to live and enough income to enable them to be adequately housed, clothed, and fed and to participate in the social, economic and political life of their society. (Barry, 2001: 305–6)

Critics of multiculturalism believe that its preoccupation with cultural inequalities detracts from the most pressing social issues facing capitalist societies, namely, socio-economic inequalities. The challenge facing multi-culturalists who wish to win over those that believe the fight for redistribu-tion is *the* important battle is to emphasize how the policies they defend will help the least advantaged members of society. So one must clarify what interests lie behind the claims about the importance of culture and provide a compelling argument to show that the particular multicultural policies one defends are those best designed to protect and promote those interests.

Discuss the following statements:

1   Requiring turban-wearing Sikhs to wear a helmet when driving a motorcycle is religious discrimination. Such a law is culturally insensitive and we should permit exemptions from the law for such religious groups.
2   I do not think that Orthodox Jews and observant Muslims should be exempt from humane slaughter regulations. If the majority of citizens believe that killing animals in this way is inhumane then why should these groups, and *only* these groups, be exempt from such laws? I thought a democracy was about majority rules and if the majority of people believe that these butchery prac-tices are inhumane and should be illegal then everyone in society should be bound by such a law. Since when did democracy become 'majority rules' with the additional clause 'provided that you don't infringe on cultural practices'?
3   The preoccupation with so-called 'cultural inequalities' and 'the politics of recognition' is really unfortunate because it deflects from the real important issue of socio-economic inequality. The main cause of suffering in society is the lack of resources for adequate housing, health care and education. If we really want to promote justice we should be investing our energy and resources into tackling the issue of poverty and not worrying about the cultural inequalities national minorities and immigrants face.

Further reading

Brian Barry, *Culture and Equality* (Cambridge, MA.: Harvard University Press, 2001).

Review Symposium on 'Culture and Equality' in *Ethnicities* 2 (2), June 2002.

Paul Kelly, (ed.), *Multiculturalism Reconsidered* (Cambridge: Polity Press, 2002).

Bhikhu Parekh, *Rethinking Multiculturalism: Cultural Diversity and Political Theory* (Basingstoke: Palgrave, 2000).

SUMMARY

- Multiculturalist critics of liberalism argue that the liberalisms of the distributive paradigm do not take *cultural plurality* seriously enough. Thus the politics of equal citizenship and redistribution is ill-equipped to tackle the myriad of issues that arise in multinational and polyethnic societies. Taylor's 'politics of recognition' requires that everyone be recognized for his or her unique identity.
- Kymlicka provides a liberal defence of minority rights. He emphasizes the importance cultural membership has for the values of autonomy and self-respect. National minorities face disadvantages (with respect to the good of cultural membership) that members of the majority culture do not face and thus they should be compensated for these unchosen inequalities. The appropriate form of compensation, argues Kymlicka, is the granting of minority rights.
- Multiculturalists also defend polyethnic rights, such as granting special exemptions from humane slaughter regulations. Liberal critics like Barry argue that multiculturalists permit people to abuse culture by utilizing it as a defence of reprehensible cultural practices. Furthermore, the emphasis on preserving group identities leads to the systematic neglect of other causes of group disadvantage.

Notes

1   As will become evident in the next two chapters, multiculturalism developed alongside debates in both feminism and deliberative democracy and thus the liberal–communitarian debate is not the sole influence on the recent debates about multiculturalism. Furthermore, recent political developments, especially the resurgence of ethnonational conflict, has spurred the interest political theorists have in these issues.

2   I will not address the issue of special representation rights as this issue will be covered in the chapter on feminism when we consider Anne Phillips's (1995) argument for gender quotas.

3   Of course one might ask how people could be expected to bid on the island's resources in such a scenario but Kymlicka asks us to imagine that this information is already available in publications or gathered by a scouting party from one ship and communicated via computer. The key point is that no one from either ship actually sees or speaks to someone from the other ship.

4   This criticism is less problematic for Kymlicka's later work as he identifies three distinct arguments for self-government rights of national minorities: the equality argument, historical agreements and the value of diversity (Kymlicka, 1995a: ch. 6).

5   This argument was made by Lord Wingley. See Poulter (1998: 293).

6 Which involve bleeding animals to death while conscious instead of stunning them prior to killing them (Barry, 2001: 41).

8 See Parekh (2000: ch. 8) for further examples dealing with dress (e.g. the controversy over turbans in the Royal Canadian Mountain Police).

9 Charles Taylor, in contrast to Kymlicka, does maintain that culture is intrinsically good (Taylor, 1995: 137).

10 'Pursuit of the multiculturalist agenda makes the refinement of broadly based egalitarian policies more difficult in two ways. At a minimum, it diverts political effort away from universalistic goals. But a more serious problem is that multiculturalism may well destroy the conditions for putting together a coalition in favour of across-the-board equalization of opportunities and resources' (Barry, 2001: 325).

7   Deliberative Democracy

Summary Contents

7.1	Introduction: the importance of democracy	137
7.2	Moving beyond the aggregative model of democracy	139
7.3	How substantive are the principles of democracy?	144
7.4	Retaining the critical edge of deliberative democracy	148
7.5	Critically assessing the ideal of deliberative democracy	150

7.1 Introduction: The importance of democracy

In the first part of this book we surveyed contemporary liberalism and the distributive paradigm. Different distributive principles are endorsed by different justice theorists (for example, the difference principle, the principle of minimax relative concession, etc.). But, as became evident in the chapter on multiculturalism, many political theorists have questioned the distributive paradigm which has dominated contemporary liberal theory. In this chapter we shall examine another theory which also questions the dominance of the distributive paradigm – deliberative democracy. Since the early 1990s the so-called 'deliberative turn' (Dryzek, 2000) in democratic theory has preoccupied debates concerning the relation between democracy and justice, a relation that was marginalized by the distributive paradigm. Ian Shapiro describes the gulf that exists between theorists of democracy and justice:

> It would be going too far to say that theoreticians of democracy and justice speak past one another, but there has been little systematic attention by political theorists to the ways in which considerations about democracy and justice are or should be mutually related. This relative inattention seems partly to have sprung from optimism among many justice theorists about what armchair reflection should be expected to deliver, a driving conviction that what is just in the distribution of social goods can be settled as a matter of speculative theory. (Shapiro, 1999: 3)

The inattention to democracy is arguably evident in all four of the liberal theories of justice examined in Part One.[1] If the demands of justice can be established by simply invoking the principles chosen in the original position, or the principle of minimax relative concession, the thesis of self-ownership or equality of resources, then what is the role of democratic politics? If we can arrive at the correct answer to what laws and policies are legitimate *independently* of any real democratic process then it seems that the latter is superfluous. As Shapiro notes, many political theorists 'appear to take it for granted that there is a correct answer to the question what principles of justice we ought to affirm; that Rawls, Ronald Dworkin, Robert Nozick, Amartya Sen, or someone else will eventually get it right' (Shapiro, 1999: 3). But if we believe that the demands of justice and the practices of a democratic polity are inextricably linked then the ideal of democracy must enjoy more prominence in our theorizing than it does in the distributive paradigm of contemporary liberalism.

Democratic theorists invoke different conceptions of democracy (for example, participatory democracy, social democracy, etc.) but I do not intend to examine these different versions of democratic theory. Our concern in this chapter is with one recent strand of democratic theory – deliberative democracy. Before we consider this ideal let us briefly consider the more general issue of what democracy is. We often invoke the ideal of democracy in many different contexts, both political and non-political. Associations or committees may seek to resolve internal disagreements by implementing democratic decision-making procedures. This usually entails deciding the issue by a show of hands and being bound by the majority decision. When applied to a political association this popular understanding of democracy requires that all citizens be entitled to an equal vote and that the will of the majority rules. But the shortcomings of this simple characterization of democracy are easily illustrated. For example, if all citizens have an equal vote but only have the option of voting for one political party we would not want to say that such an arrangement fulfilled the requirements of a true democracy. Political equality, which underlies our commitment to democracy, is not secured by simply ensuring each person is entitled to an equal vote and that the will of the majority rules. Robert Dahl (1998) provides the following comprehensive list of opportunities that must be satisfied if a decision-making process is to be called 'democratic'.

1 Effective participation.
2 Equality in voting.
3 Gaining enlightened understanding.
4 Exercising final control over the agenda.
5 Inclusion of adults (Dahl, 1998: 38).[2]

Utilizing Dahl's criteria of democracy will provide us with a useful introduction to the themes of deliberative democracy that we shall further explore in the other sections of this chapter. In the next section will shall contrast deliberative democracy with the aggregative model of democracy which will bring the first three criteria to the fore. While both models will endorse the criterion of equality in voting, the aggregative model conceives of voting as *the* primary political activity because it maintains that policy formation should be based on the preferences of the majority. This contrasts with the deliberative democrat's conception of democracy which places much more emphasis on the opportunities for effective participation and gaining enlightened understanding. The fourth criterion of exercising final control over the agenda raises a number of complex issues for deliberative democrats concerning how substantive the principles of democracy are. For Dahl, 'the policies of an association must always be open to change by the members of the association, if they so choose' (Dahl, 1998: 38). Dahl's concern is that a minority interest might be allowed to decide the political agenda if we do not ensure that the constitutional arrangements satisfy this fourth criterion. If a minority interest has control of the agenda then the association cannot be characterized as an association of political equals. This fourth criterion is the subject of much debate between procedural and constitutional democrats. The latter will be reluctant to place complete control over the political agenda in the hands of the demos for fear that unjust outcomes might occur. We have already touched on this issue in our discussion of Dworkin's defence of judicial review in Chapter 4 and we briefly revisit this issue in section 7.3 of this chapter, when we consider the issue of how substantive the principles of democracy are. In the concluding section we shall consider some of the challenges facing the ideal of deliberative democracy.

7.2 Moving beyond the aggregative model of democracy

What should the aim of a decision-making process be? Above I referred to the popular *show of hands* understanding of democracy that we often invoke when trying to resolve disagreements. According to this model of democracy, decision-making processes ought simply to aggregate the preferences of citizens in choosing public officials and parties. An outcome is thus just, according to this account of democracy, if it mirrors the preferences of the majority of people. This is what is known as the *aggregative model* of democracy. Iris Marion Young describes how the aggregative model conceives of democratic processes of policy formation:

> Individuals in the polity have varying preferences about what they want government institutions to do. They know that other individuals also have preferences, which may or may not match their own. Democracy is a competitive process in which political parties and candidates offer their platforms and attempt to satisfy the largest number of people's preferences. Citizens with similar preferences often organize interest groups in order to try to influence the actions of parties and policy-makers once they are elected. Individuals, interest groups, and public officials each may behave strategically, adjusting the orientation of their pressure tactics or coalition-building according to their perceptions of the activities of competing preferences. (Young, 2000: 19)

The aggregative model of democracy is problematic for a number of reasons. It undermines the ideal of democracy because it fails to give sufficient attention to the emphasis on effective participation and enlightened understanding, two criteria which deliberative democrats believe are vital for achieving a more just polity. According to the aggregative model of democracy citizens participate in the decision-making process primarily by making their preferences known through voting. Voting is thus conceived of as the primary political act. But deliberative democrats reject this narrow conception of participation. To fully participate in the decision-making process, argue deliberative democrats, one must participate in *authentic deliberation* and not simply express one's preferences. Such deliberation requires that parties abandon the strategic behaviour characteristic of the aggregative model of democracy and strive instead to reach a *consensus* among free and equal participants. To participate in this discursive practice is very different from participating in the decision-making process of the aggregative model of democracy. Deliberative democrats characterize participation in the democratic process as a *transformative* process. 'Through the process of public discussion with a plurality of differently opinioned and situated others, people often gain new information, learn of different experiences of their collective problems, or find that their own initial opinions are founded on prejudice or ignorance, or that they have misunderstood the relation of their own interests to others' (Young, 2000: 26).

Let us consider the following example to illustrate the differences between these two conceptions of democracy. Though the example utilizes a trivial decision – where to eat dinner – it does reveal many of the concerns that deliberative democrats have concerning the shortcomings of the aggregative model of democracy. Imagine that five friends have to decide where to go for dinner. They cannot agree on a restaurant so they decide to resolve this disagreement democratically. They believe that that is the only fair thing to do. The 'show of hands' approach of the aggregative model of democracy declares that the majority decision is the right decision and thus the friends need only indicate what their preferences are and the group should accept the preference of the majority. If three of the friends, for example, want Chinese food then that is where they should go and the two dissenters must simply accept that decision because democracy means the majority wins.

But if these friends are deliberative democrats they may not be satisfied to resolve the disagreement in this way. Before having a vote they decide that each person should have the opportunity to express their concerns for or against any of the restaurants that people have initially suggested. Each friend will then reconsider their preferences in light of those considerations. Perhaps one friend cannot afford to eat in a Chinese restaurant or is allergic to Chinese food. As a friend you may (and I hope would!) find these kinds of concerns pressing and thus they may lead you to change your initial preference. You may decide that your preference for Chinese food is less important than accommodating a friend in the kind of circumstances just stipulated. Under these circumstances you may be willing to rank an alternative restaurant as your first choice, one that is more affordable or compatible with the dietary requirements of everyone. Engaging in a deliberation about something as trivial as where to go for dinner with some friends could be a transformative process as you begin to shape your own preferences in light of the concerns of others. The friends participate in this democratic process not by simply raising their hands and expressing their existing preferences in a majority wins vote, but by listening to the concerns of others and being willing to change their minds in order to accommodate those concerns.

The more expansive conception of democratic participation that deliberative democrats endorse thus ties in well with the third criterion of democracy Dahl identifies – gaining enlightened understanding. A process of aggregating existing preferences precludes enlightened understanding as there is no attempt to understand, let alone accommodate, the concerns of one's fellow citizens. But deliberative democrats believe that their vision of democracy fosters enlightened understanding among citizens because it embodies the principle of reciprocity (Gutmann and Thompson, 1996) or the dispositions of reasonableness (Young, 2000). Elaborating on the former, Gutmann and Thompson argue that reciprocity entails mutual respect. Mutual respect is a form of agreeing to disagree.

> It consists in an excellence of character that permits a democracy to flourish in the face of fundamental moral disagreement. This is a distinctively deliberative kind of character. It is the character of individuals who are morally committed, self-reflective about their commitments, discerning of the difference between respectable and merely tolerable differences of opinion, and open to the possibility of changing their minds or modifying their positions at some time in the future if they confront unanswerable objections to their present point of view. (Gutmann and Thompson, 1996: 79–80)

By engaging in deliberation with those we disagree with we are expressing a willingness to listen to others, to take their concerns seriously and to find some common ground so that a just compromise can be achieved. Gutmann and Thompson consider a number of contentious policy issues, ranging from abortion and trade policy to welfare policy, to illustrate how the deliberative process fosters enlightened understanding and moral accommodation. But mutual respect does not mean that we must always accept the claims of those we disagree with, but it does require that we listen to their concerns and that we justify our decisions by appealing to reasons we genuinely believe all reasonable persons could accept. Gutmann and Thompson provide an example from public education to illustrate this point. In 1983 the board of education in Hawkins County, Tennessee adopted a basic reading series that was to be used in all public schools. The aim of this reading curriculum was to teach both reading skills and the values of democratic citizenship. But a group of fundamentalist Christian parents asked that their children not be required to use the books on the curriculum. The books conflicted with their religious convictions and the parents did not want their children to be exposed to other ways of life that conflict with what the Bible says. Gutmann and Thompson identify the following specific parts of the curriculum that the parents objected to:

- a short story describing a Catholic Indian settlement in New Mexico, on the grounds that it teaches Catholicism;
- a reading exercise picturing a boy making toast while a girl reads to him ('Pat reads to Jim. Jim cooks. The big book helps Jim. Jim has fun.') on the grounds that 'it denigrates the differences between the sexes' affirmed in the Bible;
- an excerpt from Anne Frank's *Diary of a Young Girl*, because Anne Frank writes that nonorthodox belief in God may be better than no belief at all; and
- a passage describing a central idea of the Renaissance as 'a belief in the dignity and worth of human beings,' because such a belief is incompatible with true religious faith. (Gutmann and Thompson, 1996: 63–4)

After discussing the parents' objections and acknowledging the sincerity of the parents' religious beliefs the board rejected their request to exempt their children from reading the textbooks. But this decision was not arrived at by simply invoking a 'show of hands' approach to public education that would consider only the relative bargaining power of the interests on either side. The principle of reciprocity requires that we take the parents' concerns seriously, which the school board did. But the reasons the parents wanted to exempt their children from the curriculum (for example, to prevent their children from making critical judgements) are reasons that actually violate the principle of reciprocity, argue Gutmann and Thompson, and this is why the parents' objections are not acceptable.

> The parents' reasoning appeals to values that can and should be rejected by citizens of a pluralist society committed to protecting the basic liberties and opportunities of all citizens. Keep in mind that the parents are trying to prevent schools from teaching their children to make critical judgements, to use their imagination, to exercise choice 'in areas where the Bible provides the answer,' and to consider the merits of the idea that all human beings have dignity and worth. If the parents were successful, their children (and perhaps others) would fail to receive the education that is necessary for developing their capacities as democratic citizens. The parents would deny the school board the authority to teach future citizens the skills and knowledge that are necessary for protecting the liberties and opportunities of all citizens, including the parents and their children themselves. (Gutmann and Thompson, 1996: 65)

The board's decision was justified, argue Gutmann and Thompson, because the curriculum is a reasonable way for a public school system to teach democratic values. The reasons for rejecting the parents' wish to have their children exempted from the curriculum are thus *public* reasons, reasons that all parents, regardless of their conception of the good, can reasonably accept. This is very different from telling the parents that their objections are rejected simply because the majority of parents do not share their concerns. Gutmann and Thompson believe that the school board's decision to reject exemptions from the reading curriculum was a reasonable policy, despite the fact that no actual accommodation took place. Mutual respect does not mean that we must always accept the claims of those we disagree with, but it does require that we listen to their concerns and that we justify our decisions by appealing to reasons we genuinely believe all reasonable persons could accept. We do not reject their demands out of hand simply because they are in the minority.

By seeking terms of agreement that are acceptable to all, the deliberative model of democracy better secures two of Dahl's criteria for democracy – effective participation and enlightened understanding – than does the aggregative model of democracy. The emphasis on voting and bargaining, which are the central political activities of the aggregative model, are replaced by the emphasis on searching for a consensus, being open-minded and respecting, and even accommodating, your opponent's position. To participate in the consensus-building process envisioned by deliberative democrats is to engage in a transformative process.

Deliberative democrats emphasize the importance of listening to the concerns of others and the willingness to change one's mind. Consider the claims of the religious fundamentalists who wanted to have their children exempted from the reading curriculum in Hawkins County:

- Should such an exemption have been given? Why/why not?
- Do you think the parents should accept the argument Gutmann and Thompson give for rejecting their claims for an exemption?
- What should the aims of education policy be in culturally diverse democracies and is such an aim compatible with respecting social and religious diversity?

Further reading

William Galston, 'Diversity, Toleration and Deliberative Democracy: Religious Minorities and Public Schooling' in Stephen Macedo (ed.), *Deliberative Politics: Essays on Democracy and Disagreement* (Oxford: Oxford University Press, 1999).

Amy Gutmann, 'Civic Education and Social Diversity', *Ethics*, 105 (3), 1995: 557–79.

Stephen Macedo, *Diversity and Distrust: Civic Education in a Multicultural Democracy*. (Cambridge, MA: Harvard University Press, 2000).

Eamonn Callan, *Creating Citizens: Political Education and Liberal Democracy* (Oxford: Oxford University Press, 1997).

7.3 How substantive are the principles of democracy?

The fourth criterion of democracy that Dahl identified above was that there must be opportunities for exercising final control over the agenda. In particular, Dahl is concerned that a minority interest might be allowed to decide the political agenda if we do not ensure that constitutional arrangements satisfy this fourth criterion. Concern for this criterion easily fits into the deliberative conception of democracy which premises the legitimacy of law on the assent of all citizens. Jurgen Habermas, for example, maintains that 'only those statutes may claim legitimacy that can meet with the assent (*Zustimmung*) of all citizens in a discursive process of legislation that in turn has been legally constituted' (Habermas, 1996: 110). Similarly Joshua Cohen claims that 'the fundamental idea of democratic legitimacy is that the authorization to exercise state power must arise from the collective decisions of the members of a society who are governed by that power' (Cohen, 1996: 95). By equating legitimacy with the outcome of an *actual* democratic process the deliberative democrat rejects the idea that the content of the law should be premised on substantive principles that are independent of such a process, such as Rawls's two principles of justice. Habermas, for example, claims that 'all contents, no matter how fundamental the action form involved may be, must be made to depend on real discourses (or advocatory discourses conducted as substitutes for them)' (Habermas, 1990: 94). According to Habermas's democratic principle the only test for the legitimacy of laws is a procedural test. 'Statutory legitimacy hangs solely on whether a law has been enacted in the correct way, not on whether it fulfils some antecedently specified substantive normative criteria for goodness or rightness' (Zurn, 2002: 510).

So proceduralists like Habermas take seriously the fourth democratic criterion put forward by Dahl – that there be opportunity to exercise final control over the agenda. The agenda is not fixed or limited in advance by appealing to some independent moral argument, such as the principles that the parties in the original position would choose. But it is worth considering what a justice theorist like Rawls might say in response to this purely 'procedural' conception of legitimacy. Recall that Rawls himself, when constructing the original position, appeals to the idea of pure procedural justice.[3] But why does Rawls construct a *hypothetical* original position in order to determine what the principles of justice are instead of simply saying that whatever principles people actually endorse by a 'show of hands' should be deemed the principles of justice? Rawls would reject the latter proposal because there is no way of ensuring that a 'show of hands' vote on the principles of justice would treat everyone as equals. Citizens could simply endorse principles that unfairly favour themselves. By invoking the veil of ignorance, for example, the original position helps better secure an impartial decision than might be the case if we simply decided what is just by asking for a show of hands. The original position helps clarify what considerations should and should not determine what the principles of justice are. So one concern that can be raised against the proceduralist conception of legitimacy advocated by theorists like Habermas is that by subjecting the demands of justice to the democratic process proceduralists run the risk of legitimizing unjust outcomes. If the majority of citizens democratically decide to limit the rights of a particular religious group, for example, then such a law must be construed as *legitimate* by proceduralists because it was arrived at via a democratic procedure. Constitutional democrats will thus want to qualify Dahl's fourth criterion of democracy by stipulating that the opportunity for exercising final control over the agenda *must be limited*. If the legislature has complete control over the political agenda then this could lead to unjust out-comes. Rights, argue constitutional democrats, have priority over the demo-cratic process and a purely procedural conception of legitimacy violates this requirement.

Deliberative democrats can respond to this kind of concern in a number of different ways. They might argue that such an unjust outcome might occur in a democratic process where legitimacy is simply equated with the will of the majority in a 'show of hands' vote but that is not what constitutes legiti-macy for proceduralists like Habermas. In order for a law to be legitimate all must be able to consent to it and the minority in question would obviously not consent to such a measure. The idealizing requirements of Habermas's 'discourse ethics'[4] thus builds in protections for certain rights and opportu-nities that rule out the kind of repressive policy just mentioned. So even pro-ceduralists like Habermas believe that it is necessary to build guarantees of basic liberty and opportunity into the ideal conditions of deliberation. Such measures are to be viewed as those necessary for a fair democratic process. In his earlier work on 'discourse ethics' Habermas lists the following as some of the inescapable presuppositions of discourse:

(3.1)   Every subject with the competence to speak and act is allowed to take part in a discourse.

(3.2)   a.   Everyone is allowed to question any assertion whatever.
        b   Everyone is allowed to introduce any assertion whatever into the discourse.
        c.   Everyone is allowed to express his attitudes, desires, and needs.

(3.3)   No speaker may be prevented, by internal or external coercion, from exercising his rights as laid down in (3.1) and (3.2) (Habermas, 1990: 89).

If the outcome of the deliberative decision-making process must meet with the assent of all participants then these participants have a right to express their views, challenge the claims of their opponents and have a say in the final decision. To engage in the deliberative process is to seek a con-sensus and persuade your opponents by argumentation, not force or coer-cion. Thus by committing oneself to deliberation one is already implicitly endorsing certain ethical principles, hence the reason why Habermas describes the theory as 'discourse *ethics*'. So even Habermas's procedural defence of legitimacy provides grounds for guaranteeing basic liberty and opportunity.[5]

But once proceduralists qualify criterion four in this way it appears that they must align themselves with constitutional democrats[6] and agree that certain rights are taken off the political agenda. By doing so they will be susceptible to the criticisms Waldron raised against Dworkin. Recall that Waldron was critical of judicial review because judges, like citizens, also disagree about rights. Waldron argues that we should not permit officials who are not elected nor accountable to resolve moral disagreements. Waldron's concern is especially problematic for deliberative democrats given their commitment to the idea that the legitimacy of law is based on the assent of all. So Dahl's fourth criterion of democracy presents something of a paradox for deliberative democrats. If they believe that all citizens should have final control over the agenda then little or no limits should be placed on democratic rule. Yet the democratic process itself requires certain things be taken off the political agenda (for example, certain rights) and thus limiting democratic rule is necessary if all are to be given the opportunity to exercise final control over the agenda.

Procedural principles do not prescribe what the content of the laws should be 'but only the procedures (such as equal suffrage) by which laws are made and the conditions (such as free political speech) necessary for the procedures to work fairly (Gutmann and Thompson, 2002: 153). Some deliberative democrats argue that the principles of deliberative democracy are *substantive* as well as procedural (Cohen 1996; Gutmann and Thompson 1996). Gutmann and Thompson (1996, 2002) are critical of the purely proceduralist approach advocated by Habermas because it does not capture the value of basic rights. 'Citizens value basic liberty and opportunity, and their mutual recognition by fellow citizens, for reasons other than the role of these values in democratic deliberation' (Gutmann and Thompson, 1996: 17). In *Democracy and Disagreement* Gutmann and Thompson defend an account of deliberative democracy that includes substantive as well as procedural principles. These substantive principles include basic liberty and fair opportunity and these principles are extended to persons not solely for the sake of democratic deliberation, but also for the sake of reciprocity, mutual respect and fairness. But if substantive principles, or even just procedural principles, are built into the deliberative account of democracy then it looks like deliberative democrats will need to engage in the same kind of armchair theorizing that they criticize justice theorists for engaging in. Indeed, echoing Shapiro's criticism of justice theorists, we could say that many democratic theorists now take it for granted that there is a correct answer to the question of what principles of democracy we ought to affirm; that Habermas, Joshua Cohen, Gutmann and Thompson or someone else will eventually get it right.

Much of the current debate between deliberative democrats is exactly this kind of armchair theorizing. Different principles, procedural and/or substantive, are defended as *the* principles of democracy by democratic theorists yet these principles themselves are not the outcome of any real democratic process. For example, in 'What Sort of Political Equality Does Deliberative Democracy Require?' Jack Knight and James Johnson examine the different kinds of equality deliberative democrats should endorse. They argue that democratic deliberation 'requires *equal opportunity of access to political influence*' (Knight and Johnson, 1997: 292). Because deliberative democrats are concerned with the effects the social distribution of power has on effective participation in the deliberative process they themselves are engaged in an 'equality of what?' debate in the same way that justice theorists are. And thus the gulf between theoreticians of justice and democracy seems to narrow significantly. Like justice theorists, deliberative democrats are concerned with the distribution of material resources. The resources individuals command have an impact on their position in the deliberative process and thus deliberative democrats must consider the effects the social distribution of power and resources have on effective participation in the deliberative process.

Even some proceduralists now endorse substantive principles. In 'Procedure and Substance in Deliberative Democracy' Joshua Cohen, who was influential in formulating the procedural account of democratic legitimacy, argues that deliberative democracy presupposes substantive principles. He argues that the deliberative view accommodates a 'principle of participation' the requirements of which are quite extensive.

> According to that principle, democratic collective choice – institutionalizing the tie between deliberative justification and the exercise of public power – must ensure equal rights of participation, including rights of voting, association, and political expression, with a strong presumption against restrictions on the content or viewpoint of expression; rights to hold office; a strong presumption in favor of equally weighted votes; and a more general requirement of equal opportunities for effective influence. This last requirement condemns inequalities in opportunities for office-holding and political influence that result from the design of arrangements of collective decision-making. (Cohen, 1996: 106–7)

Cohen's claim that the principle of participation entails a strong presumption against restrictions on the content or viewpoint of expression is particularly interesting given that that is a rather specific claim about the content of law that is derived, not from a Kantian conception of the self (recall Sandel's critique of neutrality in Chapter 5), but from the idea of democratic legitimacy. It thus looks as though deliberative democrats who endorse substantive principles of democracy end up sharing more common ground with justice theorists like Rawls and Dworkin than one might have initially suspected given the former's desire to distance themselves from the armchair theorizing of justice theorists. Both deliberative democrats and egalitarian-liberals are concerned with basic liberties, equality of opportunity and economic inequalities. But the reason deliberative democrats are concerned with these rights, opportunities and inequalities stems from their concern with the principle of democratic legitimacy. Deliberative democrats are concerned with economic inequality, for example, not because they believe justice requires that we mitigate morally arbitrary factors or strive for an 'ambition-sensitive'/'endowment-insensitive' distribution, but because structural inequalities (such as social and economic power) threaten the ideal of deliberative democracy itself.

Justice theorists could charge that deliberative democrats are simply caught up in a logical circle. On the one hand these theorists do not want to posit an account of distributive justice that would pre-empt the decisions of the democratic process itself. Yet deliberative democrats do not wish to go along with the outcomes of existing democratic arrangements as these are ones that fail to live up to the idealizing requirements of deliberative democracy. So deliberative democrats endorse substantive principles (for example, the principle of participation) that must be satisfied before the outcome of the democratic process can be deemed legitimate yet it is exactly this kind of armchair theorizing that democratic theorists criticize because it preempts the real democratic process as those principles are not ones that people have actually assented to.

7.4 Retaining the critical edge of deliberative democracy

Some deliberative democrats have sought to salvage the ideal of deliberative democracy from the apparent assimilation to liberal constitutionalism. John Dryzek (2000), for example, argues that deliberative democracy loses its critical edge when it is assimilated with liberal constitutionalism. Democracy is a dynamic and open-ended project and when the liberal state is seen as the key to facilitating authentic deliberation the changing empirical realities of the world are ignored. For example, Dryzek argues that the liberal state is increasingly subject to the constraints imposed by the transnational capitalist political economy.

> The first task of all states in this system is to maintain the confidence of actual and potential investors, to avoid capital flight. This imperative conditions policy-making, for democratic influence on policy-making introduces a dangerous element of indeterminacy, and so becomes increasingly curtailed. Public officials under the sway of such imperatives are highly constrained when it comes to the terms of arguments they can accept; it is very hard for deliberation to reach them. (Dryzek, 2000: 29)

In order to emphasize the critical strand of deliberative democracy Dryzek defends what he calls *discursive democracy*. Discursive democracy has the following characteristics:

1   It is *pluralistic* in embracing the necessity to communicate across difference without erasing difference.
2   It is *reflexive* in its questioning orientation to established traditions.
3   It is *transnational* in its capacity to extend across state boundaries into settings where there is no constitutional framework.
4   It is *ecological* in terms of its openness to communication with non-human nature.
5   It is *dynamic* in its openness to ever-changing constraints upon and opportunities for democratization. (Dryzek, 2000: 3)

Iris Marion Young is another critical theorist who seeks to distance deliberative democracy from its more liberal variants. Young (1999: 151) criticizes Gutmann and Thompson for wrongly collapsing the value of justice into the value of democracy. Furthermore, Young argues that the principles that Gutmann and Thompson propose should govern the organization and conduct of deliberation – reciprocity, publicity and accountability – need to be supplemented by a principle of *inclusion*. The criterion of inclusion is the fifth and final criterion of democracy that Dahl identified above. In the context of Dahl's analysis he simply means that all adults should have the full rights of citizens that are implied by the other four criteria. But the *norm* of inclusion, argues Young, requires that deliberative democrats reject some of their central assumptions. For example, that deliberation is culturally neutral and universal and that the process of discussion that aims to reach understanding must either begin with shared understandings or take a common good as their goal. This second assumption was implicit in Gutmann and Thompson's discussion of the school board's decision to reject the parents' argument for exclusion of their children from the curriculum. After considering the central theses of the parents' argument Gutmann and Thompson argue that the board was justified because the parents' request ran counter to the common good. The common good requires that we teach future citizens the skills and knowledge that are necessary for protecting the liberties and opportunities of all citizens. But if we assume unity as a starting point then the transformative dimension of deliberative politics is called into question. This is evident in the example Gutmann and Thompson consider. If we begin with the assumption that we all agree on the fundamental importance of protecting liberties and opportunities then it is easier to see how the board's decision is publicly justified. But if the deliberative process is supposed to be truly transformative, should we not also be prepared to question those initial opinions? In other words, if we begin by appealing to shared understandings or take the goal of deliberation to be one of achieving a common good then we may leave little room for the transformative dimension of deliberative politics.

In order to guard against this conservative consequence Young proposes seeing differences of culture and social perspectives as a resource that enriches the transformation of the deliberative process rather than something that must be overcome. She endorses a conception of *communicative democracy* (Young, 1996) that recognizes the need for a more expansive conception of political communication, one that does not construe argument in a culturally biased way. 'The deliberative ideal tends to assume that when we eliminate the influence of economic and political power, people's ways of speaking and understanding will be the same; but this will be true only if we also eliminate their cultural differences and different social positions' (Young, 1996: 123). Not all cultures express themselves in speech that is assertive and confrontational. If we are to ensure that the democratic process is inclusive of these other people and groups then we should not conceive of deliberation as a confrontation. This is the way Gutmann and Thompson present the case of the debate between the school board and the parents. Because the parents lacked a persuasive counter-argument to the proposal that their children learn these skills and knowledge they must concede defeat. For deliberative democrats like Gutmann and Thompson the main concern is that disagreement should be resolved by the force of the better argument and not economic dependence or political domination. But if a determination of the 'force of the better argument' itself privileges certain people then inclusion in the deliberative process is threatened. To guard against this exclusionary tendency Young suggests that deliberative democrats endorse an expanded conception of democratic communication, one that conceives of greeting, rhetoric and storytelling, in addition to argument, as contributing to political discussion.

7.5 Critically assessing the ideal of deliberative democracy

Providing a critical assessment of the ideal of deliberative democracy is difficult for a number of reasons. Firstly, as became evident in the previous section, theorists from diverse traditions have allied themselves with the ideal and thus any criticism of deliberative democracy must distinguish between the subtle nuances of the different versions of that ideal. Secondly, because the deliberative turn in democratic theory is a recently new development there has not, at least as of yet, emerged a mass of critical literature on the theory. But we can raise a number of concerns which challenge both the appeal and viability of the deliberative model. These challenges are not meant to serve as a refutation of deliberative democracy but instead highlight some of the challenges proponents of this ideal must consider. I shall address two related, but distinct, concerns. Firstly, that appealing to deliberation may have a destructive effect. And secondly, that the ideal of deliberative democracy is utopian.

Let us begin with the concern that the emphasis on deliberation might have a destructive effect. Recall the example of the friends who were contemplating where to go for dinner. Whilst it might sound appealing for these friends to resolve their disagreement through a process of deliberation this process could undermine the very aim it was designed to resolve. Namely, to figure out where to go for dinner. The friends, who wish to be courteous interlocutors and thus give each participant a chance to air their concerns, could spend the whole night deliberating the pros and cons of the various restaurants thus skipping dinner altogether! The transformative process of deliberation can be very time-consuming and thus we must be able to say that there comes a point when more deliberation would not resolve disagreements, in fact, it might make things worse. So how much deliberation is enough? When does the virtue of efficiency, for example, trump the virtues of deliberation? If we have to wait till a consensus emerges before decisions can be deemed *legitimate* then we will never be able to make justified decisions about the pressing policy issues that face us in everyday politics, issues ranging from the economy and health care provisions to the environment and foreign policy.

The urgency to resolve some political disagreements thus threatens to undermine the priority deliberative democrats place on the value of 'reasoning together'. Environmentalists, for example, might welcome the opportunity to debate with their opponents the pros and cons of legislation that aims to limit gas emissions harmful to the environment. However, if environmentalists believe that immediate action is necessary to avert ecological disaster then they will view a prolonged discursive process as harmful, not beneficial. Sometimes we simply cannot afford to pursue, let alone wait for, a consensus to emerge before we act. Nor is it always possible to have a genuine open debate on certain issues. As Daniel Bell (1999) notes, sound foreign policy, for example, does not readily lend itself to open debate. This point is very pertinent given the current debates about the war on terrorism that have ensued in the wake of the terrorist attacks on September 11th, 2001. Open and constructive debate requires public access to reliable information but if this information is only available to military and political elites then genuine debate on these issues will be hampered. To insist that this information be made public for the sake of having an open debate could compromise national security because it would reveal sensitive information (for example, surveillance operations or tactics) that needs to remain secret for reasons of national security. So by making deliberation the focus of their account of politics, deliberative democrats run the danger of subordinating other important values, such as efficiency and security. Deliberative democrats must make room for these other values if they are to avoid the criticism that they ignore the potentially destructive effects of deliberation.

In order to avoid the pitfalls of deliberation Bell emphasizes the preconditions that make constructive moral deliberations more likely.[7] One of these preconditions is that deliberation is more likely to be effective if the political culture values decision-making by intellectual elites. This is so, argues Bell, 'because talented elites with the motivation and the ability to understand and apply moral principles to complex political controversies with national (and international) implications are more likely to engage in constructive deliberations' (Bell, 1999: 74). Bell claims that this is a relatively controversial precondition (in a Western context) (1999: 74). Deliberative democrats are likely to reply that this is a very controversial precondition and will want to resist Bell's suggestion because it threatens to undermine the core of the idea of democratic legitimacy, namely, the idea that everyone whose basic interests are affected by policies should be included in the process of making them. But Bell's suggestion does highlight a dilemma the deliberative democrat must address. This dilemma is that the very things that make the ideal of deliberation sound inclusive, such as Gutmann and Thompson's principles of reciprocity, publicity and accountability, are the very same things that also threaten to make it exclusionary as most citizens will not have the information[8] nor the capacities needed to satisfy these diverse demands. Indeed, as Lynn Sanders (1997) points out, the endorsement of deliberation itself has not emerged through a genuinely deliberative process. So there seems to be something undemocratic about claiming that ordinary citizens ought to engage in deliberative activity the terms of which are dictated by democratic theorists!

This brings us to a second, related criticism that the deliberative democrat must address – the charge that the ideal of deliberative democracy is utopian. Is it realistic to think that we can have both deliberation *and* mass participation? Critics could argue that, given the size of the population of modern democracies, talk of citizens engaging in genuine deliberation is just impossible. Walzer, for example, says that 'deliberation is not an activity for the demos...100 million of them, or even 1 million or 100,000 can't plausibly "reason together"' (Walzer, 1999: 68). Deliberative democrats might seek to address this concern by either restricting the number of occasions when popular deliberation should occur and/or by restricting the number of people involved in the deliberation. John Rawls in *The Law of Peoples* (1999); for example, employs both strategies. He narrows the range of issues that must be deliberated by claiming that public reason only applies to fundamental political questions, such as constitutional essentials and matters of basic justice. Furthermore, Rawls restricts the number of people involved in public reasoning by distinguishing between what he calls the 'public political forum' and the 'background culture'. The former includes judges and government officials and candidates for political office. These individuals must engage in public reasoning when, for example, they decide legal cases or party platforms. But public reason does not apply to the background culture of society (for example, civil society).

Rawls's strategy for dealing with the problem of large scale is unsatisfactory. Firstly, we must ask exactly which issues qualify as the 'fundamental' issues to which the standards of public reason apply. If this list is construed too narrowly then deliberative democracy will lose its transformative dimension as it seems that we can simply appeal to the aggregative model of democracy to resolve most of the issues that come up in day-to-day politics as these issues will be deemed ones that do not raise fundamental political questions. Secondly, it presumes that we can determine which issues are matters of 'basic justice' independently of any genuine deliberation with others so we are back to the armchair theorizing that democrats wished to distance themselves from. Thirdly, if we believe that day-to-day politics does address fundamental political questions and thus think it is appropriate to hold them up to the deliberative standard then the problem of large scale is not resolved. And finally, the democratic dimension of deliberative democracy is threatened by Rawls's division between the political forum and civil society. If only judges and politicians are bound by the dictates of public reason then, as we noted above, it seems that we have abandoned the core idea of deliberative democracy – the idea that everyone whose basic interests are affected by policies should be included in the process of making them.

One novel suggestion that has recently been proposed as a way of making the ideal of deliberative democracy seem less utopian is that put forth by Bruce Ackerman and James Fishkin in 'Deliberation Day'. Ackerman and Fishkin suggest that a new national holiday be created called Deliberation Day.

> It will be held one week before major national elections. Registered voters will be called together in neighborhood meeting places, in small groups of 15, and larger groups of 500, to discuss the central issues raised by the campaign. Each deliberator will be paid $150 for the day's work of citizenship, on condition that he or she shows up at the polls the next week. All other work, except the most essential, will be prohibited by law. (Ackerman and Fishkin, 2002: 129)

Deliberation Day is meant to serve as a 'bottom-up' transformation of the democratic process. Contemporary politics is dominated by public opinion polling, sloganeering and sound-bites as political candidates sell themselves like commodities. One way of breaking this civically impoverished process is to improve the character of public opinion itself. Ackerman and Fishkin believe that many citizens actually want to take the public good seriously but the current arrangement does not have the necessary incentives in place to encourage this on a mass level. By paying deliberators for their efforts Deliberation Day will provide the incentives necessary to make such mass participation possible. But Ackerman and Fishkin believe that Deliberation Day will also generate a number of other incentives. Not only will it provide the social context necessary to engage in deliberation with other citizens, it will also transform the way political candidates run their campaigns.

> In plotting their campaign strategies and advertising, politicians and their consultants would use Deliberation Day as a fundamental reference point. They would no longer automatically suppose that candidates were best sold in eight-second bites. Throughout the campaign, their eyes would be fixed firmly on the fact that their messages would be subjected to a day-long dissection – and that millions of votes might swing as a result. (Ackerman and Fishkin, 2002: 135)

Ackerman and Fishkin cite the results of deliberative polls as evidence of the transformative potential of Deliberation Day.[9] In these polls a random sample of people are first given a questionnaire that they answer regarding issues of public policy. They then meet in small group discussions and larger plenary sessions and are given the opportunity to hear competing views and consider the evidence before making a final, more informed and reflective, decision. Engaging in extended dialogue about shared public problems often results in a dramatic change of opinion as compared to how people initially answered the questionnaire. Ackerman and Fishkin recognize that there would be problems with implementing a proposal like Deliberation Day but do not believe these obstacles are insurmountable. If deliberative democrats are seriously committed to both deliberation and mass participation then they must engage in the kind of innovative practical theorizing exemplified by Ackerman and Fishkin.

The rise of the deliberative turn in democratic theory is important for at least two reasons. Firstly, it offers us an account of democracy that is not as civically impoverished as the aggregative model of democracy and one that coheres with the practices we often associate with a democracy (for example, open discussion and debate). And secondly, the deliberative turn in democratic theory has brought justice theorists and democratic theorists closer together. The relation between justice and democracy is a complex and important relation and deliberative democrats force political theorists to take more seriously the question of how these two fundamental values are related.

Consider the following passage from 'Deliberation Day':

When you and I get together to choose a new set of leaders, we are not engaged in a private act of consumption, but a collective act of power – one that will profoundly shape the fate of millions of our fellow citizens, and billions more throughout the world. With the stakes this high, it is morally irresponsible to choose the politician with the biggest smile or the biggest handout. Rather than asking the question, 'What's good for me?,' the good citizen asks 'What's good for the *country*?' (Ackerman and Fishkin, 2002: 143)

Reflect on your own political behaviour and ask yourself if you live up to the vision of citizenship expressed by Ackerman and Fishkin:

- Do you vote? Why/why not?
- Consider the proposal for introducing Deliberation Day. Should we introduce such a holiday? Do you think it could achieve what Ackerman and Fishkin think it could achieve?
- Ackerman and Fishkin assess Deliberation Day in terms of four values: information, dialogue, deliberation and community. Do you agree with their assessment?

SUMMARY

- Deliberative democrats conceive of the democratic process as a *transformative* process, one that requires citizens to participate in *authentic deliberation* as opposed to simply expressing their existing preferences. They thus reject the aggregative model of democracy which conceives of voting as the primary political act. Instead, deliberative democrats emphasize the importance of being open-minded and respecting, and even accommodating, your opponent's position.
- Some deliberative democrats (e.g. Habermas) endorse purely procedural principles whilst others (e.g. Gutmann and Thompson) endorse substantive as well as procedural principles. Concerns about the apparent assimilation to liberal constitutionalism have led some critical theorists to re-cast the idea of deliberative democracy in a more critical light. For example, Dryzek defends what he calls *discursive democracy* and Young *communicative democracy*.
- In order to avoid the charges that deliberative democracy is potentially destructive and/or utopian deliberative democrats must provide an account of how other important values (e.g. efficiency, national security, etc.) are to be balanced against concerns for open public debate. Furthermore, given the size of democratic societies, deliberative democrats must address the concern that it is unrealistic to think that we can have both deliberation and mass participation.

Notes

1 This is debatable, especially for Rawls and Dworkin, given Rawls's later writings *Political Liberalism* (1993) and *The Law of Peoples* (1999) and Dworkin's discussion in *Sovereign Virtue* (2000) of the partnership conception of democracy.

2 When considering Dahl's criteria for democracy it is important to bear in mind that, as Iris Marion Young notes, democracy 'is not an all-or-nothing affair, but a matter of degree; societies can vary in both the extent and the intensity of their commitment to democratic practice' (Young, 2000: 5). Dahl himself admits that in the real world it is unlikely that every member of society will truly have equal opportunities to participate or influence the agenda. But this does not render these criteria useless. These criteria 'provide standards against which to measure the performance of actual associations that claim to be democratic. They can serve as guides for shaping and reshaping concrete arrangements, constitutions, and political institutions' (Dahl, 1998: 42).

3 See Rawls, *A Theory of Justice* (1999: 74–5).

4 See Habermas (1990, 1993).

5 In his later writings Habermas elaborates on the rights presupposed in his procedural model by claiming that the normative ideal of self-government, coupled with the aim of regulating human interactions through the medium of law, gives rise to five categories of rights. See Habermas (1996, ch. 3).

6 Habermas does this. See, for example, Habermas's article 'Constitutional Democracy: A Paradoxical Union of Contradictory Principles?' (2001) where he argues that constitutionalism and democracy are interdependent. But Gutmann and Thompson (1996) believe that their account of deliberative democracy transcends the dichotomy between procedural and constitutional democrats.

7 These are:

   1 A relatively fair distribution of resources.
   2 A sense of community and trust between participants.
   3 A political culture that values decision-making by intellectual elites.

8 For a comprehensive analysis of the American public's knowledge of politics, see Michael Delli Carpini and Scott Keeter *What Americans Know About Politics and Why it Matters* (1996).
9 See James Fishkin (1997).

8 Feminism

Summary Contents

8.1 Introduction   157
8.2 Liberal feminism   159
8.3 The public/private dichotomy   164
8.4 The politics of difference   169
8.5 Conclusion   174

8.1 Introduction

As a political theory 'feminism' covers a wide range of distinct issues and concerns. Some feminists align themselves with liberalism whilst others see liberalism as a thoroughly patriarchal ideology and thus they construct their normative theories in response to what they take the deficiencies of liberalism to be. Depending on which version of feminism one endorses, feminism may or may not be compatible with liberalism or other normative theories, such as communitarianism or multiculturalism. What makes a political theory 'feminist' is the emphasis it places on eliminating the oppression of women. Thus a liberal feminist believes that a liberal framework of rights, correctly conceived, could put an end to the subordination of women whilst a socialist feminist believes that class exploitation and gender exploitation are interconnected and thus the latter could not be achieved without eliminating the former.

Feminists emphasize the fact that gender distinctions are socially constructed. Gender is 'the deeply entrenched institutionalization of sexual difference' (Okin, 1989: 6). While it is an obvious biological fact that men and women will necessarily be different in some respects (for example, only women have the ability to give birth) many of the differences between men and women stem from an unjust social structure. For example, it is women who typically sacrifice their careers for parenthood, do the majority of unpaid domestic work and are made vulnerable by the institution of marriage. These differences between men and women do not stem from biological differences but from unequal power relations. Whilst feminists are united in their concern for liberating women they adopt diverse theoretical

positions for diagnosing these injustices and thus different prescriptions of
what needs to be done to create a more equal society.

In this chapter I do not attempt to survey the diverse range of theoretical
positions feminists have defended (as such an exercise would be a textbook
in itself!) but instead seek to examine some of these positions and how they
relate to the practical concern of addressing sexual inequality. In order to
accomplish this we shall focus on a number of different issues feminists have
raised which, taken together, should cover a suitable range of contemporary
arguments as well as effectively illustrate the practical significance of feminism as a political theory.

We begin by considering the position of *liberal feminism* in section 8.2. As
became evident in Part One of this book, liberalism can mean different
things to different theorists and thus the degree to which feminist concerns
are compatible with liberalism will depend not only on what one takes the
main concerns of feminism to be but also how one characterizes what liberalism is. The main proponent of liberal feminism whom we consider in the
next section is Martha Nussbaum who, in *Sex and Social Justice* (1999),
argues for a conception of feminism that is *internationalist, humanist, liberal,
concerned with the social shaping of preference and desire* and *concerned with sympathetic understanding.* Considering Nussbaum's argument is useful as it
brings to the fore feminist concerns that relate to other issues we have
addressed so far. For example, ethical universalism and Rawls's list of
primary goods.

In section 8.3 we examine the feminist slogan 'the personal is political'.
This slogan questions the public/private distinction in liberal political
thought. A public philosophy that takes seriously the goal of liberating
women must address the injustices within the family. By invoking the
public/private distinction, the liberal discourses of distributive justice are ill-
equipped to tackle the issue of the oppression of women because liberals
conceive of the family as part of the 'private' domestic sphere that is beyond
the demands of the principles of justice. Feminists argue that the belief that
the family is part of a 'private realm' is a myth, a myth that conceals the true
extent of the unjust inequalities that exist between men and women. By challenging the public/private dichotomy feminists hope to challenge the perpetuation of patriarchy, a perpetuation that is both concealed and facilitated
by the liberals' invocation of the public/private distinction.

In recent years many political theorists have sought to move beyond the
so-called *distributive paradigm* of contemporary theories of justice. As we saw
in Chapter 6, for example, the rise of debates on multiculturalism has given
rise to a new discourse of a *politics of recognition* that seeks to replace the
liberal discourse of a politics of equal citizenship and economic redistribution.
A similar trend has emerged in feminist political theory. The feminist Iris
Marion Young is one of the main critics of the distributive paradigm. In
Justice and the Politics of Difference (1990) Young argues that liberalism cannot
adequately deal with difference. She argues that it is a mistake to reduce
social justice to redistribution, as egalitarian liberals like Rawls and Dworkin

tend to do. In section 8.4 we consider Young's account of the politics of difference and the implication the emphasis on difference has for public policy.

8.2 Liberal feminism

What has become evident throughout this book is that the proponents and critics of the various theoretical positions we have examined often give quite different characterizations of the positions they defend or criticize. So it is not surprising that one finds a similar situation in the literature on feminism. In *Feminist Politics and Human Nature*, Alison Jagger, for example, claims that liberal political theory is grounded on the conception of human beings as *essentially rational agents* (Jagger, 1983: 28). According to Jagger, the liberal conception of rationality 'equates rational behaviour with the efficient maximisation of individual utility' (Jagger, 1983: 45). For this reason Jagger believes that liberal feminism contains contradictions that undermine its own philosophical foundations. A public philosophy premised on egoism is not going to liberate women. As became evident in the chapter on Gauthier, a political theory premised on the idea of maximizing utility runs counter to what many take to be a fundamental requirement of justice – that we treat everyone as equals and thus give serious consideration to the genuine human needs of all. Thus if liberal feminism means seeking to reconcile con-cerns of the oppression of women with Gauthier's project of justice as mutual advantage then it does indeed seem like a contradictory project that is destined to end in failure. But there are many versions of liberalism and some of the other variants may be more consistent with the aim of liberating women.

The concern for our shared human reason is evident in the works of early liberal feminists like Mary Wollstonecraft. In *A Vindication of the Rights of Woman* (1792) Wollstonecraft challenged the beliefs of her contemporaries who excluded women from enjoying the full rights of citizenship. Rights are based on common human reason and on common human virtues, argued Wollstonecraft, and there is no defensible reason why women should not enjoy the same rights as men enjoy. The belief that women naturally lacked the necessary prerequisites for enjoying the full rights of citizenship has long dominated human history and political thought. In *Emile* (1762), for example, Jean-Jacques Rousseau emphasized the rights of men as equal citizens of society and the importance of educating them to be independent. *Emile* also contains a section on the education of girls. Rousseau believed that females required a different education because they are naturally passive and weak. Wollstonecraft criticized such appeals to the 'natural' differences between men and women. Nurture, not nature, argued Wollstonecraft, is the cause of gender distinctions. The following passage from Wollstonecraft succinctly captures how unequal the social structure of Wollstonecraft's society was and the impact this had on how the roles of women and men were defined:

> Taught from infancy that beauty is woman's sceptre, the mind shapes itself
> to the body, and, roaming round its gilt cage, only seeks to adorn its prison.
> Men have various employments and pursuits which engage their attention,
> and give a character to the opening mind; but women, confined to one, and
> having their thoughts constantly directed to the most insignificant part of
> themselves, seldom extend their views beyond the triumph of the hour.
> (Wollstonecraft, 1995: 116)

Liberal feminists like Wollstonecraft argue that women have the same
potential for rationality that men have and thus there is no reason why
women should not enjoy the same status that men enjoy. Liberal feminists
thus emphasis the *equal worth* of all human beings, male and female, when
theorizing about what kind of society we ought to be aspiring towards and
what changes are needed to bring us closer to this more humane arrangement. As equals women should be entitled to the same benefits that men
enjoy from social cooperation. Practices of sexual discrimination, for example, contravene the demands of our shared humanity. The arbitrary or irrational use of gender in the awarding of benefits or positions is unjust and
incompatible with liberalism in the same way that discrimination based on
race or a person's religious beliefs would be.

Some liberal feminists explicitly found their theory on more than our
shared humanity and believe that justice requires more than merely the elimination of sexual discrimination. In *Sex and Social Justice*, for example, Martha
Nussbaum defends a conception of feminism that has the following five
features – it is internationalist, humanist, liberal, concerned with the social
shaping of preference and desire and concerned with sympathetic understanding. By considering the five features of Nussbaum's conception of
feminism we shall see how liberal feminists can incorporate the concerns of
the oppression of women into a liberal political theory.

The first feature of Nussbaum's feminism is that it is *internationalist*. This
means that it is a version of feminism that is informed by the fact that the
gender-related problems that women face will vary from society to society.
Feminists should not, argues Nussbaum, become inward looking and just
focus on the problems that women face in America or the United Kingdom.
While there are certain universal concerns that women face in all societies
(such as sexual harassment, rape, etc.) there are also important issues that
may be marginalized by focusing exclusively on the experiences of women
in the developed countries, issues like the denial of the right to work,
sex-selective infanticide and abortion and sex discrimination in religious
courts of family law.

The second feature of Nussbaum's feminism is *humanism*, which emphasizes the equal worth of all human beings. Her conception of feminism is
thus a version of ethical universalism. Recall from Chapter 4 Miller's contrast between ethical universalism and ethical particularism. Nussbaum's
commitment to the former is evident when she says:

The view developed here seeks justice for human beings as such, believing all human beings to be fundamentally equal in worth. It also holds that human beings have common resources and common problems wherever they live, and that their special dilemmas can best be seen as growing out of special circumstances, rather than out of a nature or identity that is altogether unlike that of other humans. (Nussbaum, 1999: 7)

Nussbaum's version of feminism is also *liberal* in that she defends a public philosophy that is premised on the equal importance, and separateness, of each human life. Furthermore, it equates a commitment to these things with a commitment to protecting those liberties which are central to the development of human life. But respecting the negative liberties of all is not sufficient for taking human development seriously. Building on the approach pioneered in development economics by Amartya Sen,[1] and from collaboration with Sen at the World Institute for Development Economics Research, Nussbaum endorses the *capabilities approach* to human development. Recall from Chapter 4 that the 'equality of what?' debate gave rise to a number of different egalitarian metrics, such as equality of welfare and equality of resources. Nussbaum favours the capabilities approach which maintains that 'the central goal of public planning should be the capabilities of citizens to perform various important functions' (Nussbaum, 1999: 42).

Unlike a standard utilitarian approach, the capability approach maintains that preferences are not always reliable indicators of life quality, as they may be deformed in various ways by oppression and deprivation. Unlike the type of liberal approach that focuses only on the distribution of resources, the capability approach maintains that resources have no value in themselves, apart from their role in promoting human functioning. It therefore directs the planner to inquire into the varying needs individuals have for resources and their varying abilities to convert resources into functioning. (Nussbaum, 1999: 34)

The capabilities approach asks What activities characteristically performed by human beings are so central that they seem definitive of a life that is truly human? Adopting a perfectionist stance inspired by Aristotle, Nussbaum puts forward the following comprehensive list of the central human functional capabilities:

1 Life.
2 Bodily health.
3 Bodily integrity.
4 Senses, imagination, thought.
5 Emotions.
6 Practical reason.
7 Affiliation.

8   Other species.
9   Play.
10 Control over one's environment (political and material). (Nussbaum, 1999: 41–2)

Nussbaum's list of capabilities is similar to Rawls's list of primary goods but Nussbaum believes that the capabilities approach is more attractive because it includes more than Rawls's list and it is more definitive than the goods Rawls identifies. Recall, for example, the way Rawls defines the least advantaged members of society. He focuses exclusively on wealth and income. But this neglects the fact that

> people have varying needs for resources: a pregnant woman, for example, needs more calories than a non-pregnant woman, a child more protein than an adult. They also have different abilities to convert resources into functioning. A person in a wheelchair will need more resources to become mobile than a person with unimpaired limbs; a woman in a society that has defined employment outside the home as off limits to women needs more resources to become a productive worker than one who does not face such struggles. In short, the Rawlsian approach does not probe deeply enough to show us how resources do or do not go to work in making people able to function. (Nussbaum, 1999: 34)

Nussbaum's endorsement of the capabilities approach will no doubt face objections from communitarians who, like Walzer, reject the idea that there is an 'objective' list of valued goods that people in all cultures will value. Take, for example, the fourth of the central functional capabilities identified by Nussbaum – senses, imagination and thought. Elaborating on this she says that this entails being able to imagine, think and reason 'in a "truly human" way, a way informed and cultivated by an adequate education … ' (Nussbaum, 1999: 41). Cultural relativists will point to cultural differences regarding things like what constitutes an 'adequate education' as a way of undermining the universal applicability of Nussbaum's capabilities approach. Determining what constitutes an 'adequate education' even within a liberal democracy is difficult enough, as we saw in the chapter on deliberative democracy, but once one extends this notion to the international arena it becomes even more rife with problems.

Nussbaum's capabilities approach brings to the fore feminist concerns at both the domestic and international level. Whether the issues are domestic ones, such as policies to eliminate sexual harassment in the workplace, or global issues such as the hunger and malnutrition of women in the developing world and practices of female genital mutilation, Nussbaum's capabilities approach provides feminists with a metric for measuring existing injustices as well as a succinct account of what the goal of public planning should be. 'What matters is that all human beings, wherever they are, should be able to develop their capabilities for choosing' (Phillips, 2001: 258).

Nussbaum's emphasis on ensuring that all people pass a threshold of capabilities has led some egalitarians to criticize her for not taking seriously the value of equality. Richard Arneson (2000), for example, claims that, for Nussbaum, 'inequalities among persons above this level [the threshold of capabilities] are a "don't care" from the standpoint of justice' (Arneson, 2000: 55). Feminists could also express similar concerns with regard to the liberating potential of the capabilities approach. If women pass the minimum threshold posited by Nussbaum's capabilities approach but still have unequal power then surely this is still unjust. But, critics would argue, the capabilities approach is not equipped to address these injustices as it only seeks to ensure that all pass a minimum threshold of capabilities.[2]

The capabilities approach faces other difficulties. 'Limited resources in the face of enormous need require that choices be made and that priorities be set' (Wolf, 1995: 111). If the capabilities approach is to provide practical guidance to policy-makers it must consider priorities and even trade-offs among the various functioning capabilities. Are all of the various capabilities Nussbaum identifies *equally* important to living a truly human life? If not, to which of those capabilities should we give priority? Susan Wolf, for example, claims that 'where people are starving it seems absurd to occupy oneself with the quality of their relationship to nature' (Wolf, 1995: 111).

Let us now consider the two final criteria of Nussbaum's conception of feminism. These are the concern with the shaping of preference and desire and the concern with sympathetic understanding. These two concerns are similar to those expressed by deliberative democrats. Deliberative democrats believe that a just public philosophy must be transformative and not simply cater to existing preferences and desires. People usually adjust their desires, argues Nussbaum, to reflect the level of their available possibilities:

> They can get used to having luxuries and mind the absence of these very much, and they can also fail to form desires for things their circumstances have placed out of reach. People from groups that have not traditionally had access to education, or employment outside the home, may be slow to desire these things because they may not know what they are like or what they could possibly mean in lives like theirs. Even at the level of simple bodily health and nutrition, people who have been malnourished all their lives may not know what it would be like to feel strong. Especially if they have been told that women are weaker than men, they may not be able to form a desire for the health and strength of which they are capable. The absence of such a desire should not convince policymakers that health and strength are not important goals to be promoted for these people. (Nussbaum, 1999: 11–12)

The transformative dimension of Nussbaum's feminist internationalism would not be possible without placing an emphasis on the need for sympathetic understanding. In emphasizing the concern for sympathetic understanding Nussbaum seeks to occupy the middle ground between feminists who characterize women's instincts to care as constructs of women's subordination and those who suggest that women's ability to care for others is part of a distinct moral ethic (that is, an ethic of care). In doing so Nussbaum has the difficult task of combining a radical feminist critique of sex relations with the possibilities of trust and understanding. Many feminists will remain sceptical about the possibilities of trust and understanding given the existing inequalities between the sexes. If genuine trust and understanding is to exist between the sexes then we must take seriously, as Okin (1989) argues, the justice of gender. This takes us into a discussion of the feminist slogan 'the personal is political'.

8.3 The public/private dichotomy

Nussbaum's version of feminist internationalism suggests that liberalism, properly conceived, can inspire a public philosophy that can make good on its promise to liberate women. But many feminists remain sceptical about the prospects of reconciling feminist concerns with liberalism. A central criticism that feminists often levy against liberal political theory is that by invoking the 'public/private' distinction liberalism cannot address the injustices that occur within the family. What, exactly, constitutes the public/private distinction is itself a source of much debate among commentators. Susan Okin, for example, claims that liberal thought takes as fundamental the dichotomy 'between the "public" world of political life and the marketplace and the "private" domestic world of the family life and personal relations' (Okin, 1989: 111).

The division between the public and private sphere is, arguably, evident in John Stuart Mill's famous defence of the 'harm principle' in *On Liberty*. Mill argued that there does exist conduct that is 'private' or 'self-regarding' and that freedom from coercion ought to be guaranteed for such actions and inactions. Take, for example, prohibitions on homosexuality. Mill's harm principle rules such prohibitions out as our sexual preferences are a private matter. Liberals believe that this protection of the private sphere is an essential commitment of a just polity. It secures the importance of individual autonomy and toleration.

Many liberals will resist, from the very start, the feminist critique of the public/private distinction by arguing that feminists mischaracterize exactly what this distinction is. Barry (2001), for example, points out that Mill did not endorse the view that *families* belong to the 'private sphere'.

> ... it is liberals who have been in the forefront of efforts to remove the legal disabilities of women, to make marital rape a punishable offence, to press for more active involvement by the police in incidents of domestic violence and for the prosecution of child-abusers, and to insist that parents should be legally obligated to provide for the education of their children.
>
> Mill is exemplary here. So far from endorsing the notion that families belong to a 'private sphere', he argued that they constitute 'a case where ... [the

sentiment of liberty] is altogether misplaced. A person should be free to do as he likes in his own concerns; but he ought not be free to do as he likes in acting for another, under the pretext that the affairs of the other are his own affairs.' (Barry, 2001: 130–1)

The feminist charge that liberalism fails to go far enough in examining how political the personal is is an important and contentious issue, so let us delve into this criticism in more detail by considering some of the different concerns feminists have expressed in this regard.

In *Justice, Gender and the Family* Okin argues that there are four major respects in which the personal is political. These are:

1   Power, a distinguishing feature of the political, can exist within the family.
2   The domestic sphere itself is the result of political decisions.
3   Domestic life is where most of our early socialization takes place.
4   The division of labour within most families raises psychological as well as practical barriers against women in all other spheres. (Okin, 1989: 128–33)

The first point emphasizes the fact that power relations can and often do exist within the family. Thus domestic and personal life cannot be beyond the reach of the demands of justice as justice is primarily concerned with power relations. If, for example, family life is such that a husband can beat his wife without fear of punishment this would obviously be unjust. But all liberals would agree with this first point. The rights of citizenship should apply to all citizens, including women. By entering into marriage women do not forfeit those rights. So the first way Okin employs the slogan 'the personal is political' is likely to be supported by both liberals and feminists.

The second way the personal is political, argues Okin, is that the domestic sphere is itself created by political decisions. The notion that family life is a 'private sphere' is a myth.

In innumerable ways, the state determines and enforces the terms of marriage. For hundreds of years, the common law deprived women of their legal personhood upon marriage. It enforced the rights of husbands to their wives' property and even to their wives' bodies, and made it virtually impossible for women to divorce or even to live separately from their husbands. (Okin, 1989: 129–30)

Okin's second point is, once again, one that many liberals would and do endorse. As we noted above, liberals like Barry point out that historically the state has unjustly interfered in family life and that it has been liberals who have been at the forefront of efforts to remove the legal disabilities against women. It is thus perhaps more accurate to say that Okin's first two points are more problematic for communitarians and conservatives than liberals. Recall Walzer's appeal to shared social meanings. Such an appeal, when applied to something like the family, may make us blind to the structural inequalities of our society that influence and shape the family. By invoking the slogan 'the personal is political' feminists are encouraging us to be wary of appeals to tradition, or so-called 'family values', as such appeals often ignore the fact that the domestic sphere is itself shaped by the political sphere so inequalities in the latter can, and often are, translated into inequalities in the former.

The debate between liberals and feminists becomes more complicated once we move on to consider the last two ways in which Okin believes the personal is political. These are the claims that domestic life is where most of our early socialization takes place and that the division of labour within most families raises psychological as well as practical barriers against women in all other spheres. Okin argues that the family is an important formative influence that shapes the gendered selves we become. When girls are brought up, for example, with the expectations that they will themselves become the primary caregiver of children and/or that they are responsible for the domestic chores in the home then the existing gender structure is simply reinforced. Okin argues that a just family is one which is *internally* regulated by the principles of justice. A humanist conception of justice is one that seeks genuine equality between men and women in terms of the paid and unpaid work they do, as well as their opportunities and obligations in general.

Many liberals have resisted Okin's suggestion that we endorse the proposal to apply the principles of justice internally to the family. Rawls, for example, while arguing that the principles of justice do impose essential constraints on the family as an institution (for example, to guarantee basic rights and liberties and fair opportunities), rejects the suggestion that they should apply directly to the internal life of the family. Such a proposal is, argues Rawls, out of place (Rawls, 2001: 165). At some point, he continues, 'society has to trust to [sic] the natural affection and goodwill of parents' (Rawls, 2001: 165). But this suggestion will not ease the concerns of feminists, who would retort that there is no basis for granting the trust Rawls speaks of. Parents may genuinely love and care for their children but unwittingly reinforce gender structures by continuing the cycle of gendered socialization that they were themselves brought up in.

Some critics of Okin seek to undermine her argument by pushing her on the issue of what it would mean to say that the family should be regulated by the principles of justice. Stephen de Wijze (2000), for example, argues that Okin's proposal would violate pluralism as there would not be just one way of justly arranging the family.

> A family may organise the division of labour according to who likes various tasks; one person loves shopping and cooking while the other prefers bathing, dressing and ferrying children to their various activities. Another family may divide labour according to who is the most competent at doing the various tasks, while another may decide that a just division is made according to shared religious beliefs about the roles of men and women in

the family. In all these examples, the division of labour within the family is not necessarily equal but each has a plausible sense of justice and fairness motivating who does what and why. (De Wijze, 2000: 279)

But once again feminists are not going to find this liberal response compelling. Firstly, the reality is that most women, even those that work outside the home, do by far the majority of unpaid labour in the home. Okin estimates 'that fully employed husbands do, at most, approximately half as much as their fully employed wives, and some studies show a much greater discrepancy' (Okin, 1989: 153). Secondly, De Wijze's appeal to the existing preferences women and men have for dividing domestic labour is problematic because those very preferences have themselves been shaped by a gendered social structure. De Wijze's description of how men and women decide on dividing domestic chores presupposes a version of the 'unencumbered self' that communitarians have criticized. Consider, for example, De Wijze's last point, the scenario where a couple decide to divide domestic chores in accordance with shared religious beliefs about the roles of women and men. According to De Wijze, if these religious roles say that a woman should do most (if not all) of the domestic labour then this is not unfair or unjust because she has 'voluntarily chosen' that end. But if we recognize, as communitarians have argued, that we are *embedded selves*, then we will not be as quick as De Wijze is to describe this family arrangement as being 'plausibly justice' or 'fair'. The women who supposedly 'consent' to taking on the bulk of domestic chores are simply fulfilling the social roles they have been encouraged (or even compelled) to take on since birth.

De Wijze's argument is further undermined once one recognizes that what counts as a 'fair division' of paid and unpaid work between women and men will reflect biased judgements about the worth of paid and unpaid work. As Okin points out, 'a husband's income and job prestige are *inversely* related to his involvement in household chores' (Okin, 1989: 153). When society places great value on paid employment and undervalues unpaid domestic labour, then these attitudes will also distort what constitutes a 'fair division' of labour between family members. A husband who brings in a large income and/or has a prestigious job is likely to be judged as doing his fair share (or even more than his fair share) and thus be exempt from domestic chores. The problem is that gender inequalities have tainted attitudes concerning the value of the different kinds of work that need to be done. De Wijze's appeal to existing attitudes concerning what constitutes a fair division of work is thus a non-starter because it merely reinforces the status quo and thus does not effectively address the unjust power relationships between men and women.

If we find Okin's argument compelling then the important practical question is – What is to be done? What, exactly, does taking the slogan 'the personal is political' entail in terms of public policy? Critics will charge that the slogan gives licence to totalitarianism as there is thus no domain which is safe from state interference. But such a concern presupposes that feminists seek to completely abolish the public/private distinction. But this is not so. What they seek to do is redefine where the divide between the public and private is. By doing this we expand the domain which the principles of justice must apply to. They apply to the family in the way liberals like Barry and Rawls acknowledge (for example, guarantee basic rights to all family members) but they also apply *within* the family. But what would this actually mean? We cannot police the family, ensuring that men and women do an equal share of paid and unpaid labour. One suggestion Okin makes is to 'have employers make out wage checks equally divided between the earner and the partner who provides all or most of his or her unpaid domestic services' (Okin, 1989: 181). This would alter the power relations in the family by giving some public recognition to the fact that unpaid labour is just as important as paid labour. This would make a significant difference to the power relations within the family, argues Okin.

> It would make a difference in cases where the earning or higher-earning partner now directly exploits his power, by refusing to make significant spending decisions jointly, by failing to share the income, or by psychologically or physically abusing the nonearning or low-earning partner, reinforced by the notion that she (almost always the wife) has little option but to put up with such abuse or to take herself and her children into a state of destitution. It would make a difference, too, in cases where the higher-earning partner indirectly exploits this earning power in order to perpetuate the existing division of labor in the family. In such instances considerable changes in the balance of power would be likely to result from the legal and societal recognition that the partner who does most of the domestic work of the family contributes to its well-being just as much, and therefore rightly *earns* just as much, as the partner who does most of the workplace work. (Okin, 1989: 181)

Okin's proposals go far beyond just this one recommendation. In order to create a genderless society public policies and law should assume no social differentiation of the sexes. More specifically, she supports making employers take the necessary measures to accommodate the reality that most workers are also parents. In order to ensure an equal division of parental responsibilities employers should make parental leave during the postbirth months available to mothers and fathers on the same terms. Furthermore, employers should permit a flexibility of hours worked so that parents can fairly balance domestic and non-domestic work.

> All workers should have the right, without prejudice to their jobs, security, benefits, and so on, to work less than full-time during the first year of a child's life, and to work flexible or somewhat reduced hours at least until the child reaches the age of seven … Large-scale employers should also be required to provide high-quality on-site day care for children from infancy up to school age. And to ensure equal quality of day care for all young

children, *direct government subsidies* (not tax credits, which benefit the better-off) should make up the difference between the cost of high-quality day care and what less well-paid parents could reasonably be expected to pay. (Okin, 1989: 176–77)

Okin also recommends changes to the education curriculum and the institution of marriage. The aspiration to create a genderless society is one that would require a diverse range of changes to existing policies. Okin is a good example of a theorist who brings out the practical significance of the feminist slogan 'the personal is political'. There is no simple solution to creating a more equal division of the benefits and burdens of social cooperation, but by challenging the public/private distinction feminists seek to draw attention to the different ways the family creates inequalities and the range of options open to us to remedy such inequalities.

Consider the following questions:

- To what degree, if any, is liberalism compatible with feminism?
- Do you agree with the feminist slogan 'the personal is political'?
- Reflecting on your own family and your upbringing, to what extent do you think the family does socialize unequal expectations in boys and girls?
- Do you think we could achieve a genderless society? What needs to be done if we are to take this aspiration seriously?

Further reading

Susan Okin, *Justice, Gender and the Family* (New York: Basic Books, 1989).
Joan Landes (ed.), *Feminism, the Public and the Private* (Oxford: Oxford University Press, 1998).
Chris Armstrong and Judith Squires, 'Beyond the Public/Private Dichotomy: Relational Space and Sexual Inequalities', *Contemporary Political Theory*, 1 (3), 2002: 261–83.
Carol Pateman, *The Sexual Contract* (Stanford, CA: Stanford University Press, 1988).
Alison Jagger, *Feminist Politics and Human Nature* (Sussex: The Harverster Press, 1983).

8.4 The politics of difference

Liberal feminists seek to inspire a public philosophy that will liberate women by emphazising the similarities between men and women. For example, that women have the same potential for rationality that men have and thus women should enjoy the same rights of citizenship that men enjoy. Okin goes so far as to argue that we should aspire to create a genderless society, one where public policies and law assume no social differentiation of the sexes. But there is an important feminist tradition that rejects the idea that we should emphasize the similarities between men and women. This tradition maintains that the only way of liberating women is to emphasize *difference*. In *Justice and the Politics of Difference* Iris Marion Young, for example, argues that liberalism cannot adequately deal with difference. Young believes that it is a mistake to reduce social justice to redistribution, as egalitarian liberals like Rawls and Dworkin tend to do. She identifies two problems with what she calls the 'distributive paradigm'. The first problem is that 'it tends to focus thinking about social justice on the allocation of material goods such as things, resources, income and wealth, or on the distribution of social positions, especially jobs. This focus tends to ignore the social structure and institutional context that often help determine distributive patterns' (Young, 1990: 15).

Young provides some examples to illustrate this concern. She considers the case of a large employer that decides to close its plant in a small city. Such an action will have a devastating impact on the small community as the plant employs a large portion of the city's workers. This example raises concerns that go beyond those of the distributive paradigm, argues Young. What is at stake in this example is not simply a concern about the justice of material distributions but the justice of decision-making power and procedures. The just remedy in situations like this might not entail achieving a certain distributive pattern but giving the workers and community the option of taking over and operating the plant themselves.

Young argues that injustices in the division of labour and of cultural imagery and symbols are further examples that cannot be subsumed within the distributive paradigm. Media stereotyping of women and ethnic minorities, for example, raises concerns that are not primarily about the distribution of income or resources. The differences between social groups are brought to the fore by making the concepts of domination and oppression, and not distribution, the central concern of justice. Young argues that 'where social group differences exist and some groups are privileged while others are oppressed, social justice requires explicitly acknowledging and attending to those group differences in order to undermine oppression' (Young, 1990: 3).

The second shortcoming of the distributive paradigm, argues Young, is that even when distributive theorists extend the demands of justice to non-material social goods like rights, opportunities and self-respect, by doing so they mistakenly ascribe material-like properties to goods that do not have these properties. Thus liberals obscure the institutional and social bases of these values. Take, for example, rights. Young asks:

> What can it mean to distribute rights that do not refer to resources or things, like the right of free speech, or the right of trial by jury? We can conceive of a society in which some persons are granted these rights while others are

not, but this does not mean that some people have a certain 'amount' or 'portion' of a good while others have less. Altering the situation so that everyone has these rights, moreover, would not entail that the formerly privileged group gives over some of its right of free speech or trial by jury to the rest of society's members, on analogy with a redistribution of income. (Young, 1990: 25)

By invoking the language of distribution liberal theories of justice focus more on end-state patterns (for example, the difference principle, equality of resources) rather than attending to social processes. But the injustices of social processes are not brought to the fore if we adopt the pattern orientation of the distributive paradigm. Young argues that two social conditions define injustice – oppression and domination. The former involves the institutional constraint on self-development and the latter the institutional constraint on self-determination (Young, 1990: 37).

Young believes that by making the concepts of oppression and domination the focus of a theory of justice one can inspire a liberating public philosophy, one that can appeal to diverse radical movements ranging from feminism to movements for Blacks, Latinos, American Indians, poor people, lesbians, old people and people with disabilities. Such a public philosophy does not seek to eliminate group differences, as the liberal ideals of equal treatment and impartiality attempt to do. It is both unrealistic and undesirable to attempt to eliminate group differences. Justice in a group-differentiated society, argues Young, 'demands social equality of groups, and mutual recognition and affirmation of group differences. Attending to group-specific needs and providing for group representation both promotes that social equality and provides the recognition that undermines cultural imperialism' (Young, 1990: 191). This emphasis on recognition is one that we examined in the chapter on multiculturalism (p. 119).

Feminists like Young do not take liberal political theory as the sole object of their critique. Young also criticizes the notion of community on both philosophical and practical grounds. The ideal of community 'presumes subjects who are present to themselves and presumes subjects can understand one another as they understand themselves' (Young, 1986: 1–2). Thus by invoking the ideal of community one denies difference between subjects. In place of the value of community Young advocates the normative ideal of political emancipation. 'A model of the unoppressive city offers an understanding of social relations without domination in which persons live together in relations of mediation among strangers with whom they are not in community' (Young, 1986: 2). The ideal city life, according to Young, embodies four virtues – social differentiation without exclusion, variety, eroticism and publicity. Let us briefly consider this forth virtue of city life – publicity – for it permits us to compare Young's argument with the communitarian argument of Sandel (1996).

As we already noted in Chapter 5, Sandel believes that politics needs to be concerned with restoring 'civic spaces', places where people can engage in debate about the common good, such as churches, schools and community centres. While Young is also concerned with preserving civic (or public) spaces, she does not embrace the ideal of community. Such an ideal paints an unrealistic picture of public spaces (for example, as a realm of unity and mutual understanding). Young argues that it is precisely because public spaces are diverse that they are exciting and vital. Streets, parks and plazas bring people of diverse groups and experiences together. When people are brought together it is not to affirm a 'common end', argues Young, but to speak and listen to each other. Public spaces are valued not because they assimilate citizens, but because they are venues for celebrating our distinctive characteristics and cultures. 'The public is heterogeneous, plural, and playful, a place where people witness and appreciate diverse cultural expressions that they do not share and do not fully understand' (Young, 1990: 241).

A democratic public, argues Young, 'should provide mechanisms for the effective recognition and representation of the distinct voices and perspectives of those of its constituent groups that are oppressed or disadvantaged' (Young, 1990: 184). In *The Politics of Presence* Anne Phillips seeks to take Young's concerns about group difference seriously by challenging the conventional understanding of democracy, what Phillips calls *the politics of ideas*. The politics of ideas conceives of difference as a matter of different ideas. This is what liberals like Rawls mean when they talk about the fact of 'reasonable pluralism'. What liberals mean when they talk about difference is that people endorse different, even conflicting, conceptions of the good life. Some people are Christian, some Muslim and others atheist. But when difference is conceived of as a matter of different ideas democratic politics is dominated by party politics where political loyalties develop around policies rather than people. The move from direct to representative democracy has shifted the emphasis, argues Phillips, 'from *who* the politicians are to *what* (policies, preferences, ideas) they represent, and in doing so has made accountability to the electorate the pre-eminent radical concern' (Phillips, 1995: 4).

One shortcoming of the politics of ideas is that it adopts a narrow conception of what constitutes political exclusion. For example, the fact that the vast majority of elected officials in legislative assemblies are white, middle-class males does not, in itself, suggest a polity is exclusionary. The key issue, for the politics of ideas, is that the policies these politicians endorse are ones that reflect the beliefs and ideals of the citizenry. But, argues Phillips, once difference is conceived

> in relation to those experiences and identities that may constitute different kinds of groups, it is far harder to meet demands of political inclusion without also including the members of such groups. Men may conceivably stand in for women when what is at issue is the representation of agreed policies or programmes or ideals. But how can men legitimately stand in for women when what is at issue is the representation of women *per se*? White people

may conceivably stand in for those of Asian or African origin when it is a matter of representing particular programmes for racial equity. But can an all-white assembly really claim to be representative when those it represents are so much more ethnically diverse? (Phillips, 1995: 6)

Phillips endorses positive action, such as quotas for women, to increase the proportion of women elected. She identifies four arguments for such policies:

1 The importance of symbolic representation.
2 The need to tackle those exclusions inherent in the party-packaging of political ideas.
3 The need for more vigorous advocacy on behalf of disadvantaged groups.
4 The importance of a politics of transformation in opening up the full range of policy options.

By advocating *the politics of presence* Phillips seeks, not to replace the politics of ideas, but rather to inspire a fairer system of representation. One that takes into consideration social characteristics such as ethnicity and gender. Changing the gender composition of elected assemblies will not, by itself, rid society of all its injustices. But Phillips believes that such a political arrangement is more likely to result in positively transforming the political landscape. Such a transformation is unlikely if we accept the status quo with its gender imbalance.

Discuss the following statements:

1 The thing that really matters is *what* politicians represent, not *who* (e.g. their gender, race, religion, etc.) they are. Of course certain personal characteristics are important. We want representatives who are intelligent, compassionate, fair-minded, etc. But once we make their personal characteristics the main focus we run into serious problems. We do not want people voting for politicians because of the colour of their skin, their gender, winning smile or hair cut. So it is imperative that we remain faithful to the central tenets of the politics of ideas.
2 Phillips's argument is a non-starter because it is susceptible to the slippery slope objection. That is, once you treat some characteristics of representatives (e.g. gender) as relevant and advocate gender quotas then you must also support similar quotas for blacks, pensioners, Christians, Muslims etc. So you end up endorsing a position which, taken to its logical conclusion, is obviously untenable.
3 Those of us who are disillusioned with contemporary politics would agree with Phillips that a politics of transformation is needed if we are to take seriously the interests of disadvantaged groups. But the emphasis on the

'politics of difference' actually undermines what is needed for substantial and lasting change to occur. Instead of dividing society into distinct 'groups', what we really need is a public philosophy that fosters, not undermines, social cohesion. If we start saying that men cannot represent women, white people cannot represent non-whites, and heterosexuals cannot represent homosexuals, all we do is divide society into hostile groups. By doing this we undermine the sense of fraternity that is needed to create a more just polity.

8.5 Conclusion

The arguments of Nussbaum and Young are interesting to compare and contrast as these feminist theorists react differently to the so-called 'distributive paradigm' of contemporary political theory. Nussbaum's liberal feminism functions from within the distributive paradigm and she premises her position on our shared humanity. The internationalist dimension of her feminism brings it into tension with (some of) the arguments developed by communitarians and multiculturalists. The capabilities approach presupposes that there are some universal goods that all people, regardless of their culture, have an interest in. For example, being able to live to the end of a human life of normal length, being able to live for and in relation to others, and being able to participate effectively in political choices that govern one's life. Furthermore, Nussbaum's emphasis on capabilities, as opposed to material goods (such as wealth), means that her theory of justice may not be as susceptible to the charge that it fails to recognize the fact that social structure and institutional context often help determine distributive patterns.

Young's feminism rejects the emphasis on sameness and redistribution. For Young the key concepts are oppression and domination. By focusing on end-state patterns (for example, the difference principle, equality of resources) justice-theorists like Rawls and Dworkin ignore social processes that undermine the equality of disadvantaged groups. Young's *politics of difference* thus shares much common ground with multiculturalist arguments, such as Taylor's *politics of recognition*. Both Young and Taylor emphasize the importance of 'group rights' and seek to inspire a public philosophy that goes beyond the vision of equal citizenship embraced by liberals. The emphasis on difference also influences, as we saw in the chapter on deliberative democracy, how Young conceives of political communication. Not all cultures express themselves in speech that is assertive and confrontational. Thus Young argues that deliberative democrats should endorse an expanded conception of political communication, one that conceives of greeting, rhetoric and storytelling, in addition to argument, as contributing to political discussion.

It is not surprising that some commentators find merits in both the appeal to redistribution *and* the emphasis on difference, and thus some argue that attention should be given to both things. Nancy Fraser (1995), for example, rejects Young's wholesale endorsement of the politics of difference. Fraser argues that some oppressions are rooted in political economy whilst others are rooted in culture. Exploitation, marginalization and powerlessness are rooted in the former whilst cultural imperialism and violence are rooted in culture. By considering some real-world applications that concern different cases of oppressed groups, such as working-class non-professionals, women, and African-Americans, Fraser argues that the politics of difference is not globally applicable.

> In some cases, such as that of nonprofessional workers, it is simply askew of the nature of the group and its oppression. In other cases, in contrast, such as gays and lesbians, the politics of difference is absolutely crucial for remedying oppression. The hardest cases, of course, are those, such as gender and 'race,' in which both redistribution and recognition are required to overcome a complex of oppression that is multiple and multiply-rooted. (Fraser, 1995: 179)

Fraser claims that some differences should be eliminated, others should be universalized, and some should be enjoyed. Fraser's conciliatory approach suggests that maybe the gulf between Nussbaum's liberal feminism and Young's politics of difference might not be that extensive after all. The difficult task then becomes one of integrating concerns of redistribution with those of recognition. The more one emphasizes the importance of recognition the more open one is to the criticism that we overlook the importance resources have in enabling individuals to function as human beings. This concern for redistribution is particularly acute when one takes an internationalist perspective. On the other hand, the more we focus on redistribution the more we are open to the criticism that some injustices cannot be resolved by appealing to the demand for redistribution. Feminists who champion the slogan 'the personal is political' or argue for gender quotas for political representatives believe that the changes needed to liberate women must be more extensive than those typically envisioned by the justice-theorists of the distributive paradigm.

The different, and sometimes competing, theoretical positions feminists adopt are due, at least in part, to the fact that the causes of social inequality are themselves varied and complex and this is reflected in both the diagnosis and proposed remedy for these injustices. Some feminists believe that the best way forward is to unite feminist concerns with a more enlightened version of liberalism whilst other feminists believe that such a reconciliation is doomed to fail as they believe that liberalism is, at best, ill-equipped to take seriously the task of liberating women, or, at worse, an instrument of that oppression itself.

SUMMARY

- Feminism is a varied political theory which is primarily concerned with the liberation of women. Liberal feminists believe that an enlightened version of liberalism can inspire a public philosophy that will seek to remedy existing social injustices. But many feminists believe that liberalism is the source of the problem and not the solution.
- The feminist slogan 'the personal is political' is often invoked as a way of bringing to the fore how deeply entrenched sexual differences are in society. In particular, the slogan requires us to consider more closely the role of the family and how it perpetuates social inequalities. Feminists reject the idea that the family is part of a 'private' realm that is beyond the demands of the principles of justice.
- Young emphasizes the importance of *difference*, something which both liberal theories of justice and appeals to 'community' are ill-equipped to deal with. Young's politics of difference links feminist concerns with the concerns of other theories, such as deliberative democracy and multiculturalism.

Notes

1 See, for example, Amartya Sen (1992).
2 In her later writings Nussbaum explicitly denies the claim that the capabilities view is indifferent to inequalities. She claims:

> A list of the central capabilities is not a complete theory of justice. Such a list gives us the basis for determining a decent social minimum in a variety of areas. I argue that the structure of social and political institutions should be chosen, at least in part, with a view to promoting at least a threshold level of these human capabilities. But the provision of a threshold level of capability, exigent though that goal is, may not suffice for justice. ...
> (Nussbaum, 2000a: 75)

Bibliography

Ackerman, Bruce and Fishkin, James (2002) 'Deliberation Day', *Journal of Political Philosophy*, 10 (2): 129–152.

Anderson, Elizabeth (1999) 'What is the Point of Equality?', *Ethics*, 109 (2): 287–337.

Arneson, Richard (1989) 'Equality and Equal Opportunity for Welfare', *Philosophical Studies*, 56: 77–93.

Arneson, Richard (1990) 'Primary Goods Reconsidered', *Nous*, 24: 429–54.

Arneson, Richard (2000) 'Perfectionism and Politics', *Ethics*, 111 (1): 37–63.

Barry, Brian (1989) *Theories of Justice*. Berkeley, CA: University of California Press.

Barry, Brian (1995) 'John Rawls and the Search for Stability', *Ethics*, 105 (4): 874–915.

Barry, Brian (2001) *Culture and Equality*. Cambridge, MA: Harvard University Press.

Bell, Daniel (1999) 'Democratic Deliberation: The Problem of Implementation', in Stephen Macedo (ed.), *Deliberative Politics: Essays on Democracy and Disagreement*. Oxford: Oxford University Press.

Beitz, Charles (1979) *Political Theory and International Relations*. Princeton, NJ: Princeton University Press.

Bentham, Jeremy (1996) 'An Introduction to the Principles of Morals and Legislation', in D. Wootton (ed.), *Modern Political Thought*. Indianapolis, IN: Hackett Publishing Company.

Braybooke, David (1987) 'Social Contract Theory's Fanciest Flight', *Ethics*, 97 (4): 750–64.

Buchanan, Allen (1982) *Marx and Justice: The Radical Critique of Liberalism*. London: Methuen.

Buchanan, Allen (1990) 'Justice as Reciprocity versus Subject-centered Justice', *Philosophy and Public Affairs*, 19 (3): 227–52.

Buchanan, James (1975) *The Limits of Liberty*. Chicago, IL: University of Chicago Press.

Christman, John (1986) 'Can Ownership be Justified by Natural Rights?', *Philosophy and Public Affairs*, 15 (2): 156–77.

Cohen, G.A. (1989) 'On the Currency of Egalitarian Justice', *Ethics*, 99 (4): 906–44.

Cohen, G.A. (1992) 'Incentives, Inequality, and Community', in Grethe Peterson (ed.), *The Tanner Lectures on Human Values*, 13. Salt Lake City, UT: University of Utah Press.

Cohen, G.A. (1995a) *Self-Ownership, Freedom and Equality*. Cambridge: Cambridge University Press.

Cohen, G.A. (1995b) 'The Pareto Argument for Inequality', *Social Philosophy and Policy*, 12: 160–85.

Cohen, G.A. (1997) 'Where the Action Is: On the Side of Distributive Justice', *Philosophy and Public Affairs*, 26 (1): 3–30.

Cohen, G.A. (2000) *If You're An Egalitarian, How Come You're So Rich?* Cambridge, MA: Harvard University Press.

Cohen, Joshua (1996) 'Procedure and Substance in Deliberative Democracy', in Seyla
    Benhabib (ed.), *Democracy and Difference*. Princeton, NJ: Princeton University Press.
Dagger, Richard (1997) *Civic Virtues*. Oxford: Oxford University Press.
Dahl, Robert (1998) *On Democracy*. New Haven, CT and London: Yale University
    Press.
Daniels, Norman (1985) *Just Health Care*. Cambridge: Cambridge University Press.
Danielson, Peter (1988) 'The Visible Hand of Morality', *The Canadian Journal of
    Philosophy*, 18: 357–84.
Davis, Lawrence (1982) 'Nozick's Entitlement Theory', in J. Paul (ed.), *Reading Nozick:
    Essays on Anarchy, State and Utopia*. Oxford: Blackwell.
Delli Carpini, Michael and Keeter, Scott (1996) *What Americans Know About Politics
    and Why it Matters*. New Haven, CT: Yale University Press.
De Wijze, Stephen (2000) 'The Family and Political Justice – The Case for Political
    Liberalisms', *Journal of Ethics*, 4: 257–81.
Dryzek, John (2000) *Deliberative Democracy and Beyond: Liberals, Critics, and
    Contestations*. Oxford: Oxford University Press.
Dworkin, Ronald (1985) *A Matter of Principle*. Cambridge, MA: Harvard University
    Press.
Dworkin, Ronald (1990) *A Bill of Rights for Britain*. London: Chatto and Windus.
Dworkin, Ronald (1995) 'Constitutionalism and Democracy', *European Journal of
    Philosophy*, 3 (1): 2–11.
Dworkin, Ronald (1996) *Freedom's Law: The Moral Reading of the American Constitution*.
    Cambridge, MA: Harvard University Press.
Dworkin, Ronald (2000) *Sovereign Virtue*. Cambridge, MA: Harvard University Press.
Elster, Jon (1986) 'Comment on Van der Veen and Van Parijs', *Theory and Practice*,
    15: 709–22.
Estlund, David (1998) 'Liberalism, Equality and Fraternity in Cohen's Critique of
    Rawls', *Journal of Political Philosophy*, 6: 99–112.
Exdell, John (1977) 'Distributive Justice: Nozick on Property Rights', *Ethics*, 87 (2):
    142–9.
Farrelly, Colin (1999) 'Justice and a Citizen's Basic Income', *Journal of Applied
    Philosophy*, 16 (3): 283–96.
Fishkin, James (1997) *The Voice of the People*. New Haven, CT: Yale University Press.
Fraser, Nancy (1995) 'Recognition or Redistribution? A Critical Reading of Iris
    Young's *Justice and the Politics of Difference*', *Journal of Political Philosophy*, 3 (2):
    166–80.
Freeman, Samuel (2002) 'Liberalism and the Accommodation of Group Claims', in
    Paul Kelly (ed.), *Multiculturalism Reconsidered*. Cambridge: Polity Press.
Galston, William (1999) 'Diversity, Toleration and Deliberative Democracy: Religious
    Minorities and Public Schooling', in Stephen Macedo (ed.), *Deliberative Politics:
    Essays on Democracy and Disagreement*. Oxford: Oxford University Press.
Gauthier, David (1986) *Morals by Agreement*. New York, NY: Oxford University Press.
Gewirth, Alan (1988) 'Ethical Universalism and Particularism', *Journal of Philosophy*,
    85 (6): 283–302.
Gutmann, Amy (1995) 'Justice Across the Spheres', in David Miller and Michael
    Walzer (eds), *Pluralism, Justice and Equality*. Oxford: Oxford University Press.
Gutmann, Amy and Thompson, Dennis (1996) *Democracy and Disagreement*.
    Cambridge, MA: Harvard University Press.

Gutmann, Amy and Thompson, Dennis (2002) 'Deliberative Democracy Beyond Process', *Journal of Political Philosophy*, 10 (2): 153–74.

Habermas, Jurgen (1990) *Moral Consciousness and Communicative Action*. Cambridge, MA: MIT Press.

Habermas, Jurgen (1993) *Justification and Application: Remarks on Discourse Ethics*. Cambridge, MA: MIT Press.

Habermas, Jurgen (1996) *Between Facts and Norms: Contributions to a Discourse Theory of Law and Democracy*. Cambridge, MA: MIT Press.

Habermas, Jurgen (2001) 'Constitutional Democracy: A Paradoxical Union of Contradictory Principles?', *Political Theory*, 29 (6): 766–81.

Hampshire, Stuart (2000) *Justice is Conflict.* Princeton, NJ: Princeton University Press.

Hampton, Jean (1986) *Hobbes and the Social Contract Tradition*. Cambridge: Cambridge University Press.

Hampton, Jean (1988) 'Can We Agree on Morals?', *Canadian Journal of Philosophy*, 18: 331–56.

Hardin, Russell (1988) 'Bargain for Justice', *Social Philosophy and Policy*, 5 (2): 65–74.

Harsanyi, John (1975) 'Can the Maximin Principle Serve as a Basis for Morality? A Critique of John Rawls's Theory', *American Political Science Review*, 69: 594–606.

Hobbes, Thomas (1996) *Leviathan*, edited by Richard Tuck. Cambridge: Cambridge University Press.

Hume, David (1978) *A Treatise of Human Nature,* edited by L.A. Selby-Bigge. Oxford: Oxford University Press.

Jagger, Alison (1983) *Feminist Politics and Human Nature*. Sussex: The Harverster Press.

Kant, Immanuel (1998) *Groundwork of the Metaphysics of Morals*. Cambridge: Cambridge University Press.

Kavka, Gregory (1982) 'An Internal Critique of Nozick's Entitlement Theory', *Pacific Philosophical Quarterly*, 63: 371–80.

Kavka, Gregory (1986) *Hobbesian Moral and Political Theory*. Princeton, NJ: Princeton University Press.

Knight, Jack and Johnson, James (1997) 'What Sort of Political Equality Does Deliberative Democracy Require?', in James Bohman and William Rehg (eds), *Deliberative Democracy*. Cambridge, MA: MIT Press.

Kymlicka, Will (1989a) *Liberalism, Community and Culture*. Oxford: Oxford University Press.

Kymlicka, Will (1989b) 'Liberal Individualism and Liberal Neutrality', *Ethics* 99 (4): 883–905.

Kymlicka, Will (1995a) *Multicultural Citizenship: A Liberal Theory of Minority Rights*. Oxford: Oxford University Press.

Kymlicka, Will (ed.) (1995b) *The Rights of Minority Cultures*. Oxford: Oxford University Press.

Levy, Jacob (2000) *The Multiculturalism of Fear*. Oxford: Oxford University Press.

Litan, Robert (1977) 'On Rectification in Nozick's Minimal State', *Political Theory*, 5 (2): 233–46.

Locke, John (1988) *Two Treatises of Government*, edited by Peter Laslett. Cambridge: Cambridge University Press.

MacIntyre, Alasdair (1981) *After Virtue*. London: Duckworth.

Mason, Andrew (2001) *Community, Solidarity and Belonging*. Cambridge: Cambridge University Press.

Mill, John Stuart (1998) *Utilitarianism*. Oxford: Oxford University Press.

Miller, David (1981) *Philosophy and Ideology in Hume's Political Thought*. Oxford: Clarendon Press.

Miller, David (1988) 'The Ethical Significance of Nationality', *Ethics*, 98 (4): 647–62.

Miller, David (1995) *On Nationality*. Oxford: Oxford University Press.

Mulhall, Stephen and Swift, Adam (1992) *Liberals and Communitarians*. Oxford: Blackwell.

Nagel, Thomas (1982) 'Libertarianism without Foundations', in J. Paul (ed.), *Reading Nozick: Essays on Anarchy, State and Utopia*. Oxford: Blackwell.

Narveson, Jan (1988) *The Libertarian Idea*. Philadelphia, PA: Temple University Press.

Nelson, Alan (1988) 'Economic Rationality and Morality', *Philosophy and Public Affairs*, 17 (2): 149-66.

Nozick, Robert (1974) *Anarchy, State and Utopia*. New York, NY: Basic Books.

Nussbaum, Martha (1999) *Sex and Social Justice*. Oxford: Oxford University Press.

Nussbaum, Martha (2000) *Women and Human Development: The Capabilities Approach*. Cambridge: Cambridge University Press.

Okin, Susan (1989) *Justice, Gender and the Family*. New York, NY: Basic Books.

O'Neill, Shane (2000) 'Liberty, Equality and the Rights of Cultures: The Marching Controversy at Drumcree', *The British Journal of Politics and International Relations*, 2 (1): 26–45.

Otsuka, Michael (2003) *Libertarianism Without Inequality*. Oxford: Oxford University Press.

Parekh, Bhikhu (2000) *Rethinking Multiculturalism: Cultural Diversity and Political Theory*. Basingstoke: Palgrave.

Pettit, Philip (1997) *Republicanism*. Oxford: Oxford University Press.

Phillips, Anne (1995) *The Politics of Presence*. Oxford: Oxford University Press.

Phillips, Anne (2001) 'Feminism and Liberalism Revisited: Has Martha Nussbaum Got it Right?', *Constellations*, 8 (2): 249–66.

Plamenatz, John (1960) 'The Use of Political Theory', *Political Studies*, 8: 37–47.

Plato (1967) *The Republic of Plato*, translated by Francis Cornford. Oxford: Oxford University Press.

Pogge, Thomas (1989) *Realizing Rawls*. Ithaca, NY: Cornell University Press.

Pogge, Thomas (1994) 'An Egalitarian Law of Peoples', *Philosophy and Public Affairs*, 23 (3): 195–224.

Poulter, Sebastian (1998) *Ethnicity, Law and Human Rights: the English Experience*. Oxford: Oxford University Press.

Rawls, John (1985) 'Justice as Fairness: Political Not Metaphysical', *Philosophy and Public Affairs*, 14 (3): 223–52.

Rawls, John (1993) *Political Liberalism*. New York, NY: Columbia University Press.

Rawls, John (1999) *A Theory of Justice*, 2nd edn. Oxford: Oxford University Press.

Rawls, John (1999) *The Law of Peoples*. Cambridge, MA: Harvard University Press.

Rawls, John (2001) *Justice as Fairness: A Restatement*. Cambridge, MA: Harvard University Press.

Ripstein, Arthur (1987) 'Foundationalism in Political Theory', *Philosophy and Public Affairs*, 16 (2): 115–37.

Sandel, Michael (1996) *Democracy's Discontent*. Cambridge, MA: Harvard University Press.

Sandel, Michael (1998) *Liberalism and the Limits of Justice*, 2nd edn. Cambridge: Cambridge University Press.

Sanders, Lynn (1997) 'Against Deliberation', *Political Theory*, 25 (3): 347–76.

Sayre-McCord, Geoffrey (1989) 'Deception and Reasons to be Moral', *American Philosophical Quarterly*, 26: 113–22.

Sen, Amartya (1992) *Inequality Reexamined*. Oxford: Oxford University Press.

Shapiro, Ian (1999) *Democratic Justice*. New Haven, CT and London: Yale University Press.

Shaw, William (1999) *Contemporary Ethics: Taking Account of Utilitarianism*. Oxford: Blackwell.

Sher, George (1997) *Beyond Neutrality: Perfectionism and Politics*. Cambridge: Cambridge University Press.

Shklar, Judith (1989) 'The Liberalism of Fear', in Nancy Rosenblum (ed.), *Liberalism and the Moral Life*. Cambridge, MA: Harvard University Press.

Skinner, Quentin (1996) *Reason and Rhetoric in the Philosophy of Hobbes*. Cambridge: Cambridge University Press.

Steiner, Hillel (1994) *An Essay on Rights*. Oxford: Blackwell.

Taylor, Charles (1985) *Philosophical Papers, Vol. 1: Human Agency and Language; Vol. 2: Philosophy and the Human Sciences*. Cambridge: Cambridge University Press.

Taylor, Charles (1990) *Sources of the Self*. Cambridge: Cambridge University Press.

Taylor, Charles (1993) 'The Politics of Recognition', in A. Gutmann (ed.), *Multiculturalism*. Princeton, NJ: Princeton University Press.

Taylor, Charles (1995) *Philosophical Arguments*. Cambridge, MA: Harvard University Press.

Tully, James (1995) *Strange Multiplicity: Constitutionalism in an Age of Diversity*. Cambridge: Cambridge University Press.

Van Parijs, Philippe (1991) 'Why Surfers Should be Fed: The Liberal Case for an Unconditional Basic Income', *Philosophy and Public Affairs*, 20 (2): 101–31.

Van Parijs, Philippe (1995) *Real Freedom for All*. Oxford: Oxford University Press.

Van Parijs, Philippe (1997) 'Interview', *Imprints: a Journal of Analytical Socialism*, 1 (3): 5–22.

Waldron, Jeremy (1995) 'Minority Cultures and the Cosmopolitan Alternative', in Will Kymlicka (ed.), *The Rights of Minority Cultures*. Oxford: Oxford University Press.

Waldron, Jeremy (1998) 'Judicial Review and the Conditions of Democracy', *Journal of Political Philosophy*, 6 (4): 335–55.

Walzer, Michael (1983) *Spheres of Justice*. New York, NY: Basic Books.

Walzer, Michael (1999) 'Deliberation, and What Else?', in Stephen Macedo (ed.), *Deliberative Politics: Essays on Democracy and Disagreement*. Oxford: Oxford University Press.

Weber, Max (1970) 'Politics as a Vocation', in H.H. Gerth and C.W. Mills (eds), *From Max Weber*. London: Routledge and Kegan Paul.

White, Stuart (1997) 'Liberal Equality, Exploitation, and the Case for an Unconditional Basic Income', *Political Studies*, XLV: 312–26.

Wolf, Susan (1995) 'Commentary', in Martha Nussbaum and Jonathan Glover (eds), *Women, Culture and Development: A Study of Human Capabilities*. Oxford: Clarendon Press.

Wolff, Jonathan (1991) *Robert Nozick: Property, Justice and the Minimal State*. Cambridge: Polity Press.

Wollstonecraft, Mary (1995) *A Vindication of the Rights of Women*. Cambridge: Cambridge University Press.

Young, Iris Marion (1986) 'The Ideal of Community and the Politics of Difference', *Social Theory and Practice*, 12 (1): 1–26.

Young, Iris Marion (1990) *Justice and the Politics of Difference*. Princeton, NJ: Princeton University Press.

Young, Iris Marion (1996) 'Communication and the Other: Beyond Deliberative Democracy', in Seyla Benhabib (ed.), *Democracy and Difference*. Princeton, NJ: Princeton University Press.

Young, Iris Marion (1999) 'Justice, Inclusion, and Deliberative Democracy', in Stephen Macedo (ed.), *Deliberative Politics: Essays on Democracy and Disagreement*. Oxford: Oxford University Press.

Young, Iris Marion (2000) *Inclusion and Democracy*. Oxford: Oxford University Press.

Zurn, Christopher (2002) 'Deliberative Democracy and Constitutional Review', *Law and Philosophy*, 21: 467–542.

Index

aboriginal people 48, 122, 126
abortion 88
accountability principle
  deliberative democracy 152
Ackerman, Bruce 153–4
agenda, final control over (democracy
    criterion) 138, 139, 144, 146
aggregative democracy model 138, 139–43
anarchism 36
Anarchy, State and Utopia (Robert Nozick)
    33, 46, 49, 51, 76
Anderson, Elizabeth 74, 90–1
apartheid 125
Archimedean point 67
Aristotle 161
armchair theorizing 146, 147
Arneson, Richard 22–3, 26, 163
assimilation 119, 121, 126
associations 115, 138
autonomy 122

Bargain of Mutual Benefit 64
Barry, Brian 11, 28, 29, 131–4, 164
basic structure of society 3, 15, 74
Beitz, Charles 23–6, 111
  David Miller distinguished 113, 114
Bell, Daniel 151–2
Bentham, Jeremy 4, 5, 76
brute luck 90, 91
Buchanan, Allen 28, 68–9, 102
Bulgaria 130
Bush, George 85

Canada 120, 122, 127
capabilities approach 161–3, 174
capital punishment 88–9
Chamberlain, Wilt (entitlement theory)
    39–41, 50
citizen democracy 87, 89
civic spaces 105, 171–2
civil disobedience 19–21
Clinton, Bill 81, 82
CM (constrained maximation) 59, 60, 61, 62
Cohen, G. A. 15–17, 44, 45
Cohen, Joshua 144, 146, 147
colour-blind society 120
commercial protective agencies 37–8
common good 149

common ownership 46
communicative democracy 150
communitarianism 97–117
  complex equality (Walzer) 98, 108, 109–10
  embedded selves 167
  feminist view 171
  liberalism 97, 99, 113–14, 115, 119, 121
    deontological 99–102
  nationalism 98–9, 110–14
  political economy 105
  Sandel, views of 97–106
  solidarity 115
  state neutrality 102–6
community
  criticism of notion 171
  cultural 120
  ideal 115, 172
complex equality 98, 108, 109–10
compliance problem (mutual advantage,
    justice as) 57–63
comprehensive liberalism 75
conception of self *see* self, conception of
conditions matching argument (justice)
    28, 102
conflict
  rationality account 55
'conscious-state' theories 76
constitutionalism 19–20, 87, 88, 89, 148
constrained maximation (CM) 59, 60, 61, 62
cooperative surplus 66
cultural diversity 120, 126
cultural heritage 122, 123
culturalism *see* pluralism
Culture and Equality (Brian Barry) 131
curriculum, school *see* education curriculum

Dahl, Robert 138, 141, 144
Danielson, Peter 65
De Wijze, Stephen 166–7
Deliberation Day (proposed national
    holiday) 153–4
deliberative democracy *see* democracy:
    deliberative
deliberative turn 137
democracy
  agenda, final control over 138, 139,
    144, 146
  aggregative model 138, 139–43

democracy *cont.*
  citizen 87, 89
  communicative 150
  constitutional 19–20, 145
  criteria 138
  deliberative 137–56
    accountability principle 152
    armchair theorizing 146, 147
    authentic deliberation 140
    and feminism 163, 174
    ideal, critical assessment 150–5
    procedural test 144, 145, 147
    publicity principle 151, 152
    reciprocity principle 141, 142, 152
    'show of hands' approach 139, 140,
      142, 144, 145
    as transformative process 140, 143, 149
    utopian ideal 152
  discursive 148–9
  enlightened understanding 138, 141, 143
  ideal 138
    assessment of 150–4
    utopian 152
  importance of 137–9
  and justice 137, 154
  majority decision 138
  participation, effective 138, 140, 143, 147
  partnership conception (Dworkin) 86,
    87, 89
  and political equality 85–9, 92
    democratic wager 86, 87
  substantive principles 139, 144–8
Democracy and Disagreement (Amy
  Gutmann/Dennis Thompson) 146
Democracy's Discontent (Michael Sandel) 97, 102
democratic discourse 87
democratic equality 12, 13, 91–2
deontological theories 4–5
  liberalism 99–102
difference
  politics of 158–9, 169–73, 174, 175
difference principle (of justice)
  defined 3
  domestic justice 26, 114
  egalitarian critique 15–16
  and equality of welfare 78
  global justice 26, 114
  least advantaged 21
  moral implications 10
  and order of principles 4
  overlapping consensus 29
  rectification principle 49
diffidence
  as source of conflict 55
discourse ethics 145–6
discursive democracy 148–9
distributional equality 75, 77, 85, 92

distributive justice
  'ambition-sensitive'/'endowment-
    insensitive' 89, 126, 148
  complex equality 98, 106–7
  entitlement theory 39, 48–9
  neutrality 83
distributive paradigm 158, 170, 174
diversity, cultural 120, 126
division of labour
  feminism 167, 170
dominant protection agencies 37, 38
dress codes 122, 129–30, 131
Dryzek, John 148
duties (natural)
  distinguished from obligations 17–18
Dworkin, Ronald
  auction tale (shipwrecked survivors)
    78–9, 123, 126
  and constitutionalism 87, 88, 89
  and democracy 85–9
  and equality 73–93
    political 85–9
    of resources 73, 75–80, 81, 82, 83
  and health 79, 80, 107, 108
  hypothetical unemployment insurance
    scheme 79, 80, 81, 82, 90
  and judicial review 87, 88, 89
  and luck egalitarianism 89–92
  and strategic problem 81
  Waldron, Jeremy (critique by) 88
  and welfare reform 80–5

education curriculum
  exclusion of pupils from 141–3, 149
efficiency 5–6, 13–15, 44
egalitarianism
  common assumptions 75
  luck 74, 89–92
  Rawls on 13, 35, 73
    critique by Cohen 15–17
  see also equality; equal opportunity
Emile (Jean-Jacques Rousseau) 159
enlightened understanding
  deliberative democracy 138, 141, 143
entitlement theory (of justice) 33–52, 53
  and community 115
  'enough and as good' proviso 42–3
  eye lottery example 34–5, 49, 50
  initial acquisition principle 41–6
  minimal state, argument for 33, 37, 49
  monopoly element 36
  property rights 34
  rectification principle 46–9
  redistributive element 36, 38
  self-ownership, and private property 49–51
  side constraints 34, 50, 53
  Wilt Chamberlain on 39–41, 50

environmentalism 151
equal basic liberties principle 3
equal citizenship principle 120, 121
equal concern principle 84, 85, 90, 91
equal importance principle 75, 77, 79
equal opportunity 10–15
    efficiency 13–15
    egalitarian critique (G. A. Cohen) 15–17
    formal 10, 11
    liberal equality 11, 12
    lotteries (three) 11
    luck egalitarianism 74, 89–92
    natural liberty 10, 12, 101
    principles of justice 3
    and talents 10
equality
    citizen 87, 89
    complex 98, 108, 109–10
    democratic 12, 13, 91–2
    distributional 75, 77, 85, 92
    Dworkin on 73–93
    and freedom 34
    justice (initial position) 7, 8
    liberal 11, 12, 101
    and liberty 34, 73
    moral 73
    of outcomes 13
    political (and democracy) 85–9
    of resources 73, 75–80, 81, 82, 83, 138
        see also self-ownership
    of welfare 75, 77, 78
    see also equal opportunity; inequality
ethical communities
    nations as 112
ethical particularism/universalism 111, 113, 160–1
Exdell, John 46
eye lottery example
    entitlement theory of justice 34–5, 49, 50

fair equality of opportunity principle 3
fairness, justice as 3–31
    assumptions, shared 6–7
    basic structure of society 3, 15, 74
    civil disobedience 19–21
    efficiency 5–6, 13–15
    egalitarian critique (G. A. Cohen) 15–17
    equal opportunity see equal opportunity
    least advantaged, identity of 10, 21–3, 74
    nearly just society 19
    original position 7–10, 100, 144–5
    political conception 26–30
        consensus, overlapping 29–30
    right and good 4–6
    theory (John Rawls) 6–7, 53
        criticism 15–17, 22
    utilitarianism 4, 5–6
    see also principles of justice

families
    and feminism 164–8
fear, liberalism of 130, 131
Federal Election Commission 85
feminism 157–76
    capabilities approach 161–3, 174
    and complex equality 110
    deliberative democracy 163, 174
    distributive paradigm 158, 170, 174
    and equal worth of human beings 160
    and families 164–8
    gender distinctions 157–8, 159, 164
    human life, development of 161
    and humanism 160
    internationalist 160, 163, 164, 174
    labour, division of 167, 170
    liberal 158, 159–64, 166, 175
    and marriage 169
    Nussbaum on 158, 160–4, 174
    Okin on 110, 157, 164–9
    politics of difference 158–9, 169–73, 174, 175
    public/private dichotomy 158, 164–9
    and rights 170–1
    women, domination of 110, 157, 171
    Young on 139, 149–50, 158, 170, 174
Feminist Politics and Human Nature
    (Alison Jagger) 159
Fishkin, James 153–4
Foole, Hobbesian theory 58–9, 62
foundationalism 53–4, 58, 62, 65
France
    headscarves affair 129
Fraser, Nancy 175
free exchange principle 107
free-riders 68, 84
freedom 34, 82–3
Freedom's Law: The Moral Reading of
    the American Constitution (Ronald
    Dworkin) 88

Gauthier, David 53–71, 73, 115
    and compliance problem 57–63
    and liberal feminism 159
gender distinctions 157–8, 159, 164
genderless society, creation 168
Glaucon 58
global justice 23–6, 111, 113
good, the (ethical theory) 4–6, 99
goods
    competition for 55
    primary 9, 107, 122, 123, 125, 162
Gore, Al 85
'greatest happiness' principle 76
Gutmann, Amy 108, 141–3, 146, 149, 150, 152

Habermas, Jurgen 144, 145–6
Hampshire, Stuart 97

Hampton, Jean 55
handicapped people 69, 74, 77, 80
harm principle 164
Harsanyi, John 9–10
Hawking, Stephen 79
headscarves affair (France) 129
health care 107, 108
health coverage, universal 79, 80
hedonism 76
helmet law 122, 127–8, 131
heritage, cultural 122, 123
hijab 129–30, 131
Hobbes, Thomas 36, 53–6, 57–9, 63, 64
homosexuality 164
household chores 167, 170
humanism 160
Hume, David 4, 112

ideas, politics of 172
immigrants 120, 124, 125
impersonal preferences 77
incentives 14, 16, 153
inclusion principle
    deliberative democracy 149
inequality
    and efficiency 13, 14
    immigrants and 124, 125
    natural 80
    Pareto argument for 15
informed preferences 77
initial acquisition principle
    entitlement theory (of justice) 41–6
initial bargaining position 63
injustice 20, 171
insurance scheme analogy (Dworkin) 79,
    80, 81, 82, 90

Jagger, Alison 159
Jews, Orthodox 127, 132
Johnson, James 147
judicial review 87, 88, 89, 139, 146
justice
    and democracy 137, 154
    descriptive claim 5, 29
    distributive *see* distributive justice
    entitlement theory *see* entitlement theory
        (of justice)
    as fairness *see* fairness, justice as
    Gauthier on *see* Gauthier, David
    global (Charles Beitz on) 23–6, 111, 113
    as human construction 98
    and injustices 20, 171
    as mutual advantage *see* mutual
        advantage, justice as
    normative claim 29
    Nozick on *see* Nozick, Robert
    pie-cutting approach 39, 40, 51

justice *cont.*
    political conception 26–30
    principles *see* principles of justice
    Rawls on *see* Rawls, John
Justice, Gender and the Family (Susan
    Okin) 165
Justice and the Politics of Difference (Iris
    Marion Young) 158–9, 170

Kant, Immanuel 4, 19, 27, 112
    Kantian interpretation of justice 28, 102
Kavka, Gregory 48
Knight, Jack 147
Kymlicka, Will 119–20, 121, 122–7,
    130, 132–3

Law of Nature 36
Law of Peoples (John Rawls) 25, 152
least advantaged, identity of 10, 21–3, 74
    examples 22–3
Lee, Robert E. 100
Leviathan (Thomas Hobbes) 53, 54–5
Levy, Jacob 130–1
liberal feminism 158, 159–64, 166, 175
liberalism
    comprehensive 75
    cultural membership 122
    deontological 99–102
    egalitarian 73
    and equality 11, 12, 101
    of fear 130, 131
    liberal-communitarian debate 97, 99,
        113–14, 115, 119, 121
    neutrality doctrine 83
    political 74–5
        see also Political Liberalism (John Rawls)
Liberalism, Community and Culture (Will
    Kymlicka) 101
Liberalism and the Limits of Justice (Michael
    Sandel) 97
libertarianism 33–4, 45
liberty 10, 12, 34, 40, 73, 101
Locke, John 4, 36, 42, 99
    Lockean proviso 64, 65, 67
luck egalitarianism 74, 89–92
    brute luck 90, 91

MacKinnon, Catharine 104
majority rule 87, 88
marriage 169
Mason, Andrew 115
maximin rule
    principles of justice 9, 10
Mill, John Stuart 4, 76, 99, 164
Miller, David 98–9, 110–14
    Charles Beitz distinguished 113, 114
minimal state, argument for 33, 37, 49

minimax relative concession (MRC) 66–7, 137–8
minorities, rights of 122–7
monism 121
Morals by Agreement (David Gauthier) 54, 67, 70
MRC (minimax relative concession)
    66–7, 137–8
multiculturalism 119–36
    Barry on 131–4
    national minorities, rights of 122–7
    politics of recognition 119–22
    polyethnic rights 120, 127–31
Multiculturalism of Fear (Jacob Levy) 130
Muslims 127, 132
mutual advantage, justice as 53–71
    compliance problem 57–63
    constrained maximization (CM) 59, 60,
        61, 62
    cooperative surplus 66
    free-riders 68
    and liberal feminism 159
    limits of 67–70
    moral intuitions 54
    non-moral premises 54
    opacity 60
    and poker game 59–60
    rational bargain, defined 63–7
    reciprocity thesis 68, 73
    rough equality clause 57–8, 68, 69
    state of nature 54–7
    straightforward maximization (SM) 59,
        60, 61, 62
    translucency 60, 61
    transparency 60
mutual protection agencies 37
mutual respect 141, 143, 146

nation
    meaning 112
nationalism 98–9, 110–14
natural resources 34
    global justice 23–4
natural rights tradition 36
naturalism 121
nature-nurture debate
    feminism 159
neutrality doctrine 83, 84
Northern Ireland
    Orange Order 132
Nozick, Robert
    and community 115–16
    and 'conscious-state' theories 76
    entitlement theory of justice *see*
        entitlement theory (of justice)
    and Rawls's theory contrasted 53
    and utilitarianism 73
    and Walzer 107
Nussbaum, Martha 158, 160–4, 174

obligations
    distinguished from natural duties 17–18
Okin, Susan 110, 157, 164–9
On Liberty (John Stuart Mill) 164
opacity 60
oppression concept
    feminism 171
option luck 90
Orange Order (Northern Ireland) 132
original position (justice as fairness
        theory) 7–10
    as appropriate initial status quo 8, 53
    communitarianism 100
    democracy, substantive principles 144–5
    formal constraints of the right 8
    rationality of parties 8–9
    veil of ignorance 8, 54, 123

Parekh, Bhikhu 120, 121, 125–6, 129–30
Pareto optimal/Pareto argument for
        inequality 14, 15
participation, effective
    deliberative democracy 138, 140, 143, 147
particularism 106
    ethical 111, 113, 160
partnership conception 86, 87, 89
personal preferences 77
Phillips, Anne 172–3
pie-cutting justice theory 39, 40, 51
Plato 58
pleasure principle 76
pluralism 6, 120, 121, 166, 172
political conception of justice 26–30
political economy 105
political equality 85–9, 92
    constitutionalism 87, 88, 89
    democratic wager 86, 87
    judicial review 87, 88, 89
    partnership conception 86, 87, 89
political liberalism 74–5
Political Liberalism (John Rawls) 3, 26, 27
political preferences 77
Political Theory and International Relations
        (Charles Beitz) 23
politics of difference 158–9, 169–73, 174, 175
politics of ideas 172
Politics of Presence (Anne Phillips) 172, 173
politics of recognition 120–1, 133
    feminism 158, 174
polyethnic rights 120, 127–31
popular sovereignty 87
pornography, law against 104
preferences, and welfare 76–7
presence, politics of 172, 173
primary goods 9, 107, 122, 123, 125, 162
principles of justice
    argument for 9–10

principles of justice *cont.*
  defined 3
  difference principle *see* difference
      principle (of justice)
  domestic 24
  duties/obligations 17–18
  and families 166
  formal constraints of the right 8
  individuals, applicable to 17–21
  initial acquisition 41–6
  justifications 27–8
  lexical order 4
  maximin rule 9, 10
  original position 7–10, 100, 144–5
  rationality 54
  reflective equilibrium 6–7
  and self-respect 18
  veil of ignorance 8, 54, 123
  see also fairness, justice as; justice
principles matching justification (justice)
      28, 102
Prisoner's Dilemma 54, 55–6
private property
  natural rights to 45
  and self-ownership 49–51
private sphere
  families belonging to 164–5
procedural republic 97–8
property rights 34, 42, 50, 51
  see also private property
publicity principle
  deliberative democracy 151, 152

racism 103, 104, 125
rational bargain, defined 63–7
  Bargain of Mutual Benefit 64
  cooperative surplus 66
  initial bargaining position 63
  Lockean proviso 64, 65, 67
  minimax relative concession (MRC)
      66–7, 137–8
rational preferences 77
rationality account of conflict 55
rationality of parties
  justice as fairness theory 8–9, 54
Rawls, John
  and deliberative democracy 152, 153
  and egalitarian theory 13, 35, 73
      critique by Cohen 15–17
      see also equal opportunity; equality
  and ethics 4–5, 99
  on least advantaged, definition 10, 21–3, 74
  methodology 6–7, 53
      criticism 15–17, 22
  and morality 54
  and pluralism 172
  primary goods 9, 107, 122, 123, 125, 162

Rawls, John *cont.*
  and principles of justice 54
      see also principles of justice
  and property rights 34
  and rectification principle 49
  and self-ownership 50
  and social goods 9, 107, 108
  and state neutrality 104
  utilitarianism, critique of 4, 5–6, 9, 34, 73
  see also fairness, justice as
reciprocity principle
  deliberative democracy 141, 142, 152
reciprocity thesis 68, 73
recognition, politics of *see* politics of
      recognition
rectification principle
  entitlement theory (of justice) 46–9
      distributive justice 48–9
      intragenerational and intergenerational
          rectification 47
reflective equilibrium 6–7
refugees 125
religious beliefs 127–8, 141–3, 149
Republic (Plato) 58
resources
  equality of 73, 75–80, 81, 82, 83, 138
      see also self-ownership
  natural 23–4, 34
respect, mutual 141, 143, 146
right, the (ethnical theory) 4–6, 99
Ripstein, Arthur 53
Robinson Crusoe 64–5
rough equality clause (Thomas Hobbes)
      57–8, 68, 69
Rousseau, Jean-Jacques 4, 159

Sandel, Michael 97–106, 110, 171
Sanders, Lynn 152
Sayre-McCord, Geoffrey 61–2
Second Treatise (John Locke) 42
self, conception of 99
  unencumbered 97, 100, 101, 102, 103
self-defence, right to 36
self-determination, national 113
self-government rights 122, 125
self-ownership 34, 35, 39, 53
  and democracy 137–8
  and private property 49–51
  see also common ownership
self-respect 122
Sen, Amartya 161
September 11th, 2001 attacks 151
Sex and Social Justice (Martha Nussbaum)
      158, 160
sexual discrimination 160
sexual preferences 164
Shapiro, Ian 137–8, 146

Shaw, William 4
Shklar, Judith 130
'show of hands' approach
    deliberative democracy 139, 140, 142,
        144, 145
Sidgwick, Henry 5
Sikhs
    and helmet law 127–8, 131
Skokie controversy (1977–8) 103
slaughter regulations 122, 128–9, 131
SM (straightforward maximization) 59,
    60, 61, 62
Smith, Adam 4, 10
social contract 4
social goods 9, 107, 108
Socrates 58
solidarity 115–16, 133
South Africa 125
Sovereign Virtue (Ronald Dworkin) 74, 75,
    79, 92
sovereignty
    popular 87
special responsibility principle 75, 77–9
state
    dominant protective association as 38
    minimal, argument for 33, 37, 38
    necessity for 35–9
    ultra-minimal 38
state of nature
    entitlement theory of justice 36
    mutual advantage theory 54–7
    and original position 7
    theorems 56–7
state neutrality
    communitarianism 102–6
straightforward maximization (SM) 59,
    60, 61, 62

taxation of earnings 35, 49, 50, 79, 83
    tax cuts 15, 16
Taylor, Charles 126
teleological theory 4, 5
terrorism 151
Thatcher, Margaret 15, 16
Theory of Justice (John Rawls) 3, 4, 17, 23,
    26, 28, 100
Thompson, Dennis 141–3, 146, 149, 150, 152
translucency 60, 61
transparency 60
Tully, James 133
Turkish names, use of 130, 131
Two Treatises of Government (John Locke) 36

unemployment insurance scheme
    (hypothetical) 79, 80, 81, 82, 90
United Kingdom
    helmet law 127–8, 131

United States
    aboriginal population 122
    American Civil War 100
    complex equality 109
    contemporary politics, public philosophy
        97–8, 102
    democracy in 87
    health care 108
    political economy 105
    political equality 85–6, 87–8
    productive employment in 108
    state neutrality 103–4
    welfare reform 82–3
universalism 106
    ethical 111, 160–1
utilitarianism
    description 76
    Nozick's critique 73
    Rawls's critique 4, 5–6, 9, 34, 73
utility
    preference-satisfaction account of 76
    utilitarians on 4

Van Parijs, Phillipe 82–4, 90
veil of ignorance 8, 54, 123
Vindication of the Rights of Women (Mary
    Wollstonecraft) 159
voting 138–9, 140

Waldron, Jeremy 88, 133, 146
Walzer, Michael
    and communitarianism 97, 98, 106–10, 116
    and democracy 152
    and feminism 162, 165–6
Wealth of Nations (Adam Smith) 10
Weber, Max 36
welfare
    Bentham on 76
    equality of 75, 77, 78
    preferences 76–7
    success theories 76
welfare reform
    and basic income proposal 80–5
Welfare Reform Act (1996) 81, 82
welfare state 38, 39
Wolf, Susan 163
Wollstonecraft, Mary 159, 160
women
    domination of 110, 157, 171
    quotas for 173, 175
    see also feminism
World Institute for Development
    Economics Research 161

Young, Iris Marion 139, 149–50, 158,
    170, 174